CAPITALISM, CONFLICT AND INFLATION

CAPITALISM, CONFLICT AND INFLATION

Essays in Political Economy

BOB ROWTHORN

LAWRENCE AND WISHART
LONDON

Lawrence and Wishart Ltd
39 Museum Street
London WC1A 1LQ

First published 1980
Copyright © Bob Rowthorn, 1980

Printed and bound in Great Britain at
The Camelot Press Ltd, Southampton

Contents

Acknowledgements

I am grateful to the following publications for allowing me to reproduce articles which originally appeared in their pages: *New Left Review* for 'Neo-classicism, Neo-Ricardianism and Marxism', 'Imperialism in the Seventies' and '"Late Capitalism"'; *Marxism Today* for 'Inflation and Crisis'; and the *Cambridge Journal of Economics* for 'Conflict, Inflation and Money'. I am also grateful to the Cambridge Political Economy Group for allowing me to republish 'Britain and the World Economy' which first appeared in their pamphlet, *Britain's Economic Crisis*. Publication details and dates of all these articles are given in the text.

Introduction

The essays in the present collection were written during the nineteen seventies and reflect my main areas of interest during the period. Although covering a fairly wide range of topics, they all deal with classical themes of political economy such as imperialism, capitalist development, or inflation; to this extent they form a coherent whole. Moreover, they are united by a common thread, which is their emphasis on the importance of power and conflict in capitalist economies. This emphasis places the essays outside the mainstream of orthodox economics which, despite periodic challenges, is still dominated by a harmonious vision of the world in which power and conflict play only a minor role – they are regarded as 'frictions' which impede the smooth operation of economic laws, but do not affect in any fundamental way either the character of these laws or the way in which the economy as a whole functions. Like most Marxists, I reject such a harmonious vision and find myself more in sympathy with the famous dictum of Marx and Engels that 'the history of all hitherto existing society is the history of class struggles'. Most of the essays in the present collection have already been published elsewhere and, with the exception of one article which has been extensively rewritten, are reproduced in more or less their original form. There is, however, some new material, namely a long essay dealing with Marx's theory of wages, and a shorter essay on Rosa Luxemburg and the political economy of militarism.

The first essay in this collection was written in response to the debate which followed the publication of Piero Sraffa's book *The Production of Commodities by Means of Commodities*.[1]* Sraffa's book had a profound effect on the left in the Cambridge Economics Faculty; a vast amount of energy was expended in mastering its intricacies and implications, and it was widely acclaimed as a revolutionary new approach to economics. Like everyone else I was caught up in this enthusiasm for a time, but

* See notes at end of each article.

then I began to experience serious doubts. I found myself increasingly irritated by the messianic character of this new school of thought, and unsatisfied by the extremely narrow vision it offered. So, to clarify my thoughts, I wrote an article which is reprinted here, 'Neo-classicism, Neo-Ricardianism and Marxism', in which I tried to identify the main achievements and failings of the Sraffian approach. This article had quite an impact. It annoyed many of Sraffa's followers, who interpreted it, incorrectly, as an attack on everything they stood for. There are, I admit, one or two isolated sentences which might support such an interpretation, but in general the article was rather generous towards them. Its main point was not that Sraffa and his followers, or 'Neo-Ricardians' as I called them, were completely wrong, but rather that they were very limited in their approach, and that their exclusive emphasis on the distribution of income had led them to ignore the social aspects of production. Some of Sraffa's followers, such as Ian Steedman, have since accepted this criticism and have extended their analysis to take these social aspects into account. The reader may notice that throughout the article I use words such as 'he' and 'him' to refer in general terms to both men and women. I do not believe that this represents a sexist bias on my part, but it does reflect an implicit sexism in the language conventional at the time. If I were to write the article again I should take care to avoid such a mistake.

The next essay 'Imperialism in the Seventies' is a revised version of a paper originally delivered to a conference at the Catholic University of Tilburg in the Netherlands. It is concerned with the dynamics of the multinational enterprise; it charts the rise of such enterprises and considers their significance for the world economy. It shows how the pattern of overseas expansion was very uneven during the fifties and sixties. The big firms of some countries, such as Britain and the US, relied mainly on overseas investment as a way of penetrating foreign markets, whereas those of other countries, such as Germany and Japan, relied mainly on exports to achieve this objective. However, the essay predicted that such differences were temporary and that the nineteen seventies would see a dramatic change when German, Japanese and other hitherto national firms began investing on a large scale overseas. Events have amply confirmed this prediction. The essay also predicted that overseas investment would lead to friction between the major capitalist powers, and concluded that the seventies would be a period of growing inter-imperial rivalry. Events have not really confirmed this prediction and, although there has been growing friction between the capitalist powers, this has not been primarily concerned with the question of overseas investment or multinational enterprise. When this essay first appeared it was criticized for neglecting the role of anti-imperialist movements in the Third World, and for exaggerating the extent of inter-imperial rivalry. I accept this criticism, and I should add that the essay also neglects the role of socialist countries whose existence has profoundly modified the character of the world imperialist system.

Imperialism is also a theme of the essay 'Britain and the World Economy'. This essay was my contribution to a pamphlet entitled *Britain's Economic Crisis* which was produced by a group of economists in Cambridge immediately after the Labour Government took office in 1974.[2] The pamphlet attacked the right-wing policies of the Labour leadership, and argued that only a bold left-wing alternative could reverse Britain's economic decline and overcome the crisis facing the country. As part of such an alternative, it proposed a whole range of measures for dealing with Britain's external economic relations, to loosen the hold of imperialism on the British economy, so as to give a hypothetical left-wing government the freedom to pursue radical internal policies.

The fourth essay ' "Late Capitalism" ' is an extended review of Ernest Mandel's book of the same name. In this essay I develop some of my own views about post-war economic growth and prospects for the future. My main area of disagreement with Mandel concerns the rate of profit and the factors which caused it to decline from the mid sixties onwards. Like many other Marxists, Mandel places great emphasis on the organic composition of capital as the factor which governs the broad character of capitalist development and determines whether the epoch in question will be one of economic expansion or stagnation. Specifically, he argues that the post-war boom was brought to an end by a rising organic composition of capital which made investment unprofitable and caused the pace of accumulation to decline. In my essay I criticize both the general proposition that the organic composition is *always* such a decisive factor as Mandel claims, and the specific proposition that post-war growth was brought to an end by a rising organic composition. And, having criticized Mandel's view of the present crisis, I suggest an alternative explanation. It is interesting to note that in his latest book *The Second Slump*, Mandel no longer even tries to demonstrate statistically that the organic composition of capital rose during the nineteen sixties and seventies, and now merely asserts this proposition as an article of faith.[3]

The next three essays in the collection are all in some way concerned with the question of wages. The first of them, 'Inflation and Crisis', was written as a contribution to the debate on this subject in the theoretical journal of the Communist Party *Marxism Today*. It spells out in simple terms some of the main issues involved in this debate, and considers the question of inflation in the wider context of capital accumulation and its regulation by the modern state. Briefly, the argument is that inflation is the outcome, sometimes deliberate and sometimes not, of attempts by the state to promote capital accumulation, through expansionary monetary and fiscal policies, at a time when the rate of profit is tending to fall. By creating conditions under which firms can raise prices, the state either prevents the rate of profit from falling or else reduces the extent of this decline, and thereby avoids or contains the crisis which otherwise follow a reduction in the rate of profit. However, as the essay argues, the inflationary process is inherently unstable, and to keep up the rate of profit prices will have to rise at an ever faster rate. Sooner or later, when the inflationary dynamic gets out of control, the priorities of the state will begin to change, and currency stability will become more important than economic expansion. At this point the state will adopt a more restrictive financial policy which brings the boom to an end and brings prices back under control.

The same theme is explored in a more formal, mathematical way in the article 'Conflict, Inflation and Money'. This article, which originally appeared in a slightly more technical form in the *Cambridge Journal of Economics*, was strongly criticized by a number of left Keynesians who found it offensive. They objected to its suggestion that wages and prices may be influenced by supply and demand, and that market forces may act as a discipline which holds both workers and capitalists in check.

The article suggests that unemployment may undermine the strength and determination of trade unions, and thereby reduce the ability of workers to defend themselves or to gain higher wages. It also suggests that firms may be less willing or able to raise prices when they are facing a saturated market. Both of these propositions are anathema to left-Keynesians, for whom it is self-evident that in the modern world wages and prices are determined 'institutionally' by trade unions and monopolies whose behaviour is quite unaffected by market forces. I find this proposition anything but self-evident and, in my opinion, the power of trade unions and monopolies is most definitely limited by the market conditions under which they operate.

Many left Keynesians also objected to my suggestion that monetary policy may provide an effective instrument of demand management, and to my illustration of this proposition by means of a crude version of the Quantity Theory of Money. On my use of the Quantity Theory, I can only repeat what I said in the article, that it is used for purely *illustrative* purposes and is not meant to be taken as an accurate picture of how the world really works. On the question of money and demand, I can only say that there is considerable evidence that monetary policy does influence demand, and that the state can influence the course of economic events through its control of the money supply. I must, however, agree with those Keynesians who argue that monetary policy is not very good at promoting economic recovery during a depression, and that fiscal policy provides a more effective way of increasing demand.

As already mentioned, the essay 'Marx's Theory of Wages' is published here for the first time. It arose out of my dissatisfaction with existing Marxist literature on this subject, which is usually quite uncritical of Marx and fails to consider his writings on wages against the background of his classical predecessors such as Ricardo. I found this an extremely difficult essay to write because Marx's own views are very obscurely presented and are by no means consistent. Nevertheless, there is a wealth of stimulating material in his writings on wages, and I have tried to summarize these writings and explore their implications. I am only too aware of the defects in this essay, but I hope the reader will persevere and find something interesting.

The next essay, 'Skilled Labour in the Marxist System', is a substantially revised version of an earlier article of the same name. It has been greatly shortened and simplified, but the basic argument has not been altered. The essay is easy enough for readers with a mathematical training, but others may find it difficult. The main point of the argument is that skills are produced with human labour, and that the superior value-creating capacity of skilled workers is due to the labour embodied in their skills. Teachers and others employed in the educational sector therefore contribute to the value of ordinary commodities because they produce the skills used by the workers who make such commoditites. If education is organized privately, on a profit-making basis, it is just like any other capitalist sector. Educational workers are exploited and perform surplus labour which is appropriated by their employers in the form of profit. If, on the other hand, education is organized on a non-profit making basis by the state, things are rather different. Educational workers are still exploited, but the surplus labour they perform is no longer appropriated by their own employers. It is instead *transferred* to capitalists in the non-educational sector. The mechanism of this transfer is as follows. As a non-profit making body the state supplies education at cost-price to the rest of the economy. The more the state exploits its workers, the lower is the cost of education, the lower is the price of skilled labour-power, and the higher are the profits of capitalists who purchase this labour-power. Thus, by forcing its workers to perform surplus labour the state reduces the price of labour-power and thereby increases the amount of capitalist profit. This additional profit represents the surplus or unpaid labour of educational workers in the state sector. Because such workers contribute indirectly to capitalist profits they may be described as *indirectly* productive. Clearly, educational employees are not the only workers in this category and the surplus labour of many kinds of state employee may be indirectly appropriated by capital. In a modern capitalist economy, therefore, the distinction between productive and unproductive labour is not always very useful, and where state employees produce inputs which are used in capitalist production they have much in common with productive workers.[4]

The last essay in this collection, 'Rosa Luxemburg and the Political Economy of Militarism', has not previously been published. It criticizes conventional interpretations of Rosa

Luxemburg and points out that her writings on militarism, although rather obscure, are very interesting and contain an embryonic theory about the role of the modern state in promoting capitalist development. This aspect of her writings has been largely ignored by conventional interpretations, which have focused exclusively on the questions of underconsumption and aggregate demand.

NOTES

1. P. Sraffa, *The Production of Commodities by Means of Commodities*, Cambridge, 1960.
2. M. Ellman, B. Rowthorn, R. Smith and F. Wilkinson, *Britain's Economic Crisis*, Nottingham, 1974.
3. E. Mandel, *The Second Slump*, London, 1978.
4. This question is explored at some length in Ian Gough's *The Political Economy of the Welfare State*, London, 1979.

Bob Rowthorn
Cambridge, 1979

1

Neo-Classicism, Neo-Ricardianism and Marxism*

This essay will discuss the system of thought known as Neo-Classical economics, the criticisms made of this system by the Neo-Ricardian school, and finally and especially, the relationship of Neo-Ricardianism to Marxism. The treatment of Neo-Classical and Neo-Ricardian economics has been made deliberately general, in order to keep the argument clear and avoid confusion. At present academic economics in the capitalist world is in a state of confusion, as its dominant system of thought – Neo-classicism – comes under attack. Despite the elaborate mathematical reformulations it has undergone in recent years, this kind of economics differs very little in its fundamentals from what Marx, a century or more ago, contemptuously described as 'vulgar economy' – the systematization of what is immediately visible in the sphere of market relations: individual preferences, prices and exchange. Throughout this paper, therefore, the terms 'vulgar economy' and 'neoclassical economics' will be used interchangeably. Vulgar economy can be characterized in the most general terms as follows.[1]

I VULGAR ECONOMY

In the first place, it is *individualist*, and *subjectivist*, seeing society as a collection of individuals whose nature is, for analytical purposes, assumed to be given or predetermined, quite independently of the social phenomena under consideration. Its object is to explain these social phenomena by relating them to the psychological characteristics of the given individuals and the initial situation in which they find themselves. In vulgar economy the individual plays a precisely analogous role to the atom in Newtonian mechanics. Just as Newtonian mechanics

* First published in *New Left Review*, July–August 1974.

sees material reality as the interaction of unvarying or eternal atoms, so vulgar economy sees social reality as the interaction of individuals whose natures are invariable or permanent. Society is explained in terms of the individual, rather than the individual in terms of society. This stands in sharp contrast to the view of Marxists and such non-Marxists as Durkheim, who see the individual as the product of society and who seek to explain social phenomena in terms of social laws which do not derive from the individual. Indeed, in Marx's work the individual appears merely as the representative or bearer (*Träger*) of specific social relations. The accumulation of capital, for example, is not seen as the result of capitalist greed or subjective time-preference, but as an expression of the immanent laws of capitalist development, which can be understood without any reference to the subjective characteristics of the individual capitalist.

In the second place vulgar economy suffers from what might be described as *naturalism*. Since even the most superficial description of what are generally regarded as economic phenomena cannot escape the fact that things are produced, production must somehow or other be included within the scope of vulgar economy. The way in which production is treated, however, is remarkably similar to the way in which the individual is treated. Just as the individual is assumed to be asocial, so too is production. Instead of seeing production as a social process in which human beings combine together within a specific framework of social relations, vulgar economy sees production as an asocial or natural process in which inputs of labour, land and means of production, misleadingly described as capital, are mysteriously transformed into outputs of material and non-material goods.

In so far as property relations enter into this picture, they relate not to the labour process, or what Marx called the appropriation of nature, but to the distribution process, or what Marx called the appropriation of the product. Thus, when Debreu talks of a private ownership economy he is referring, not to the fact that the capitalist employs the worker and organizes production, but to the fact that some people have a claim to part of the social product, deriving from their 'ownership' of the means of production.[2]

Finally, vulgar economy is characterized by the primacy it

accords to market phenomena or *exchange*. This is hardly surprising. Given the fact that society is seen as an agglomeration of individuals whose nature is fixed, who do not combine together in a social production process and whose only link with each other is through the buying and selling of commodities, market phenomena must inevitably assume primary importance.

Thus, vulgar economy or neoclassical economics is characterized by *subjective individualism, naturalism* and the primacy it awards to *exchange*. The effects of vulgar economy have been twofold: at a scientific level it has inhibited, if not entirely prevented, serious study of the capitalist mode of production and the 'economic law of motion of modern society'; and at an ideological level it has provided a moral justification of the existing social order.

These two effects, although related to each other, are analytically distinct, and it would be a mistake to assume that every Neo-classical economist is an apologist for the capitalist system. The individual practitioner of Neo-classical economics may be motivated by the purest spirit of scientific curiosity or may even be a socialist who finds the present social order morally repugnant. This fact does not, however, alter the objective effects of Neo-classical economics as a system of thought. No matter what the aspirations of its more progressive practitioners, the conceptual framework and starting point of Neo-classical economics render virtually impossible a scientific analysis of the capitalist or any other mode of production. Once these concepts and starting point are accepted, the main lines of analytical development are predetermined, and attempts to modify this development in the name of 'greater realism' take on an inevitably eclectic character. Genuine scientific advance becomes possible only to the extent that the original system of thought is, implicitly or explicitly, abandoned. To use Bachelard's expression, Neo-classical economics constitutes an 'epistemological obstacle' whose significant effect on a scientific plane is simply to inhibit the development of an authentic science of modes of production.[3] Despite a formidable mathematical apparatus, the contribution of Neo-classical economics to such a *social* science has been negligible. Of course, the mathematical methods found in modern Neo-classical economics have been of great importance in such fields as linear programming, where the aim is to develop the science of rational choice or, as it has been called, 'praxiology'. But the fact that Neo-classical economics and praxiology share the same mathematical methods and, within limits, the same conceptual framework, does not in any way validate the pretensions of Neo-classical economics, when it claims to be the general starting point from which a science of the capitalist mode of production should begin. The relationship between these two systems of thought may be polemically compared to that between astrology and astronomy, which share the same vocabulary and, within limits, the same concepts. But this in no way validates astrology as a science which enables us to understand human destiny.

Although useful as a system of thought serving to justify the capitalist mode of production and inhibit fundamental inquiry into its functioning, Neo-classical economics is incapable of handling the problems of social control and organization confronting capitalist enterprises or the State. As a result, there has arisen a series of practical disciplines, some of which reject certain elements of Neo-classical theory, and others of which base themselves pragmatically upon observed statistical regularities, whose explanation is only tenuously related to this theory. Keynesianism, for example, partially rejects individualism, seeking, although not always finding, laws which cannot be directly deduced from the behaviour of individuals with given preferences and perceptions – uncertainty, expectations and their *formation* play a central role in this approach. Scientific management, to take another example, rejects the notion of production as a natural process and, within the confines laid down by bourgeois property relations, examines the rational (profitable) organization of the labour-process and control of the work-force. What all of these practical disciplines have in common, however, is the lack of any grand vision comparable in scope to that of vulgar economy, being all more or less eclectic in approach. Despite the mushrooming of applied economics and related disciplines in recent years, vulgar economy remains the dominant, indeed to all intents and purposes the only, general system of thought within the world of academic economics. At one time, Keynesianism appeared capable of providing an alternative, but after twenty-five years of successful application it has been reduced to the status of a practical discipline and provides no real challenge to vulgar economy. Indeed, a watered-down version of Keynesianism has been incorporated into what Samuelson has called 'the grand Neo-classical synthesis'.

Neutrality and Apology

Vulgar economy achieves its ideological impact in two distinct ways: through the picture of the world given by its apparently neutral variants, and through the openly apologetic use made of certain of its findings. The apparently neutral variants analyse the capitalist system as if it were an inherently stable and smoothly self-regulating mechanism. Unemployment, crises, uneven development and similar negative features of the system are regarded as deviations from 'equilibrium', or as secondary phenomena and their existence is *for analytical purposes* ascribed to 'frictions' or 'imperfections', such as monopoly or imperfect information. Quite apart from its inhibiting effect on scientific work, such an approach has direct political implications. In consistently treating such negative features as deviations from equilibrium or as secondary phenomena, vulgar economy assumes that they play no fundamental role in the capitalist system. It is but a short step to conclude that they can be eliminated by the introduction of more competition, better information or some other piecemeal change designed to remove imperfections in an otherwise perfect mechanism.

Apologetic uses of vulgar economy frequently derive from its emphasis on the correspondence between the subjective preferences of individual participants and the technical configuration of the economy. In simpler versions, the equilibruim conditions – expressing this correspondence – take the form of a series of equalities between the 'subjective' rates of substitution of one good for another, and the corresponding 'objective' or technical rates of substitution. In more sophisticated versions, certain of these equalities are replaced by inequalities, to allow for the possibility of boundaries, corners or other irregularities. Since apologetic uses rely largely upon simpler versions of the theory, let us assume that all equilibrium conditions take the form of equalities. The argument which follows can be modified to cover the case of inequalities.

The apologetic possibilities of the above correspondence can be seen with the aid of a simple example. Suppose the technology is such that the use of one additional unit of a good, say corn, as an input to the production process will, if efficiently utilized, cause the output of the same good in the following year to rise by $1 + x$ units, all other inputs and outputs remaining constant—then, in the language of vulgar economy, x is the 'marginal product' of corn. Under the assumed conditions, any individual who reduces his current corn consumption by one unit can, if he wishes, receive in return an amount of corn in the following year equal to $1 + x$ units. In other words the 'corn rate of interest', measuring the return in terms of corn to the individual saver, is equal to the marginal product of corn.

Now since the system is in equilibrium, there can be no individual consuming corn who would prefer $1 + x$ units in the following year to 1 unit in the current year. for, should such an individual exist, he would make use of the possibility of substitution offered by the corn rate of interest, reducing his current consumption, and the configuration of the economy would change, contrary to the assumption that the system is in equilibrium. Indeed, since the equilibrium conditions are assumed to be equalities, one can go further and say that every single individual, without exception, will be just at the margin of choice, just indifferent between the consumption of one unit of corn in the given year and $1 + x$ units in the following year. If he gives up the consumption of an additional unit of corn he will need exactly $1 + x$ units in the following year to restore him to his original level of satisfaction. Any less and he will be worse off, any more and he will be better off. In the language of vulgar economy, x is his 'subjective rate of time-preference' in the consumption of corn, and is taken to be a measure of the subjective loss he experiences when postponing his consumption of corn.

Thus, provided the equilibruim conditions take the form of equalities, and we consider only changes in the production and consumption of a single commodity, which we also take as a numéraire, we find that *marginal products, rates of interest,* and *subjective rates of time-preference* are all equal.

Now, although these equalities are unlikely to hold in practice, their assertion does not of itself constitute an open apology for the capitalist system. To convert them into such an apology something more is needed, and this is provided by the manner in which the various terms are interpreted in apologetic writing. The postponement of consumption is described as a *sacrifice* to be measured by the relevant subjective rate of time-preference, the receipt of extra commoditities is described as a *reward* to be measured by the relevant rate of interest, and finally marginal products are described as the *marginal contribution to production* of capital in the particular form it happens to take. With this terminology the above equalities can be re-expressed as: the saver receives a reward in the form of interest, proportional both to his sacrifice and to the marginal contribution of his capital to production.

Even when equilibrium conditions take the form of inequalities rather than equalities, this apologetic terminology can be used. Interest remains the reward for sacrifice or abstinence, and it is still related, although not necessarily proportional, to the sacrifice involved and the marginal contribution of capital to production. More generally, the various categories of income are described as rewards for various kinds of sacrifice, each of which provides a necessary contribution to production: the capitalist forgoes the consumption of his capital, receiving interest (or profit) as his reward; the landlord forgoes the use of his land, receiving rent as his reward; and, finally, the worker forgoes his leisure, receiving wages as his reward. Having described the situation in this way, it is but a short step to seeing the relationship between the capitalist, the landlord and the worker as an essentially *harmonious* one, in which each makes his distinct contribution to production, and receives his appropriate award. Marx expressed this very clearly in the following rather lengthy passage. 'This, moreover, renders a substantial service to apologetics. For [in the formula] land-rent, capital-interest, labour-wages, for example, the different forms of surplus-value and configurations of capitalist production do not confront one another as alienated forms, but as heterogeneous and independent forms, merely different from one another but *not antagonistic*. The different revenues are derived from quite different sources, one from land, the second from capital and the third from labour. Thus they do not stand in any hostile connection to one another because they have no inner connection whatsoever. If they nevertheless work together in production, then it is a harmonious action, an expression of harmony, as for example, the peasant, the ox, the plough and the land in agriculture, in the real labour process, work together *harmoniously* despite their dissimilarities. In so far as there is any contradiction between them, it arises merely from competition as to which of the agents shall get more of the value they have jointly created. Even if this occasionally brings them to blows, nevertheless the outcome of this competition between land, capital and labour finally shows that, although they quarrel with one another over the division, their rivalry tends to increase the value of the product to such an extent that each receives a larger piece, so that their competition, which spurs them on, is merely the expression of their harmony.'[4]

The Aggregate Production Function

Note the double harmony between the factors – in production they co-operate, and in distribution their competitive struggle is merely the manifestation of a deeper community of interest. This harmony of interest is most simply expressed in popular versions of vulgar economy based upon the marginal productivity theory associated with the so-called 'aggregate production function'. In this theory it is assumed that commodities can be reduced to a common standard in such a way that, for analytical purposes, the existence of many different commodities can be ignored and, therefore, income distribution, equilibrium and other features of the system can be analysed as though there existed only one homogeneous commodity, such as the corn we used in the above example. This commodity appears both as an input, where it is called *capital*, and as an output, where it is called *income*. Inputs are transformed into outputs by means of a *production function*, which determines the amount of output produced with given inputs of land, labour and capital.

There are a number of reasons for the popularity of this theory. It is simple, being suitable for teaching and more openly propagandist purposes, lending itself readily to diagrammatic exposition. Moreover, although simple, it purports to be based upon the more complex 'general equilibruim' theory, in which an unlimited number of commodities can appear. Indeed, until, recently, it was claimed that nothing significant was lost in the transition from the multi-commodity world of general equili-brium theory to the single-commodity world of the aggregate production function. Finally the apparent success of the theory in practical application has been an important factor in its popularity. A whole range of supposedly scientific work has been based on the aggregate production function, in particular that of Solow, Denison and others, dealing with the causes of economic growth and the contribution of non-material inputs to production.

When dealing with questions of equilibrium and income distribution, certain assumptions are usually made about the shape of the aggregate production functions and the preferences of individuals. The production function, for example, is assumed to exhibit constant returns to scale and uniformly diminishing marginal products with respect to the three factors of land, labour and capital. Provided the preferences of the participants display certain well-known properties, these assumptions will be sufficient to ensure that corresponding to each initial endowment, specifying the resources possessed by each individual participant, will be a unique equilibrium position. In this position every factor is rewarded according to its contribution to production, which is, in turn, equal to the subjective sacrifice the owner of a factor makes when he allows the latter to be used for production rather than consumption.

It also follows from the conventional aggregate theory that in a competitive economy the working class cannot improve its collective position by organising at the economic level to raise wages, improve conditions, or control the production process. According to this theory, all such organization will cause some kind of inefficiency, in the form of either the under-employment or misallocation of some factor.[5] Even where one group of workers does improve its position by organization it can only be at the expense of other workers, who will be forced either to accept lower wages or worse conditions, or else lose their jobs.

This does not mean that workers cannot redistribute income towards themselves. What it does mean, however, is that such redistribution should be achieved through taxation – preferably lump-sum, so that marginal equalities are not disturbed. Taxes may be levied on either income or wealth. Since taxes cannot be changed through the economic struggle of workers against their own employer or a group of employers, it follows that in this theory workers have no real need to organize themselves at the work-place level, except perhaps to help the competitive process by putting pressure on the backward employer. If they must organize, workers should do so at the political level, perhaps even forming their own political party to fight for their interests.

Superficially, this view appears consistent with a militant class politics—workers could, after all, use their party to press for the most radical social changes. Its real content, however, is quite the opposite. The basis of any class politics is the day-to-day struggle of the worker at his place of work, against his employer. Only by spreading and unifying these specific struggles, do workers learn to act as a class. Without such a foundation, working-class politics, no matter what their beginning, degenerate to a point where the working class ceases to act as a class. To the extent that he remains politically active, the worker then fights, not as a member of his class, but as an individual, as a *citizen*. Thus, no matter how radical its slogans, the practical content of a theory which argues that all changes should be affected by means of taxation and property redistribution, is ultimately the political participation of the worker as an individual citizen and the dissolution of the working class on an organizational level. In a nutshell, workers must abandon class struggle and devote themselves to bourgeois politics.

It follows quite naturally that many radical exponents of marginal productivity theory, who advocate a drastic redistribution of wealth and income through taxation, should at the same time be bitter opponents of trade-unionism and all other kinds of working-class struggle outside of the traditional framework of bourgeois politics. Thus, bourgeois reformers can in one breath expose and condemn widespread poverty and unequal distribution of property, advocating redistribution to establish a property-owning democracy, and, in the next breath, rant against the trade-union movement as the fundamental cause of present economic ills.

More conservative exponents of marginal productivity theory, of course, do not even go this far. For them the existing distribution of property is sacrosanct, representing the reward for past effort. If workers want property, they should save! However, amongst academic economists this view is no longer very fashionable, and the mainstream opinion is that property and income should be redistributed via the means offered by the bourgeois political process – taxation. Naturally, redistribution must not go to the point where it destroys 'incentives', nor must state intervention be so drastic that it threatens individual 'freedom'. Moreover, even if few academic economists still believe that Neo-classical economics provides a complete justification for the existing state of affairs, there can be no doubt that this kind of economics continues to legitimate reactionary views which remain fashionable in the wider society. In providing an apparently scientific basis for these views, Neo-classical economics continues to exert a reactionary influence. From a scientific point of view, of course, the main objection to this kind of economics centres around its function as an epistemological obstacle, inhibiting fruitful scientific study of the capitalist and other modes of production.

II NEO-RICARDIANISM

Vulgar economy has been severely criticized by a school of economists, who are best described as Neo-Ricardians, as much of their work takes the form of a more or less conscious return to the method, if not the exact propositions, of Ricardo.[6] They have also been called the Cambridge or Anglo-Italian school. The main characteristics of the economists of this school are their rejection of subjective individualism, of supply and demand as determinants of income distribution, and the explicit inclusion of economic classes in their analysis. From this position they have undertaken an *immanent* critique of vulgar economy, showing that many of its central propositions are not consistent with its own assumptions, and in particular that marginal productivity theory based on the aggregate production function cannot be derived from the general equilibrium system.

The starting point of their critique is the observation that means of production in a capitalist economy have a dual nature. On the one hand, they are physical objects and as such their use in the production process leads to the creation of greater output. On the other hand, they are the property of certain individuals, and as such their ownership entitles these individuals to a certain portion of the total product. As physical objects, means of production, or capital as they are called, cannot be reduced to any economically meaningful common standard. Of course, they could be measured by their weight, volume or some other physical attribute, but such a reduction would be irrelevant to the study of such questions as income distribution or equilibrium. As property, however, means of production can be reduced to a common standard, namely their price or, as the Neo-Ricardians misleadingly say, their value.

This opposition can be expressed in Marxist terminology by saying that capital is both a heterogeneous collection of use-values and a homogeneous collection of exchange-values. With this distinction in mind, the Neo-Ricardians show that, in the marginal productivity theory based on the aggregate production function, the reduction of all commodities to a common standard must be done on the basis of exchange values, rather than weight, volume or any other physical attribute. Now as the rate of profit varies, exchange-values will generally alter and, as a result, the exchange-value or price of any given collection of commodities may alter. In other words, the reduction of commodities to a common standard depends on the rate of profit. It is not, therefore, generally possible to perform this reduction before the rate of profit is known.

This result is used by the Neo-Ricardians to discredit the aggregate production function, which vulgar economists supposed could be constructed from technological data alone, and which possessed the property that 'capital' per man was inversely related to the rate of profit. The Neo-Ricardians show that it may be impossible to order production techniques according to their 'capital intensity' – the exchange-value of capital per man. One technique may be more capital intensive than another at both high and low rates of profit, yet be less capital intensive at intermediate rates of profit. Under these circumstances, there can be no monotonic relationship between capital intensity and the rate of profit, or, for that matter, between capital intensity and the wage rate. Associated with this is the famous 'reswitching paradox'. Capitalists may prefer one technique when the rate of profit is low, prefer another technique at intermediate rates of profit, and finally at high rates of profit they may again prefer the orginal technique. At both high and low rates of profit, therefore, capitalists choose the same technique, but at intermediate rates they choose another. More generally, it may happen that, even though the necessary monotonic relationship exists, it is 'perverse', with capital intensity rising as the rate of profit rises. Significantly, these conclusions of the Neo-Ricardians are not mere curiosities, for reswitching or perverse relationships can occur under quite plausible assumptions.

Finally, the Neo-Ricardians have stressed the already known fact that if capital is interpreted as a homogeneous fund of exchange-value, the marginal product of capital may not be equal to the rate of profit or interest, even though all the necessary continuity and other conditions of the simpler versions of general equilibrium theory are satisfied.[7]

These achievements of the Neo-Ricardian school are real and substantial, and ought not to be underestimated. They amount to a complete demolition of the aggregate production function and marginal productivity theory based on it. As a result vulgar economy, in so far as it retains any scientific pretensions, is now forced to rely upon general equilibrium theory. This theory is far less suitable for teaching and propagandist purposes than the old aggregate theory. Moreover, stressing as it does the dependence of everything on everything else, general equilibrium theory has the disadvantage of appearing vacuous and irrelevant to all but the most committed of observers. Finally, this theory is unable, except under the most restrictive assumptions, to show that equilibrium is unique. When there exists more than one equilibrium, it is quite possible to maintain that working-class struggle at the economic level could shift the system from one equilbrium to another, thereby improving the position of the working class as a whole. Thus, in contrast to its discredited aggregate version, general equilibrium theory is less deterministic in its view of the capitalist system.

The Resistance of General Equilibruim Theory

Having listed the achievements of the Neo-Ricardian school, perhaps I should say something about the more exaggerated claims made by some of its adherents. The work of Sraffa has not proved that the distribution of income is independent of supply and demand. By their nature, supply and demand can only take effect in a situation where there exists the possibility of variation in either production, consumption, or supply of labour. In Sraffa's system such variations are explicitly excluded, as the author's stated objective is to study properties of the economy which do not depend on variations other than those of prices, wages and the rate of profit. As a result, supply and demand play no role in Sraffa's system. To conclude from this, however, that supply and demand play no role in the real world is to make the most elementary error. It is to confuse the world, as we think about it, with the world as it really is, or, if you like, to confuse the object of knowledge with the real object. The fact that Sraffa, with good reason, chose to hold production, consumption, and supply of labour constant *in his analysis*, says nothing whatsoever about how these elements behave in *reality*. If, in reality, production, consumption or supply of labour alter in response to changes in wage-rates or rates of profit, then it is conceivable that supply and demand may determine the level at which the actual wage or profit rate settles.

Under these circumstances, the correct scientific procedure is not to deny that supply and demand may exert such an influence, but to seek for the fundamental laws of which supply and demand are merely a manifestation. Even Marx, a bitter opponent of vulgar economy, admitted that supply and demand had a proximate effect on wages when he said; 'As to the *limits* of the *value of labour*, its actual settlement always depends upon supply and demand, I mean the demand for labour on the part of capital, and the supply of labour by the working men.'[8] Naturally Marx did not leave the question here. Much of his work was devoted to revealing the objective determinants of capital's demand for labour and its supply by the working men.

In this context it should be said that the analysis of the Neo-Ricardian school may be formally consistent with general equilibrium theory. This theory does not depend upon the possibility of measuring capital independently of the rate of profit. Moreover, the fact that capital, considered as a homogeneous fund of exchange-value, does not receive its marginal product in the general equilibrium system, has no bearing whatsoever on the existence or non-existence of an equilibrium. Moreover, if an equilibrium exists where average rates of profit in each industry are equal, all the Neo-Ricardian equations will be satisfied at this point. If this equilibrium happens to be unique, wages and the rate of profit will be uniquely determined, and we shall have a case in which Sraffa's equations have been combined with the determination of distribution by individual preferences.[9]

Finally, it should be noted that, although capital as a homogeneous fund of exchange-value may not receive its marginal product, certain marginal equalities may still hold within the general equilibrium system. Provided sufficient continuity assumptions are made to ensure that all equilibrium conditions take the form of equalities, rather than inequalities, the following marginal quantities will be equal: the degree of subjective 'loss' involved in saving, the 'reward' received for saving, and the 'contribution to production' of saving. This equality was illustrated in our earlier example where saving, interest and extra production consisted of a single commodity – corn. It is possible to extend this equality to the general case in which more than one commodity may vary. Thus, within the general equilibrium framework, there remain certain apologetic possibilities. Interest can still be seen as a reward for a sacrifice which leads to greater production. The apologetic possibilities are, of course, limited by the fact that there may exist many different equilibrium positions, each of which is equally sanctioned by the moral standards of bourgeois justice.

III   MARX'S THEORY

During the last decade or so, there has been a considerable revival of interest in Marxist political economy, and valuable work has been done on such topics as imperialism and the role of the state. On the level of fundamental or 'high' theory, however, Marxists still find themselves trapped within a debate whose terms of reference were laid down by vulgar economists such as Böhm-Bawerk, on the one hand, and Neo-Ricardians such as Bortkiewicz, on the other. This debate, which has dominated the interpretation of Marx's political economy throughout the entire 20th century, has received a powerful stimulus from the recent growth of Neo-Ricardianism.

In the Anglo-Saxon world at least, Marxists have mainly addressed themselves to such topics as: is the choice of techniques based on values or prices; what is the role of demand in determining prices; what is the formally correct solution to the transformation problem; when is the average rate of profit equal to the ratio of surplus-value to the value of capital advanced; when is the rate of surplus-value equal to the ratio of profits to wages? In some cases their answers have been rather different from those of the Neo-Ricardians, but in general these differences have not been very great. Indeed, many Marxists (an illustrious example is Dobb in his later writings) regard Sraffa's work as providing both the solution to a number of problems, whose treatment by Marx was unsatisfactory, and perhaps an alternative, more modern version of the labour theory of value.[10]

Now, important though some of these questions may be, Marxist political economy, as a distinct system of thought, cannot be understood in terms of the answers it gives to them. So long as the theoretical work of Marxists is restricted to such questions, Marxism, with good reason, will appear as a rather eccentric wing of Neo-Ricardianism – its specific characteristics being a somewhat tedious insistence of the need for an 'historical approach', a frequent dogmatic insistence on the explanation of prices by values, and a particularly militant class rhetoric. Indeed, this is reflected in the widespread identification of Neo-Marxism with Neo-Ricardianism, an identification which follows Bortkiewicz in seeing the specific characteristics of Marxism as a harmless, but useless, eccentricity.

This view of Marxism, or rather of the system of thought of Karl Marx himself, is in my view mistaken. Marx's problematic differs fundamentally from that of Ricardo and the Neo-Ricardians. I shall now proceed to examine crucial ways in which these two problematics differ.

The Capitalist Mode of Production

It is well known that Marx criticized Ricardo (and other classical economists) for thinking of capitalist production as something 'eternal' or 'natural'. This has been widely interpreted to mean that Ricardo was unhistorical in his approach, and that the main distinction between Marx and Ricardo is that Marx saw capitalism as a mere passing phase in the history of human society, whereas Ricardo did not. In other words, Marxism is seen as Ricardianism plus history.

The trouble with this view is not so much that it is wrong, but that it is superficial. Marx did indeed criticize Ricardo for failing to analyse capitalism as a system which grew out of an earlier form of society and will in turn be replaced by another form, and for failing to analyse or describe the historical development of this system. But he also admired Ricardo's analytical and, in the first instance, a-historical method. Where Ricardo failed, in Marx's opinion, was in his characterization of the capitalist system, and as a result in his analysis of 'the economic law of motion of modern society'. Moreover, the intellectual reason he failed to characterize the capitalist system adequately is quite simply that he lacked a concept – the concept of a 'mode of production'. Virtually every one of Marx's specific criticisms of Ricardo can be traced back to the absence of this concept in the latter's work – his confused treatment of prices and values, his failure to distinguish adequately between production and circulation, between surplus-value and profit, or between labour and labour-power.

Thus, when Marx says Ricardo thought of the capitalist system as something 'eternal' or 'natural', he is not so much criticizing Ricardo for his unhistorical analysis, but saying that, because Ricardo thought of capitalism in this way, he failed to see it as a mode of production with specific features differentiating it from other modes of production. Marx's use of the concept of a 'mode of production' marks a radical shift in problematic, which has been largely unacknowledged or ignored by Marxist political economists.

Seen in its most general terms, a mode of production is simply the set of social relations within which men produce. In his famous *Preface to a Contribution* Marx says; 'In the social production of their life, men enter into definite relations that are indispensable and independent of their will, relations of production which correspond to a definite stage of development of their material productive forces. The sum total of these relations of production constitutes the economic structure of society, the real foundation, on which rises a legal and political superstructure and to which correspond definite forms of social consciousness. The mode of production of material life conditions the social, political and intellectual life process in general.'[11] Any mode of production has two distinct aspects or levels: the mode of appropriation of *nature*, and the mode of appropriation of the *product*. This distinction can be seen clearly in the following passage where Marx describes the capitalist labour process. 'The labour-process, turned into the process by which the capitalist consumes labour-power, exhibits two characteristic phenomena. First, the labourer works under the control of the capitalist to whom his labour belongs; the capitalist taking good care that the work is done in a proper manner, and that the means of production are used with intelligence, so that there is no unnecesssary waste of raw material, and no wear and tear of the implements beyond what is necessarily caused by the work. Secondly, the product is the property of the capitalist and not that of the labourer, its immediate producer.'[12]

In their appropriation of nature, men combine together in a definite set of social relationships specified by such characteristics as production techniques, organization of the labour-process, divison of labour, authority and control. Notice that the appropriation of nature, as it is defined here, is a *social* affair. It is not man in the abstract acting upon nature, nor is it the 'non-human world of technology' as the Neo-Ricardian Baradwaj has described the labour process.[13] It is social man producing within a definite set of social relationships.

The manner in which the product, and therefore the surplus product, is appropriated varies from one mode of production to another. In feudal or slave society, for example, surplus product is directly appropriated by extra-economic force. In capitalist society it is appropriated on the basis of apparent freedom, according to the *economic* laws of commodity exchange. This aspect of a mode of production is widely acknowledged to involve social relationships. Indeed, under the name 'distribution' the Neo-Ricardians treat it as the only level at which social relations occur, and, as Baradwaj's phrase reveals, treat the equally important appropriation of nature as an asocial or natural process. The two levels of a mode of production are relatively autonomous and cannot be reduced one to another. The laws of motion of a mode of production are based upon the articulation and interaction of the two levels, and these laws can, therefore, only be understood by means of an analysis which takes account of both levels.

With these distinctions in mind, let us examine Marx's characterization of the capitalist mode of production. To understand his characterization, one must perceive that Marx was seeking, on the one hand, to contrast the capitalist mode with slave, feudal and other modes of production, in which the labourer is permanently tied to an individual owner or master and does not have the freedom to dispose of his labour-power as he wishes, and, on the other hand, he was seeking to contrast industrial capital with merchant, usurers' and other forms of capital. Capitalist production proper is characterized by two things: it is the production of commodities – goods are produced for exchange and social production is spontaneously organized by means of this exchange; and every element in the labour process has become a commodity, including labour-power itself – the capacity of the labourer to work. Thus, capitalist production is commodity production, generalized to the point where labour-power has become a commodity. The worker cannot, of course, sell himself for an indefinite length of time, for then he would cease to be a freeman.

As a commodity owner, the worker is free to sell or not sell his labour power, as he chooses, subject only to the economic constraints imposed by the exchange of commodities. This is in contrast to feudalism and slavery, where the worker does not possess such freedom. Marx says in the *Grundrisse*, 'In the slavery relationship the worker belongs to an individual, particular owner, whose labour machine he is . . . In the bondage relationship, the worker is an element of landed property; he is a chattel of the earth just as cattle are . . . Labour power seems to the free worker to be entirely his property, one of his elements which he as a subject, controls, and which he retains in selling it.'[14] This freedom is, however, formal rather than real, for, although the worker is not compelled by direct coercion to work for others, he does not possess the means to work on his own account, and therefore must out of economic necessity work for others. He is, as Marx says: 'free in the double sense, that as a free man he can dispose of his labour-power as his own commodity, and that on the other hand he has no other commodity for sale, is short of everything necessary for the realization of his labour-power.'[15]

In other words, he must work for others, or he starves. Unlike the slave or the serf, he has some freedom to choose the individual who will control his labour-power – he can, within limits, choose the capitalist for whom he works. But, although he can free himself from the individual capitalist, he cannot free himself from the despotism of capital as a whole. He must still work for some capitalist. Hence the formal rather than real nature of his freedom. Even so, it remains true that the constraint on the free labourer is the economic law of commodity exchange, rather than the extra-economic force of slave or feudal society.

The Specificity of Industrial Capital

For our purposes, however, the more important contrast is between industrial capital and other forms of capital. Many 'vulgar socialists', such as Proudhon, sought the explanation for capitalist profit and surplus-value in what Marx called the realm of 'circulation' – the buying and selling of commodities, and the lending of money for interest. Merchant capital, which acquires its profits by buying cheap and selling dear, relies upon some monopoly position or form of extra-economic power in the circulation of commodities. Indeed, it is characterized by the fact that its profit derives from the sale and purchase of commodities at prices which differ from values or, more generally, from prices of production.[16] Usury capital is characterized by the fact that it derives profit from the lending of money for interest.

The vulgar socialists looked upon industrial capital – capital directly exploiting labour-power by employing workers to produce commodities – as a form of merchant or usurers' capital. The implication of this view is that surplus-value could be eliminated simply by making the exchange of commodities competitive and banning the lending of money for interest. Labour-power could remain a commodity. Marx took just the opposite view. In his eyes, the capitalist mode of production is characterized by the fact that surplus-value is actually created outside of the sphere of circulation, and does not stem fundamentally from monopoly or extra-economic force in the sphere of circulation, nor from the lending of money for interest. On the contrary, the capitalist mode of production is characterized by competition in the sphere of circulation, and by the 'exchange of equivalents'. Moreover, usurers' and merchant capital are no longer independent forms, but must be seen as derivative forms of industrial capital which is the dominant form in modern society. 'Both merchants' capital and interest-bearing capital are derivative forms, and at the same time it will become clear, why these two forms appear in the course of history before the modern standard form of capital.'[17]

The contrast between merchants and industrial capital, and thereby the specific characteristics of industrial capital, can be made clearer by comparing the labour-process (production) and the exchange of commodities (circulation) in three different *hypothetical* situations. The first situation is that of simple commodity production, where independent producers such as peasants or artisans exchange freely and competitively their commodities. In this situation both production and circulation are characterized by freedom and equality. In the labour-process the worker is independent, being under the control of no other person, and is free to do what he wants within the limits laid down by the natural world. In the circulation process he sells his wares freely, without interference, and like any other commodity seller receives the competitive price.

Next consider a situation where individual producers must sell or buy through intermediaries who hold a monopolistic position. We can consider such a situation as the combination of merchant capital in the sphere of circulation with simple commodity production in the labour-process. Historically this was often the form in which independent producers were compelled to trade. In this combination, production, as before, is characterized by freedom and equality. Circulation, however, is characterized by unfreedom and inequality. The monopoly of the intermediaries denies to the individual producers the right, or at least the opportunity, of trading with anyone else. Moreover, the intermediary and the individual producers do not confront each other as equals, as they did before. The intermediary is in a privileged position as a trader.

Finally, consider capitalist production in its pure form, where free competition reigns. In their capacity as commodity traders, all participants, capitalists and workers, are free in the sense that they can sell to anyone willing to buy, and buy from anyone willing to sell. This applies to the worker's sale and the capitalist's purchase of labour-power just as much as it applies to transactions in any other commodity. As traders, capitalists and workers participate equally, each having commodities to exchange, each being unable to bear any extra-economic power to alter the ratios at which they must exchange commodities. Thus, as in the case of simple commodity production, circulation is characterized by freedom and equality – the significant difference, of course, being that labour-power is now a commodity and the worker sells not his products, but himself. Having sold himself, the worker must now work for the capitalist. In the labour-process he works under the control of the capitalist, producing what the latters wants, submitting to capitalist labour discipline and performing the kind of work the capitalist desires. The labour-process is, therefore, characterized by unfreedom and inequality. The worker must do as he is told, and the capitalist stands over him as a superior, rather than confronting him as an equal, as he does in the sphere of circulation.

The three situations just described can be summarized thus:

	Merchant Capital Plus Simple Commodity Production	Simple Commodity Production	Capitalist Production
Circulation	unfreedom and inequality	freedom and equality	freedom and equality
Production	freedom and equality	freedom and equality	unfreedom and inequality

It is clear that in these examples, merchant capital and industrial capital are related to the pure form of simple commodity production in diametrically opposite ways. Merchant capital represents the introduction of unfreedom and inequality in the realm of exchange. Industrial capital represents the introduction of unfreedom and inequality in production. It is also clear that no amount of freedom and equality in the realm of circulation will convert capitalist production into simple commodity production. Now, bourgeois equality applies exclusively to the circulation process, where individuals participate as commodity buyers and sellers. It does not relate to the labour-process. Thus, capitalist production is consistent with bourgeois equality, and, for that matter, with bourgeois freedom which allows every commodity-owner to dispose of his commodity as he wishes. Finally, bourgeois justice sanctions the unfreedom and inequality in production. As a seller of labour-power, the worker has freely consented to work for the capitalist for a given length of time, under known conditions. In making him work, the capitalist is only exacting his due as a commodity purchaser. The fact that the worker is compelled to sell himself to the capitalist, because he has been dispossessed at some stage in the past, or else was bred a proletarian, is of no concern to bourgeois justice, which concerns itself exclusively with the actual act of exchange and not the circumstances which bring about and condition this exchange. Thus, capitalist production is consistent with bourgeois equality, freedom and justice. Merchant capital, on the other hand, is not. In introducing monopoly or non-economic coercion into circulation, it is violating these standards. So long, therefore, as we are considering the situation of the simple commodity producer, facing feudal or other monopolies, the application of bourgeois standards represents a liberation for the labourer.

When we consider capitalist production, however, this is not the case. On the contrary, it is the application of bourgeois standards to circulation which is the foundation of the worker's unfreedom and inequality in the labour-process. Indeed, it is the existence of free and unfettered commodity exchange which makes the 'law of value' act upon the individual capitalist as an external coercive force, which compels the individual capitalist to behave as he does in the labour-process, which leads him to revolutionize the labour-process so that the worker becomes a mere appendage to the machine. As Marx remarked on the relationship between freedom (anarchy) in exchange and unfreedom (despotism) in production, 'in a society with capitalist production, anarchy in the social division of labour and despotism in that of the workshop are mutual conditions of the other'.[18]

Now, the crucial point about the vulgar socialists was that they thought that the worker could be liberated by the application of bourgeois morality. As we have seen, however, this is not the case. Indeed, in its purest form, capitalism is the very embodiment of bourgeois morality, since all commodity sellers receive their rights as commodity sellers. In putting forward their demands for freedom and equality in the realm of circulation, the vulgar socialists were putting forward the demand of small artisans and other simple commodity producers, seeking to free themselves from domination by merchant capital, which in many cases was gradually impoverishing them and converting them into proletarians. To these workers, the demands of the vulgar socialists promised a short term if not a long-term salvation. To the proletarian, however, who was already compelled to sell his labour-power they promised nothing. Indeed, many of the great struggles of the working class, over such questions as the limitations of the working day or the formation of trade unions, have been struggles against bourgeois freedom in exchange, for they have sought to deny to the individual worker the right to dispose of his labour-power as he wishes. The freedom of the individual worker has been curtailed in the interests of the working class as a whole.

The basic position of Marx is summed up in the following celebrated passage from *Capital,* describing the sphere of circulation. 'This sphere that we are deserting, within whose boundaries the sale and purchase of labour-power goes on, is in fact a very Eden of the innate rights of man. There alone rule Freedom, Equality, Property and Bentham. Freedom, because both buyer and seller of a commodity, say of labour-power, are constrained only by their own free will. They contract as free agents, and the agreement they come to, is but the form in which they give legal expression to their common will. Equality, because each enters into relation with the other, as with a simple owner of commodities, and they exchange equivalent for equivalent. Property, because each disposes only of what is his own. And Bentham, because each looks only to himself. The only force that brings them together and puts them in relation with each other, is the selfishness, the gain and the private interests of each. Each looks to himself only, and no one troubles himself about the rest, and just because they do so, do they all, in accordance with the pre-established harmony of things, or under the auspices of an all-shrewd providence, work together to their mutual advantage, for the common weal and in the interest of all. On leaving this sphere of simple circulation or exchange of commodities, which furnishes the "Free-trader Vulgaris" with his views and ideas, and with the standard by which he judges a society based on capital and wages, we think we can perceive a change in the physiognomy of our dramatis personae. He, who before was the money-owner, now strides in front as capitalist; the possessor of labour-power follows as his labourer. The one with an air of importance, smirking, intent on business; the other, timid and holding back, like one who is bringing his own hide to market and has nothing to expect but –

a hiding.'[19] On this basis, let us now examine three basic points where Marx diverges from Ricardo and his modern followers: the origin of surplus-value, the concept of labour-power, and the distinction between variable and constant capital.

1. The Origin of Surplus-Value

Marx stated that surplus-value orginated in production and not in circulation, and that surplus-product represented the surplus or unpaid labour of workers. This has been interpreted by many, including Bortkiewicz and other Neo-Ricardians, to mean that profits or the surplus product represent a *deduction* from the product of labour, and that the capitalist is able to deduct this surplus product because he owns the means of production, without which production is impossible.

As it stands this interpretation of Marx is either incorrect or incomplete. If by 'deduction', it is meant that the capitalist obtains his profit by making use of a monopoly position in circulation and cheating the worker, the interpretation expresses a view diametrically opposed to that of Marx who, as we have seen, did not locate the orgin of profit within the realm of circulation. Alternatively, the expression 'deduction from the product of labour' may simply mean that workers provide the only human factor in the production process and, therefore, create the entire product. From this point of view, all output is the product of labour and it follows *definitionally* that surplus product is a part of labour's product and is, therefore, a deduction from this product. Although correct, and accepted by Marx, this view is superficial and certainly does not demand his long analysis to sustain it. Indeed, there is something rather circular in the argument which first defines *all* output as the product of labour, and then truimphantly exclaims that it has shown surplus product to be a deduction from the product of labour. Of course, for propagandist purposes, it is useful to make such an argument against the apologetic versions of vulgar economy, which see the 'sacrifice' of the capitalist as a contribution to production.

Against more sophisticated Neo-classical economists, such as Debreu, however, such an argument is useless. They would agree that, considered from a technical point of view, the only human contribution to production is labour, and that capitalists get a part of the total product because they own the means of production. Indeed, they would go further and say that all this takes place on the basis of competition, of bourgeois justice. The argument could be given more weight by pointing to the origins of the present distribution of property, how workers were dispossessed in the process of primitive accumulation, and how the capitalist system has mechanisms for ensuring that sufficient proletarians will be available for exploitation. Even with this addition, however, the interpretation fails to come to grips with Marx's specific characterization of the capitalist mode of production and the form of exploitation within it. Indeed, it fails to distinguish any significant differences between the capitalist mode of production, where the worker labours under the direct control of the capitalist, and certain other modes of production, such as the domestic system in which the labourer works at home, using materials and perhaps means of production owned by the entrepreneur, or alternatively, simple commodity production where workers are in debt to the money lender. In all but capitalist production, the worker is not paid a wage for his labour-*power*, but receives payment in the shape of the *product* of his labour. This distinction does not, however, play any great role in the main deduction theories, which pay very little attention to the labour-process and the social relations under which it is conducted.

This distinction does, however, play a crucial role in Marx and one must interpret him literally, when he says that surplus-value is created in production and not in circulation, for then one is compelled to take into account the specific feature of capitalism as a mode of *production*, not merely as a mode of distribution, as the deduction theorists, particularly those of the Neo-Ricardian school, tend to think of it. In particular, one must begin with the fact that, in this mode of production, the labourer works under the control of the capitalist, who *compels* him to work, to produce value. Moreover, the worker is compelled to work for longer than is necessary merely to replace the means of subsistence he consumes. Thus, he is compelled to perform *surplus* labour, which is embodied in a surplus product, which being a commodity is surplus-value. It is this emphasis on the labour-process which characterizes Marx's analysis, and which, more than anything else, distinguishes him from all main schools of bourgeois economics, both Neo-classical and Neo-Ricardian, as well as most modern Marxist writers, who display much the same faults as the Neo-Ricardians.

This emphasis is particularly clear when Marx discusses Ricardo's treatment of wages. Ricardo, like the Neo-Ricardians of today, took the intensity and duration of the working-day as given, and considered merely changes in the rate of wages per unit of time. In doing so, he removed production, as a social process, from the picture. Surplus-value is seen, not as something intimately related to the social power of capital within the labour-process, but as the result of two factors: on the one hand, the real wage rate which reflects the subsistence needs of workers, together with their bargaining power, and, on the other hand, the productivity of labour, which in the Ricardian tradition, reflects the ingenuity of the capitalist, rather than the struggle between capital and labour within the production process.

The effects of this perspective are described by Marx in the following passages: 'The labourer must first be *compelled* to work in excess of the necessary time, and this compulsion is exerted by capital. This is missing in Ricardo's work, and therefore also the whole struggle over the regulation of the normal working-day.' Then further: 'The *origin of surplus-value* does not become clear and consequently Ricardo is reproached by his successors for having failed to grasp and expound the nature of surplus-value. That is part of the reason for their scholastic attempts at explaining it. But because thus the origin and nature of surplus-value is not clearly comprehended, the surplus-labour plus the necessary labour, in short, the *total working-day*, is regarded as a fixed magnitude, the differences in the amount of surplus-value are overlooked, and the productivity of capital, the *compulsion to perform surplus-labour* – on the one hand (to perform) absolute surplus-labour, and on the other its innate urge to shorten the necessary labour-time – are not recognized, and therefore the *historical* justification for capital is not set forth. Adam Smith, however, had already stated the correct formula. Important as it was, to resolve into labour, it was equally important to resolve surplus-value into surplus-labour, and to do so in explicit terms.'[20]

In contrast to Ricardo, Marx initially took the daily wage as fixed and considered variations in the duration and intensity of work. This enabled him to concentrate on what he considered to be the crucial aspect of capitalist exploitation – that, behind the façade of freedom and equality in the exchange of commodities, lies the harsh reality of compulsion and inequality in the labour-process. Later, both in *Capital* itself and *Wages, Price and Profit*, Marx allows the daily wage to vary and builds up a picture which includes both the struggle over wages in the sphere of circulation and the struggle over the duration and intensity of work in the labour-process.

Provided our sole aim is to study certain formal relationships between technology, real wages and the rate of profit, there is little to choose between the approaches of Marx and Ricardo. *Ex-post* they lead to the same result. Workers perform surplus labour in either case and the same equations will describe the relationship between the various market magnitudes – prices, wages, and so on. Indeed, the Ricardian approach is perhaps simpler. If, however, our aim is to understand capitalism as a mode of production and to 'reveal the economic law of motion of modern society', it is ridiculous to ignore certain fundamental determinants of this motion and concentrate exclusively on the quantities which appear in the equations of Sraffa and other Neo-Ricardians. For they, like the Neo-classicals, consider production to be an asocial or natural process. For them, capital is, as I have already said, a social relationship only when it concerns the appropriation of the product, or as they put it 'the distribution of income'. For them, all social relations are focused on the process of circulation. The fact that capital also organizes and enforces the production of commodities, and the production of surplus-value, is of no importance to them. Their equations, indeed their whole theory, could, with minor changes, be modified to fit a society in which workers hired their equipment from capitalist owners, who took no part in the production process. Provided the real wage was defined to mean what the workers retain after the payment of hire-charges to the capitalists, the formal relationships would be unchanged. Moreover, capitalists would still derive their income from the ownership of the means of production, and they would still 'deduct' their profit from the product of labour. The fact that Neo-Ricardian theory can, with so little modification, be adapted to suit such different modes of production, suggests that it is seriously deficient.

2. The Value of Labour-Power

Marx criticized the classical economists for talking of the 'value of labour', which he considered to be an irrational expression for the 'value of labour-power'. He himself gave a variety of reasons why the latter was the correct expression. In the first place, it corresponded to the fact that exploitation in the capitalist system is based upon bourgeois justice, that workers sell their capacity to work at its value – they are not cheated. As Marx says in his *Marginal Notes on Wagner*: 'Now in my presentation profit on capital is in fact also not "only a deduction or 'theft' from the labourer". On the contrary, I represent the capitalist as the necessary functionary of capitalist production, and indicate at length that he does not only "deduct" or "rob" but enforces the production of surplus-value and thus first helps to create what is to be deducted; I further indicate in detail that even if in commodity exchange only *equivalents* are exchanged, the capitalist – as soon as he has paid the labourer the real value of his labour-power – quite rightfully, i.e. by the right corresponding to his mode of production, obtains surplus-value.'[21] In the second place, it resolved the classical problem that labour, unlike any other commodity, appeared to have two distinct values, one corresponding to the labour contained in the workers' subsistence, and the other corresponding to the worker's actual labour. To overcome this, the classics distinguished between living and dead labour, suggesting that living labour should have one value, and dead or embodied labour another value. This distinction between living and dead labour destroyed the unity of their value theory, and Marx's replacement of 'labour' by 'labour-power' served to restore this unity.

Thus, the introduction of the concept 'labour-power' served both to emphasize that exploitation in capitalist society is based upon bourgeois justice, and to unify the theory of value so that every commodity has a unique value. Neither of these, however, is the fundamental reason for the change. This, once again, concerns the characterization of capitalism as a mode of production. So long as the classical economists used the concept 'value of labour', they were able to avoid discussing the social relations of the labour-process itself, or at least to avoid giving these relations a central part in their analysis. The significance of this can be seen from the following passage from *Capital*: 'That which comes directly face to face with the possessor of money on the market, is in fact not labour, but the labourer. What the latter sells is his labour-power. As soon as his labour actually begins, it has already ceased to belong to him; it can therefore no longer be sold by him. Labour is the substance, and the immanent measure of value, but *has itself no value.*'[22] By the time the worker enters the production process, he has already sold himself to the capitalist, even if his payment actually comes later, even if he works on piece-rates. His labour-power no longer belongs to him. He no longer controls his own labour.

It was the absence of the concept 'labour-power' which prevented the classical economists from seeing capital in its entirety, as a social relationship. 'Instead of *labour*, Ricardo should have discussed labour-*power*. But had he done so, *capital* would also have been revealed as the material conditions of labour, confronting the labourer as power that had aquired an independent existence and capital would at once have been revealed as a *definite social relationship*. Ricardo thus only distinguishes capital as "accumulated labour" from "immediate labour". And it is something purely physical, only an element in the *labour-process*, from which the relation between labour and capital, wages and profits, could never be developed.'[23] Note the dual nature of the social relationship which is capital. On the one hand, as a relation between capital and labour, it concerns the subordination of the worker to the capitalist during the appropriation of nature, and, on the other hand, as a relation between profits and wages, it expresses their relations during the appropriation of the product.

In the last analysis, the significance of the distinction between labour and labour-power is that, in purchasing labour-power, capital establishes its despotism in the labour process. And through this despotism capital constantly revolutionizes the techniques of production, raises the productivity of the worker and brings together ever greater number of workers, thereby laying the material foundation for a new society and stimulating the resistance of the class which will bring this new society into being. This concept of the social relation 'capital' is, it will be noticed, markedly different from that of either Ricardo or the Neo-Ricardians. For the latter, capital is a social relationship only in so far as it represents a claim to a part of the product.

3. Variable and Constant Capital

Amongst a wide variety of economists, there has been considerable confusion about the distinction between, or even the meaning of, the terms 'variable' and 'constant' capital. Some economists have immediately identified these with circulating and fixed capital respectively. Others have identified variable capital directly with the wage fund, so that if workers are paid at the end of the production period, as Marx said they usually were, variable capital is not in fact capital, since it is not advanced.

To understand the distinction, we must begin with the simple fact that variable capital is fundamentally the worker himself or rather his labour-power. It is true that Marx used the term to describe the wage fund, but such a use is derivative and by no means fundamental. Thus, variable capital is labour-power – the living or subjective element in the labour-process. Constant capital, by contrast, is the dead or the objective element in the process. The reason that each of these is capital, has nothing whatsoever to do with whether they are paid in advance or not. What matters is that during the production process both constituents are under the control of the capitalist. Both means of production and the worker are incorporated into capital itself. 'On entering that process, they become incorporated with capital. As co-operators, as members of a working organism, they are but special modes of existence of capital. Hence, the productive power developed by the labourer when working in co-operation, is the productive power of capital. This power is developed gratuitously, whenever the workmen are placed under given conditions, and it is capital that places them under such conditions. Because this power costs capital nothing, and because, on the other hand, the labourer himself does not develop it before his labour belongs to capital, it appears as a power with which capital is endowed by Nature – a productive power that is immanent in capital.'[24]

Thus, constant capital is means of production and variable capital is labour-power. Each of these is to be interpreted first of all, not as components of the fund expended in purchasing them, but rather as qualitatively distinct elements within the labour-process itself, in other words as elements of what Marx called 'productive' capital in contra-distinction to money or commodity capital. By calling labour-power 'variable' capital, Marx established a conceptual connection between the creation of surplus-value and the despotic nature of the capitalist production process. The surplus-value created by workers in this process is not determined simply by the means of consumption needed to sustain them, but also by the amount and intensity of the labour they are compelled to perform. By increasing the amount or intensity of labour his workers perform, the individual capitalist is able to extract additional surplus-labour. If powerful enough, therefore, he can *vary* the amount of surplus-value his workers create. Thus, the term 'variable' draws attention to the fact that the surplus-value actually created varies according to the relative power of combatants within the production process.

These definitions are so simply and so clearly given by Marx, that it would seem impossible for anyone who has read the First Volume of *Capital*, to misunderstand them or fail to see their importance. Yet generations of economists, both Left and Right, have done just this. Such is the power of tradition over people's minds, a tradition that insists on reading Marx as though he were an English classical economist.

NOTES

1. For sophisticated expositions of Neo-classical theory, See K. Arrow and F. Hahn, *General Competitive Analysis*, Edinburgh 1971, and G. Debreu, *Theory of Value*, New York, 1959. For cruder versions, see C. Ferguson, *The Neo-Classical Theory of Production and Distribution*, Cambridge, 1969, or virtually any conventional economics textbook.

2. Debreu, *Theory of Value*, pp. 78–80.

3. See Gaston Bachelard, *La Formation de l'Esprit Scientifique*, Paris, 1938, especially Chapter 1.

4. *Theories of Surplus-Value*, Vol. III, London, 1972, p. 503.

5. For the classic statement of this view, see J. Hicks, *The Theory of Wages*, London, 1963, especially Chapter 11.

6. The major work of this school is, of course, P. Sraffa, *Production of Commodities by Means of Commodities*, Cambridge, 1960. A number of important cognate articles – in particular, P. Garegnani, 'Heterogeneous Capital, the Production Function and the Theory of Distribution'; L. Pasinetti, 'Switches in Technique and the "Rate of Return" in Capital Theory'; and J. Robinson, 'The Production Function and the Theory of Capital' – are reprinted in G. Harcourt and N. Laing, *Capital and Growth*,

or E. Hunt and J. Schwartz, *A Critique of Economic Theory*, both London, 1971.

7. The exchange value of any bundle of commodities depends on two factors: its physical composition and the price of each individual commodity in terms of the numéraire (money). In any comparison between two states of an economy, therefore, differences in the exchange value of capital or output may reflect either or both of these factors. Let us assume that an equal amount of labour is performed in the two states and that each state is, in the conventional technological sense, efficient. By comparing one state with the other, we can define the *marginal product of capital* as the difference in output divided by the difference in constant capital, where all magnitudes are reduced to a common standard by expressing them in current prices, i.e. in terms of their exchange-value relative to the numéraire commodity. It is clear that this marginal product will reflect, not only physical differences between the two states, but also differences in relative prices. The exchange value of capital, for example, may be higher in one state than another, not because its physical components are different, but because they have different prices. It is this shift in relative prices which accounts for the possible non-equality of the rate of interest and the marginal product, even when appropriate neo-classical assumptions are made. To get by this difficulty, neo-classical economists use a different definition of marginal product, and proceed as though relative prices in the two states were identical. As a device for micro, partial or efficiency analysis, this approach is acceptable. In the study of income distribution, however, it is not, and differences in relative prices between the two states must be taken into account. The role of relative prices in this context was first perceived by K. Wicksell, *Lectures on Political Economy*, Vol. I, London, 1934. For good discussions of the whole subject, see L. Metzler, 'The Rate of Interest and the Marginal Product of Capital', *Journal of Political Economy*, August 1950, pp. 289–306; and E. Malinvaud, 'Capital Accumulation and Efficient Allocation of Resources', *Econometrica*, Vol. 21, 1953, pp. 233–68.

8. Marx-Engels, *Selected Works in one Volume*, London, 1968, p. 226.

9. Both Garegnani and Pasinetti, in their above-cited essays (see note 6), base their rejection of supply and demand theories, including general equilibrium theory, on the fact that aggregate 'capital' may not be a continuous function of the rate of profit. It is not clear from their arguments, however, why supply and demand theories must necessarily depend upon such continuity. It is true that traditional aggregate theory required this kind of continuity, but no such assumption is made by general equilibrium theory, which allows for the possibility of aggregate capital being a discontinuous function of the rate of profit. Whatever its other failings, and they are many, general equilibrium theory is not open to this particular objection.

10. See Maurice Dobb, 'The Sraffa System and Critique of the Neo-Classical Theory of Distribution', *De Economist* 1970, pp. 347–62, reprinted in Hunt and Schwartz, *A Critique of Economic Theory*.

11. Marx-Engels, op. cit., p. 182.

12. *Capital*, Vol. I, Moscow, 1961, pp. 184–5.

13. K. Bharadwaj, 'Value through Exogenous Distribution', *Economic and Social Weekly*, Bombay, 24 August 1963, pp. 1450–4; reprinted in Harcourt and Laing, *Capital and Growth*.
14. See *Grundrisse*, Pelican/NLR edition, London, 1973, pp. 464–5.
15. *Capital*, Vol. I, p. 356.
16. Marx used the term 'merchant capital' in two different senses: sometimes to denote commercial capital in general, even when it operated under competitive conditions, and at other times to denote capital which made a profit by fraud or monopoly in the sphere of exchange. In this essay, the term is used in the second and more restricted sense.
17. *Capital*, Vol. I, p. 165.
18. *Capital*, Vol. I, p. 357.
19. *Capital*, Vol. I, p. 176.
20. *Theories of Surplus-Value*, Vol. II, Moscow, 1968, p. 406.
21. See the translation in *Theoretical Practice*, No. 5, 1972.
22. *Capital*, Vol. I, p. 536.
23. *Theories of Surplus-Value*, Vol. II, p. 400.
24. *Capital*, Vol. I, p. 333.

2

*Imperialism in the Seventies — Unity or Rivalry ?**

This essay will discuss the effects of recent economic trends on the unity of the imperialist bloc and on the autonomy of its constituent elements—the individual nations.[1] Three broad possibilities may be distinguished:

US super-imperialism in which all other capitalist states are dominated by the United States and have comparatively little freedom to choose their policies and control their economies in ways opposed by the American state. America acts as the organizer of world capitalism, preserving its unity in the face of socialism. This domination may not, of course, operate smoothly – for antagonisms will not be eliminated but merely contained.

Ultra-imperialism in which a dominant coalition of relatively autonomous imperialist states performs the organizing role necessary to preserve the unity of the system. For this to work the antagonisms between the members of the coalition must not be so severe that they overcome the interest they have in maintaining the coalition.

Imperial Rivalry in which the relatively autonomous states no longer perform the necessary organizing role, or perform it so badly that serious conflicts break out between them and the unity of the system is threatened. For this to happen the antagonisms between states must be severe.

Recent Marxist writers have been divided in their views on which of these three variants of imperialism is most likely. The majority, amongst whom are to be found Sweezy, Magdoff, Jalée and Nicolaus, believe that the United States is not only the dominant imperial power today, but that it will become increasingly dominant in the future.[2] Their argument runs, with variations, roughly as follows. American firms are much bigger, more advanced and faster growing than their foreign rivals.

* First published in *New Left Review*, September–October, 1971.

They are using this strength to take over key sectors of European industry, and are using American state power to force their way into Japan. Eventually American firms will dominate the economies of Europe and Japan, and, as a result, large sections of the national bourgeoisies of these countries will be denationalized, becoming objectively – if not subjectively – representatives of American capital. Moreover, European and Japanese capital surviving this process will be weak and completely subordinate to American capital. Even today, they argue, a coalition of dominant American and subordinate foreign capital is creating a unified imperialism under the hegemony of the United States and the contradictions between national capitalisms are becoming of increasingly little significance. The significant contradiction is more and more between a unified imperialism and the 'third-world'. These writers have been criticized, in my opinion fairly, as 'third worldists' by Ernest Mandel. For convenience I shall also use this term.

On the opposite side stand Mandel and perhaps Kidron, who believe that the hegemony of the United States is being challenged by the Europeans and the Japanese.[3] Mandel argues as follows. A combination of mergers, accumulation and rationalization is destroying the size advantage of American firms, and as a result non-American productivity levels are catching up with those of the Americans. The formation of a supranational state in Europe would speed up this process considerably, but even in the absence of such a state the Europeans are closing the gap. Since non-American wages are much lower than American wages, increases in productivity could make goods produced in Europe and Japan so cheap that exports from these countries could flood American markets, creating severe contradictions within that country as American capitalists try to hold down wages in an attempt to stem this flood. Moreover, American penetration of Europe or Japan has by no means reached the point where the bourgeoisies of these countries have been denationalized. National states still defend the interests of national capital. Neither Europe or Japan are anywhere near to being neo-colonies. As the struggle for world markets intensifies there will be increasing conflict between nation states as they attempt to defend their respective firms. In particular, the non-Americans will come into conflict with the

Americans. Indeed the European states may even form an alliance or perhaps a supranational state to enable them to stand up to the Americans on equal or near equal terms. Internally, within the non-American nations, contradictions will become increasingly severe as states try to hold down wages to enable their firms to compete more effectively. Thus Mandel's view is of an imperialism increasingly racked by internal contradictions, although he does not believe these will be severe enough to break out into wars. The need to defend the system as a whole will be too great to allow this to happen.

Somewhere in between these two poles hovers the Soviet economist Varga who, appealing to the law of unequal development, argues that European and Japanese capital will break the hegemony of American capital, and that the United States will be forced to share its leadership of the imperialist world.[4] Antagonisms between national capitals, however, will be of comparatively little importance in determining the future of the imperialist system. They will be adequately, if not smoothly, contained by the rapidly proliferating supranational institutions, whose aim is both to resolve the economic antagonisms between national capitals and to preserve the unity of imperialism against the challenge posed to it by the revolutionary movements of the third world. Apart from his notion that the leadership of imperialism will be shared by a number of states, Varga's ultra-imperialism does not differ greatly in content from the super-imperialism of the third-worldists.

Points of Difference

It is clear that there are three central issues on which the various schools of thought differ: 1. the relative strength of US capital and the related question of the degree to which it can dominate Europe and Japan by capturing most key industrial sectors; 2. the severity and nature of the antagonisms between different national capitals; 3. the extent to which the common fear of socialism can overcome those antagonisms which do exist.

It is impossible in the space of this article to discuss in depth all of these points of difference. On the third, I shall content myself with the following observations. The degree to which the common fear of socialism can overcome antagonisms depends

on the nature and severity of these antagonisms, and the extent
to which states perceive that in pursuing the interests of their
national capitals they are putting the entire system in jeopardy.
China and Eastern Europe would never have been invaded if the
Japanese and German imperialists had realized that the outcome would not be the colonization of these areas but their
detachment from the imperialist system as a whole. To ascribe
this myopia to madness, as does Varga when he says that
capitalism will no longer be dominated by madmen like Hitler,
is to ignore the objective conditions which determine whether
or not 'madmen' are in control. Amongst these objective
conditions must be counted the nature and extent of the
antagonisms between national capitals. A high degree of
antagonism may induce a high degree of myopia. Indeed this
may even be 'structural' myopia in the sense that those
concerned may individually understand what is happening but
be powerless to prevent it. We do not, of course, need to take
such an extreme example as that of imperialism and war. The
system may put in jeopardy by contradictions between capital
and labour within the imperial countries, contradictions
brought to explosion-point by antagonisms between national
capitals. A crisis caused by the collapse of the international
monetary system might, for example, lead to a socialist
revolution in Italy or France. So might competitive attempts by
the imperialist states to contain inflation, attempts which had
their roots not in a contradiction between imperialism and the
third world but in antagonisms between national capitals.
Rather than pursue such an obvious, if neglected, line of
argument, let us pass on the remaining two questions at issue.

The Strength of US Capital

The relative strength of US capital and its advantages in the
struggle for world markets have been greatly exaggerated by the
'third-worldists'.

First, although Americans firms are still, on average, larger
than their foreign rivals, mergers, takeovers and high rates of
accumulation in Europe and Japan have done much to close this
gap. In many industries such as chemicals, machinery, oil or
steel the differences in size have ceased or are rapidly ceasing to
be significant. In others, such as computers or automobiles, the

differences are still significant, although in most cases they are being lessened by the continued concentration and centralization of capital in Europe and Japan. Indeed, if the Common Market, with or without Britain, can develop a common company law facilitating mergers between European firms of different nationalities, all but a few of the existing inequalities in size will be eliminated or reduced to the point where they no longer matter.

Secondly, although it is true that American firms are the leading innovators and have monopolies or near-monopolies in the production of many advanced or 'modern' products, the third-worldists' almost exclusive focus on these products and the research and development expenditures associated with them is seriously misleading. It ignores both the temporary nature of technological monopolies and the faster growth of European and Japanese capital in products other than the most advanced. As leaders, American firms must spend enormous amounts making mistakes which others can avoid and discovering things which others can imitate or adapt cheaply. Within a few years of their introduction, 'modern' products in which the Americans initially have a monopoly become 'traditional' and are produced efficiently and in bulk by European and Japanese firms. To maintain their lead, therefore, or to prevent it being eroded too rapidly, American firms are forced to spend far more on research and development than their rivals overseas. This is the price they pay for being leaders.

As the gap between the Americans and the non-Americans closes, the scope for catching-up will, of course, diminish and the non-Americans will be increasingly forced to become innovators themselves and competition will become increasingly centred on advanced products. Indeed the growing chorus of demands in Europe and Japan for technological cooperation and for more state expenditure on research and development suggests that this is already happening, and that non-American capital is preparing to challenge the Americans in areas where they have, until now, reigned supreme. It is quite wrong, therefore, to see these demands as evidence of a desperate last-ditch attempt on the part of weakening European and Japanese capitals to resist 'technological colonization' by the Americans. Their growing need to become innovators themselves and not merely imitators is a direct consequence of their past dynamism and the increasing sophistication of both their markets and products. If the European and Japanese challenges fail these firms will, of course, be compelled to tail along behind the Americans. However, their failure is by no means a foregone conclusion, as the third-worldists seem to believe. On the contrary, the growing strength of European and Japanese capital, caused by mergers and accumulation, together with the growing size and sophistication of their markets, suggests that they will be able to mount an effective challenge in most, if not all, advanced products.

Finally, the third-worldists have over-emphasized the offensive aspects of American direct investment overseas and under-emphasized its defensive aspects. With the exception of a brief period in the late sixties, when the United States experienced a boom at the same time as Germany experienced a recession, continental Europe has grown substantially faster than the United States during the last two decades. Japan has grown even faster than continental Europe, its GNP rising from one twentieth of the American GNP in 1953 to nearly one sixth in 1968. This growth has affected American firms in two ways. On the one hand, growing markets overseas have offered them the chance to expand overseas, often in products for which American demand has begun to level out as domestic markets become saturated. On the other hand, growth of overseas economies has enabled many foreign firms to strengthen themselves to the point where they have begun to threaten the world position of American giants. American investment in Europe and other areas can only be appreciated if both these aspects of non-American growth are taken into account. In addition to increasing the sales of American firms, overseas investment has served to frustrate foreign competition and preserve American monopolies. If American firms had not taken over actual or potential foreign rivals and established subsidiaries overseas, they would have been forced to rely upon exports – not a very effective means of penetrating foreign markets – and today would be faced with an even greater foreign challenge.

Despite their phenomenal expansion overseas, however, big American firms are having and will have increasing difficulty in keeping ahead of their foreign rivals. The fast growth of

American firms in the late sixties was based largely on an accelerated growth of the US economy and a rapid increase in the level of concentration in that economy, neither of which is likely to last. The US economy is once again stagnating and American giants will experience increasing difficulty in raising their share of the domestic economy. Thus, viewed in a longer perspective, the cause of the American invasion of Europe must be seen as the erosion of a previously impregnable position. So long as they were absolutely superior, American firms could rely mainly on exports, and could regard European and Japanese recovery with a certain indulgence. With European and Japanese recovery, however, the firms of these countries have become dangerous challengers and American firms are forced to invest overseas for their own defence. Hence their massive investment in Europe and their increasing pressure on Japan to allow the entry of foreign capital. So much for the supposedly overwhelming and increasing superiority of American capital. Let us now turn to the question of antagonisms.

Antagonisms

Relations between capitals are always to some extent antagonistic, the degree of antagonism depending both on the area of actual or potential competition and on its intensity. Thus, in the present case, where we are concerned with relations between capitals of different nationalities, it is important to know: 1. over what areas the firms of North America, Europe and Japan are or will be in competition with each other; 2. what form this competition will take – will, for example, Continental and Japanese capitals create or at least attempt to create international firms of their own or will they rely mainly on exports as a means of penetrating foreign markets? To answer these questions, let us begin by discussing international trade and investment.

1. International Trade and Investment

The post-war economic growth of advanced capitalist countries has been accompanied by an increasing dependence on international trade as both imports and exports have risen considerably faster than output. Much of this increase has consisted of manufactured goods either sold to or imported from other advanced capitalist countries. As a result, trade within the advanced capitalist bloc is now three times as large as between this bloc and the rest of the world, and exports account for a significant proportion of the output of many manufacturing firms.

Exports have not, however, been the only way in which firms, particularly big firms, have penetrated foreign markets. Direct investment, whereby firms establish and operate production and distribution facilities overseas, has played an important role in the penetration of foreign markets by the firms of at least five countries – Britain, the United States, the Netherlands, Canada and Switzerland. Indeed it has been more important than exports in the case of Britain and the United States. Between 1957 and 1965 direct investment accounted for five-sixths and three-fifths respectively of the overseas expansion of the average American and British manufacturing firm (see Table 1).

TABLE 1

Expansion Overseas of Manufacturing Firms, 1957–65

percentage of sales increase accounted for by:

	Exports	*Overseas production*	*Overseas sales*
US	2	13	15
UK	12	20	32
France	6	1	7
Germany	14	2	16
Italy	24	5	30
Netherlands	27	17	43
Canada	33	13	46
Japan	17	2	20

Source: Robert Rowthorn, *International Big Business* 1957–67, CUP 1971, Table 22.

Moreover, since big firms account for the bulk of overseas investment, the proportions given in Table 1, which reflect the experience of the *average* firm, understate the extent to which big firms in the major investing countries rely on overseas production for their expansion. For these firms, overseas investment has become the characteristic means of serving important markets. Exports are reserved for lesser markets or products for which overseas demand is not yet large enough to justify local production. For the firms of the remaining countries, such as France, Italy, Germany and Japan, overseas investment has not until recently played a significant role in the penetration of foreign markets. Even the big firms have relied mainly on exports.

Overseas investment has enabled the firms of certain countries to establish powerful and sometimes dominant positions in foreign markets, even where their export performance has been poor. Indeed, it is only by looking at overseas production as well as exports that one gets an idea of the penetration of American or British firms into such areas as Europe, South Africa, Australia or Canada.

The role of investment becomes particularly clear when one examines the economic relations between the United States and other advanced capitalist countries. In 1966 American exports to Europe were not much different from European exports to the United States (see Table 2). American penetration of European markets by means of exports was thus more or less

TABLE 2

Exports and Local Production ($ millions)

	X	P	P/X	X	P	P/X
Out of US	1957			1966		
Europe	6,940	10,762	1·55	14,440	36,000	2·50
Japan	1,851	555	0·30	3,545	2,000	0·62
Into US	1959			1966		
UK, Netherlands, & Switzerland	2,320	4,657	2·01	3,740	7,400	1·97
Other Europe	4,580	559	0·12	8,050	1,271	0·16
—France	690	92	0·13	1,050	123	0·12
—Germany	1,380	47	0·03	2,700	138	0·05
Japan	1,543	29	0·02	4,444	50	0·01

Source: For European figures see R. E. Rowthorn and S. Hymer in C. P. Kindleberger, The International Corporation (Harvard University Press, 1970). Japanese figures have been calculated in the same way.

Definitions:

X = exports
P = manufacturing and petroleum sales of local subsidiaries.

matched by European penetration of American markets by means of exports. When we look at investment, however, the situation is quite different. The sales of American manufacturing and petroleum affiliates in Europe were equal to approximately $36,000 millions, a figure which is two and a half times as large as the total value of all American exports to Europe including food and raw materials. The sales of European manufacturing and petroleum affiliates in America were, by contrast, fairly small, being equal to less than $9,000 million, which is considerably less than the value of European exports to America, and less than one quarter of the sales of American affiliates in Europe. As a result of this imbalanced investment the total sales of American firms in Europe, including both exports and local production, were two and a half times the total sales of European firms in the United States. In absolute terms this meant that American firms extended their markets by a *net* amount of around $30,000 millions, i.e. US sales in Europe exceeded European sales in United States by this amount.

A more detailed breakdown of the figures by country would reveal wide variations in the degree to which American penetration of particular foreign markets had been matched by non-American penetration of the American markets. British, Dutch and Swiss firms have invested heavily in the United States and their affiliates account for the bulk of European production in that country. Indeed the Netherlands and Switzerland have positive investment balances with the United States, with the result that Swiss and Dutch firms actually sell more in the United States than American firms sell in Switzerland and the Netherlands. Other European countries such as France, Germany or Italy have not invested much in the United States, and American sales in these countries are considerably greater than the sales of their firms in the United States.

Turning now to Japan, we find a completely different picture. Foreign investment in Japan has been restricted and until recently Japanese firms did not invest much overseas. Moreover, trade with the United States is *roughly* balanced, just as it is in the case of the Europeans. Indeed, Japan exports slightly more to the United States than the United States exports to Japan. The result of this combination – roughly balanced trade and little investment – has been that American firms have not been able to penetrate Japanese markets to any great extent, and what gains they have made have been more or less offset by Japanese gains in American markets.

The significance of overseas investment in international competition goes far beyond the example we have just been discussing. An examination would reveal:

(i) Trade in manufactures between industrialized capitalist countries is usually in rough balance. Collectively, the manufacturing firms of each of these countries lost about as much of their domestic markets to foreign imports as they gain by exporting to other industrialized capitalist countries. Only in trade with underdeveloped and other resource-producing countries do industrialized countries have substantial surpluses in manufactures.

(ii) Overseas investment is becoming the most effective means of penetrating the world's major markets. It is becoming increasingly important both as a means of defending existing markets and of capturing new ones.

(iii) Direct investment, unlike trade, is often highly unbalanced. Britain, the United States, the Netherlands and Switzerland have invested far more overseas than foreign firms have invested in these countries. As a result, their big firms have made considerable net gains, capturing markets overseas without sacrificing an equivalent amount of home markets in return.

If Lenin's words were something of an exaggeration when he wrote them in 1916, they have become true today: 'Under the old capitalism when free competition prevailed, the export of *goods* was the most typical feature. Under modern capitalism, when monopolies prevail, the export of *capital* has become the typical feature.'[5]

2. European and Japanese Capital

A well-established, if not so well understood, feature of capitalism is the tendency for capital to expand outwards and seek new markets overseas. Since European and Japanese firms are manifestly not exceptions to this rule, it follows from the above conclusion regarding the role of direct investment in overseas expansion that these firms will be forced to rely increasingly on overseas investment if their objectives are to be attained.

As well as what might be called the universal reasons for overseas expansion, however, European firms have an added reason in the form of an already massive American investment in Europe. As we have shown above, this investment has enabled American manufacturing and petroleum firms to penetrate European markets to such an extent that their sales in Europe exceeded European sales in the United States by $30,000 millions a year in 1966. Clearly, American firms derive a considerable advantage from this net penetration of European markets and to eliminate or greatly reduce the deficit will be one of the future objectives of European big capital.

The deficit can, in principle, be tackled in one of two ways: *defensively* by reducing the size and growth of American sales in Europe, or *offensively* by increasing European sales abroad, both in the United States and elsewhere. Since American capital is already well-established in Europe, a defensive approach would have to based on drastic state intervention if it were to have any real effect. The result would be a confrontation with America on a scale which, for obvious reasons, European capital wants to avoid; although, as we suggest below, such a confrontation may eventually come about if America protects its domestic capital against the incursion of European and other foreign capital. We can assume, however, that European capital will not initiate such a confrontation and that, until the American state initiates it, American firms will be allowed to operate fairly freely in Europe. In so far as European capital attempts to reduce the American advantage it will adopt, therefore, an offensive approach and counter-attack overseas either by exporting more or by establishing more overseas subsidiaries.

Exports cannot, however, provide anything like the necessary increase in overseas sales. Quite apart from what might be called the micro-reason of rising European wage costs (see Table 5 below), there is a crucial macro-reason relating to the equilibrium of the world monetary system. Annual European *exports* would have to increase by a gigantic amount, $20,000 millions to $30,000 millions over and above any offsetting increase in *imports*.

Europe as a whole would have, therefore, to run massive currrent account surpluses with the rest of the world. Moreover, since the bulk of non-European purchasing power is located in America, a large proportion of the extra exports would have to be bought by that country, and America would have to run massive current account deficits. Thus, if the Europeans were successful in their export drive, the result would be European surpluses and American deficits of unprecedented magnitude, qualitatively larger than the surpluses and deficits which have plagued the capitalist world during the last few years. Within a short time either the world monetary system would collapse and with it trade, or else a major realignment of currencies, in which some were revalued and others devalued, would take place, thereby destroying the cost advantage of European firms and restoring the equilibrium of the world monetary system. In other words, the very success of the export drive, by creating huge surpluses and deficits, would undermine the conditions which made it successful. This argument, it should be noted, applies quite generally to the question of overseas expansion by means of exports. Any country which exports so successfully that it obtains massive surpluses tends to undermine the conditions of its own success.

It seems then that a defensive approach, although technically possible, would do more harm than good to European firms and that an offensive approach based on exports could not provide surpluses large enough to compensate for more than a small proportion of the enormous American sales in Europe. Only by investing heavily overseas, establishing production facilities in other countries, could European firms hope to compensate for losses to American firms in Europe.

Thus for both general reasons relating to the outward expansion of capital and particular reasons relating to the already massive American stake in Europe, European firms must invest heavily overseas. For the same general reasons Japanese firms will have to follow suit. As yet, however, the incentive for the latter to do so is not quite so great, for they have managed to pursue a successful defensive strategy in which the operation of American capital in Japan has been severely circumscribed. American pressure is, however, causing Japan to relax some of its restrictions and, should the stage be reached where American capital has more or less free entry into Japan, Japanese firms will be forced to adopt an offensive strategy which seeks to compensate for domestic losses by investing overseas.

It is important to notice that any compensation for American sales in Europe must come about through sales outside of Europe. If, for example, the manufacturing firms of one European country increase their sales in another European country, the gains of the firms of the first country are exactly cancelled by the losses of those of the second. Taking in each other's washing in this way, whether its other vices or virtues, does nothing to compensate for the American presence in Europe. If American firms succeed in penetrating the Japanese economy, then collectively European and Japanese firms will only be able to compensate for American penetration by expanding into areas other than Europe or Japan. Since the bulk of the world's markets outside of these two areas are to be found in America, any substantial improvement in the net position of European and Japanese firms would imply a massive penetration of American markets. Thus an offensive strategy, which aimed to compensate for a large part of the American gains in Europe and perhaps one day Japan, would entail massive expansion into American markets, which could only come about through direct investment.

The overseas expansion of Continental and Japanese firms by means of direct investment has, in fact, already begun. The overseas investment of German, Italian and Japanese firms has increased dramatically in recent years (see Table 3). Between them these three countries invested an average of $230 millions a year during 1957–60. By 1961–4 the figure had risen to $480 millions a year, in 1967 it was $600 millions, and by 1968 it had reached $840 millions. Between them these three countries invested as much overseas as Britain in 1968. Germany provides the most striking case. After rising steadily for the last few years, German direct investment overseas was substantially more in 1969 than foreign direct investment in Germany.

These are, however, no more than signs. Annual American direct investment overseas is still far greater than that of Japan and the major Continental countries combined. Moreover, much of their investment is going to countries other than the United States, so that exports still provide their main way of penetrating American markets.

The question is, therefore, whether European and Japanese direct investment overseas will continue to grow rapidly and whether much of it will be directed towards the United States? Before attempting to answer this question, it is necessary to

TABLE 3

Direct Investment Overseas ($ billions)

	1957–60	1961–64	1967	1968
USA	2·83	3·21	3·15	3·03
UK	0·51	0·67	0·74	0·89
Subtotal	3·34	3·88	3·89	3·92
Germany	0·12	0·22	0·25	0·39
Italy	0·06	0·17	0·23	0·23
Japan	0·05	0·09	0·12	0·22
Subtotal	0·23	0·48	0·60	0·84
Belgium	—	—	0·05	0·03
France	0·01	0·10	0·20	—
Netherlands	0·71	0·12	0·21	0·22
Canada	0·06	0·10	0·08	0·16

Sources: IMF, OECD.

make clear at what level the response will be cast. A complete answer could take into account a whole range of political and other factors, such as the reaction of the American state to heavy foreign investment in the United States. Since, however, it is part of our aim to understand the forces which may lead the American state to act against foreign capital, we shall assume that the existing liberal policies are maintained. This will enable us to understand the economic tendencies at work within the current situation, although it will not, of course, tell us the extent to which these tendencies will be realized in practice.

The problem has both macro and micro aspects. On a macro level, if Europe and Japan are to finance heavy overseas investment, they must be able to guarantee a substantial surplus somewhere else in the balance of payments. Only a world banker such as America (or, at one time, Britain) can finance direct investment overseas by accumulating short-term and portfolio liabilities. During the last few years such a surplus has appeared. Between them Germany, Italy and Japan now have on current account alone a surplus of over $6,000 million dollars a year (see Table 4). This is over twice the annual net

TABLE 4

Current Account Balances ($ millions)[1]

	1966	1967	1968	1969
Japan	1,254	−190	1,048	2,185
Germany	119	2,464	2,838	1,770
Italy	2,117	1,599	2,627	2,368
Total	3,490	3,873	6,513	6,323

For comparison

Net US Direct Investment Abroad[2]	−3,639	−3,154	−3,025	−3,060

Source: OECD.

Notes: 1. − indicates deficit.
2. − indicates a net outflow of US direct investment.

direct investment overseas of all American firms combined. Thus if only half of the European and Japanese surplus was channelled into direct investment, the firms of these countries would invest overseas as much as American firms. So far, however, this has not happened. The surplus has instead been devoted to the accumulation of short-term dollar liabilities and gold, and the purchase of American securities. Indeed, European holdings of American corporate stocks alone now stand at $13,000 millions (1968) and are almost enough to offset the enormous American direct investments in Europe. To understand how this situation has arisen we must look at the problem on a micro-level. Until fairly recently there were two reasons why Continental or Japanese firms did not invest very much overseas, and relied mainly on exports to serve foreign markets. First, wage costs were lower at home than in many other countries, in particular than in the United States. Although these were partially offset by the higher cost of capital goods, it was still cheaper to produce at home. A survey conducted amongst American firms on behalf of the National Industrial Conference Board, for example, revealed that for the year 1960 costs in the European Common Market were only about 0·85 of costs in the United States.[6] Secondly, to invest overseas a firm must be able to establish an efficient-sized plant and must be able to sell the output of that plant. To build or buy a large plant may be very expensive, and to be sure of selling its products the firm must either have already built up a market by exporting or must have the funds to finance a costly programme of sales promotion and to cover the losses incurred whilst demand for its products grows. Until a few years ago, all but a few Continental and Japanese giants were unable to command the necessary funds, hence had not penetrated overseas markets to any great extent. As a result, they had no alternative but to export when they could and forgo markets when they could not. Moreover by exporting these firms could exploit cheap labour and economies of scale at home, whereas by producing overseas, particularly in North America, they would have been compelled to pay high wages and would have been unable to exploit economies of scale.

In recent years, however, the situation has begun to change. Money wage costs in Europe and Japan are rising rapidly (see Table 5 below), so that the advantage of cheap labour is being lost. Continental and Japanese firms have established markets for many of their products by exporting. Mergers and high rates of accumulation have strengthened them to the point where many can now afford to build efficient-sized plants overseas and can finance the promotion of their products where necessary.

The notion of an efficient-sized plant depends not only on technical conditions but also on the scale of production of rival firms. In a small economy like Australia, for example, a firm may be able to operate quite happily with a scale one-fifth, one-tenth, or even less of what would be necessary for survival in the United States. Thus initially the growing ability of Continental and Japanese firms to finance overseas investment will manifest itself, indeed is already manifesting itself, in an expansion into areas other than the United States. As the process of merger, rationalization and accumulation continues, however, it is inevitable that these firms will turn increasingly to the United States itself. To help them they may have state aid, disguised wherever possible to prevent American retaliation. If international mergers such as that between Dunlop and Pirelli become the fashion, European investment in America will take place on an enormous scale. Similarly, if Japanese industry consolidates still further and the Japanese economy continues growing at its present rate, Japanese firms will invest heavily both in the United States and elsewhere.

We may sum up this argument by saying that rising costs at home, greater strength, and established overseas markets for European and Japanese products are all combining to make the big firms of these countries move towards investment as the most effective way of penetrating foreign markets, both in America and elsewhere. European-wide mergers would accelerate this process but it will occur even without them. This does not, of course apply to all products or all firms. It is likely that we shall see both a more intensive export drive by some firms, particularly those too small to invest, and a massive investment drive by others.

This discussion has been concerned with manufacturing firms. For obvious strategic and economic reasons, however, a similar growth of non-American investment overseas will occur in the field of natural resources. Indeed, it is already beginning.

3. Conclusions

The above discusson, although by no means definitive, points to the following conclusions:

(i) European and Japanese capital is strong enough not only to fight back against American capital but also to counter-attack by expanding overseas.

(ii) The overseas expansion of big European and Japanese firms will increasingly take the form of direct investment in other countries, including the United States itself. Exports will, however, continue to be important both for small firms and certain products.

(iii) Continent-wide mergers in Europe and further consolidation in Japan would accelerate the process considerably and enable the firms of these countries to invest overseas on an enormous scale.

These conclusions, it will be noticed, are broadly similar to those of Ernest Mandel, who stresses the growing challenge of European and Japanese capital to American hegemony. One important difference, however, lies in the emphasis given here to direct investment by the Europeans and Japanese, in contrast to Mandel's emphasis on exports. Mandel's view on this subject are discussed below, in the Appendix.

Capital and the Nation State

Before discussing what the above conclusions imply about the future development of the capitalist system, it will be helpful to discuss the relationship between the strength of capital and the autonomy of a state *vis-à-vis* other states. All of the writers mentioned above, no matter whether they believe in US super-imperialism, ultra-imperialism or imperial rivalry, take for granted that the autonomy of a nation state is determined by the strength of capital based on that nation – i.e. that a state with strong capital is autonomous and that one with weak capital is subordinate. Thus, those who believe that American capital is overwhelmingly stronger than European or Japanese capital see Europe and Japan being and remaining subordinate to the United States, and, conversely, those who believe that European and Japanese capital is challenging American capital see Europe and Japan becoming increasingly autonomous. In reality, however, things are not so simple; for although strength and autonomy are related to each other, there is no one-to-one correspondence between the strength of capital and the autonomy of the state.

British *big* capital is still among the strongest in the world. Of the 100 largest businesses in the world 11 are British, compared with 18 for the EEC as a whole; of the 200 largest non-American companies 53 were British at the end of the sixties, compared with 43 Japanese, 25 German and 23 French.[7] British companies have always operated on a global scale and are flanked by a major banking and financial centre in the City. Yet the British *state* has not aggressively pursued the interests of a specifically British capitalism. The economic policies of British governments have, on the contrary, been highly sensitive to the advice of the international institutions of the capitalist world and of the largest imperialist power, the United States. The policies adopted by British governments during the recurrent balance of payments crises were, in fact, quite different from those which would have been pursued by a more independent capitalist state and have aggravated the stagnation of British capitalism. Paradoxically the weakness of the British state is to be explained not by the simple decline of British capitalism as such, but by the very *strength* of the cosmopolitan activities of British capital, which has helped to undermine further its strictly domestic economy. British big capital has always had a major international dimension and the conditions of the post-war world led to an *accentuation* rather than modification of this pattern. While capital in Europe and Japan had less experience and few facilities for direct investment overseas, combined with great opportunities in a rapidly growing home economy, British big capital found itself with unexciting domestic prospects but a plethora of overseas opportunities and contacts. The relative decline of the home-base of British capitalism was thus reinforced and the relative independence of the British state further undercut. Between them, these trends – the international expansion of British big capital coupled with the contraction of the British state and the domestic economic base of British capitalism – have led to a situation where many British companies now conduct a large part of their business in areas where the British state exercise no control and little influence, and where it can offer them little or no protection. As a result both they and British capitalism generally become extremely vulnerable to retaliation should Britain follow economic policies not to the liking of other imperialist powers.

Coherent policies for advancing the indigenous interests of British capitalism would in the last decades have entailed such measures as import controls, severe restrictions on overseas investment and the freezing of certain sterling balances. Each of these would have in turn inhibited the international operations of British firms, either by interfering with their ability to move capital freely across frontiers and perhaps denying them the funds necessary for investment, or else by provoking retaliation on the part of other capitalist states. In return, British companies would have been offered the benefits of growth in their home economy. However, the dubious and difficult prospects of growth in the single domestic market could not match those of expansion into varied overseas markets. Thus as the British economy became more integrated into a global capitalism over which the British state had no control, it became increasingly vulnerable internationally and the potential benefits to big capital of a straightforwardly aggressive nationalist development dwindled accordingly. Thus, faced with the threat of massive losses in their foreign business in exchange for doubtful gains in their domestic business, those sections of British capital which operate internationally, and

this includes the bulk of finance capital and many large industrial companies, have opposed the measures necessary for dyna-
mizing British capitalism, preferring – if not actually liking – the
alternative of stagnation and deflation in response to the
demands of the other imperial powers.

Thus, leading sections of the British bourgeoisie have been
effectively 'denationalized', not through their own weakness but
through the weakness of the British state and their own home
base. The overseas strength of British *capital* has compounded
the debility of British *capitalism*. If the dominant British
corporations had been smaller they would not have been able to
expand overseas to anything like the same extent. Overseas
production and international finance would now account for a
far less important part of their income, British companies and
the British economy would be less vulnerable to retaliation,
and, as a result, the benefits and possibilities of domestic growth
would be much greater. Alternatively, if the British state and the
domestic British economy had retained their former power,
foreign retaliation would be far less likely and attempts to
stimulate and restructure the domestic economy would not
jeopardize the international operations of British firms. British
firms would not then have to choose between domestic and
overseas expansion. They could have both. *If the discussion of
Europe and Japan above showed that there are inherent limits to
expansion solely through exports, the British case demonstrates the perils
of expansion via direct investment unsustained by a sufficiently strong
sponsoring state and home base.*

Perspectives

Let us now return to the prospects for the European Economic
Community and Japan. As European and Japanese firms
expand overseas, they will increasingly threaten the position of
American firms, both in the United States and elsewhere.
Initially the American state is likely to respond to this threat,
indeed is already responding, by restricting certain kinds of
imports, aiding domestically controlled firms and attempting to
obtain or maintain American privileges in overseas markets. If
these measures prove inadequate, as they probably will in the
face of heavy European and Japanese investment, the American
state will be tempted to restrict the operations of foreign capital

in the United States, and where possible persuade its more dependent allies to do the same.

Thus, as non-American capital counter-attacks, the American state will intervene more vigorously on behalf of American capital. To penetrate the United States and other areas under its hegemony non-American capital will, therefore, be forced to rely increasingly on the use of its own state power: financial and technological support to lower costs of production and to provide the funds for expansion; economic or even military inducements to weaken America's grip on its satellites; and, finally, counter-threats against American capital in Europe. If these measures fail, European and Japanese expansion in the United States and its satellites will be severely hampered, and European and Japanese capital will be forced to operate mainly outside the US sphere of influence. Thus, the medium-term prospect is one of increasing intervention by the American state in the face of a growing non-American challenge, threatened or actual retaliation by non-American states, and perhaps a partial reversal of existing tendencies towards interpenetration as the capitalist world fragments into more self-contained regions.

The extent to which the American state can be deterred from intervening on behalf of American capital depends on the extent to which non-American states are able to act in a concerted fashion and to form effective alliances. A European bloc, for example, embracing virtually the whole of Western Europe would have tremendous bargaining power with the United States. With sales in Europe of over $60,000 million a year, American subsidiaries would be extremely vulnerable to retaliatory action by the combined European powers in the event of a conflict with the United States, and at the present time the loss of a substantial proportion of these sales would far outweigh the benefits to American firms of vigorous state intervention on their behalf. Thus, although not enough to guarantee that America would continue to follow liberal policies, the threat of retaliation by the combined European powers would, in the short run, be enough to guarantee the existence of a powerful liberal lobby in the United States. In the medium run, however, the formation of a European bloc would have the opposite effect, for by facilitating European-wide mergers and mobilizing massive state resources on behalf of European firms, this bloc would so strengthen European capital that it could expand overseas on an enormous scale, both into the United States and elsewhere. Before long the Europeans would pose such a serious threat to the operations of American firms in Latin America, Canada, Australia, the Middle East and even the United States itself that many firms of formerly liberal views would be forced to call upon the American state to defend their interests in these areas, even if the price of such defence was a restriction of their activities in Europe. Thus, although in the short run the formation of a European bloc might deter the American state from acting too vigorously on behalf of American capital, in the medium run it would have the opposite effect and would only serve to intensify the pressures for state action.

It is clear from the above discussion that the ability of firms to compete internationally, both in capturing new markets and sources of supply and in defending existing ones, will come to depend increasingly on the use of state power. If, for one reason or another, the state power available to capital is nowhere near commensurate with its needs, then not only will this capital be at a serious disadvantage in world competition, but even the state power it does command will not be exploited to the full for fear of provoking retaliatory action by other states.

To overcome this disability there are several obvious courses of action. The state concerned can ally itself or even merge with other states, thereby placing greater state power at the disposal of its capital. Britain's application to join the Common Market, for example, is intended to serve both of these objectives. British capital, being highly international in its operation and perspectives, needs a greater state power than Britain alone can provide, and at the same time is frightened that, if Britain remains outside the Common Market, the state power of continental countries will be used against it. Alternatively, failing an alliance or merger of states, capital can change its nationality. For example, provided the British state agreed, certain British firms operating mainly within the US sphere of influence might change their nationality and become American. Under certain circumstances even the agreement of the British state would be unnecessary.

These two courses of action are not, of course, mutually exclusive. Indeed alliances may actually facilitate changes of nationality. Within the Common Market, for example, it may become relatively easy for say a French firm to merge with a German firm and gradually shift the balance of its activities and eventually its headquarters into Germany, becoming thereby effectively and one day legally German. Given a merger between states, on the other hand, the situation is less simple, for then all capitals adopt the 'nationality' of the new unit. This change will not however, affect the original nations and national capitals equally and the degree to which it can be considered a true change of nationality will vary from country to country.

Although changes of nationality may eventually turn out to be important, alliances or mergers of states are likely to be of more immediate significance in view of the growing unity of the Common Market and Britain's application for membership. At its widest, an extended Common Market might cover virtually the whole of Western Europe, and, at its most complete, so many basic economic and military decisions would be irreversibly centralized that the resulting 'United Europe' would be a single nation. As well as increasing considerably the state power at the disposal of European capital, this unification would have the effect of 'renationalizing' the operations of many European firms and of giving them a much greater interest in the health of the newly created 'home' economy. All West European markets would be brought under the control of what amounted to a single state power, and, from the point of view of European firms, many formerly overseas markets, i.e. those located in other European countries, would become home markets. Many firms which were previously international under the old system of separate European states would become 'national' under the new system – most of their production and sales would be located within the 'national' boundaries of a United Europe. As a result, these firms would have a strong interest in a fast-growing 'national' economy, even where the price of this growth was conflict with America or some other capitalist state. This does not imply, of course, that all of these firms would have a corresponding interest in their growth of their original national economies. On the contrary, capital based on the more backward areas of Europe or those where the working class was particularly militant would migrate to more prosperous or more congenial parts of Europe, with possibly disastrous consequences for the areas left behind.

Since European big capital would depend closely on the health of the West European economy and would derive considerable benefits from the use of European state power, it would act as a 'nationalist' force, supporting an autonomous economic development for Western Europe and relying on the use of state power overseas. The relationship of European capital to the European 'state' would be much the same as that of American capital to the American state and this European state would, therefore, be autonomous *vis-à-vis* other states and would act vigorously on behalf of its own capital when necessary. Thus, a United Europe would constitute what, for want of a better name, we may call an 'imperialist metropolis', i.e. it would be autonomous and imperialist.

It is not necessary to assume such an all-embracing West European unity in order to deduce the existence of imperialist metropolises other than the United States. If the existing Common Market unified to the point where crucial economic and military decisions were irreversibly centralized, then capital would have much the same relationship to the 'state' as we observed in the case of a United Europe, and the Common Market would constitute a single imperialist metropolis.

At the present time of writing, of course, a number of existing nations constitute imperialist metropolises in their own right. Most firms, big or small, based on such countries as France, Germany or Japan are and will remain closely dependent on their home economies for some years to come. In times of economic crisis these firms will have an overriding interest in domestic growth and will, therefore, support an autonomous economic policy. Moreover, these states are able to extend substantial, if not entirely adequate, protection and support for the relatively limited overseas operations of their firms, either in the form of direct economic and even military aid, such as Japan is likely to offer its firms in South East Asia, or else in the form of retaliatory measures against foreign interest in the home economy, such as continental Europe may take if America restricts imports from Europe. Thus, even in the absence of European unification, an ideal solution from the point of view of most big European firms, there will be autonomous non-American states which will use their power vigorously on behalf of their own capital.

Conclusions

We shall make no attempt to summarize what is contained above, other than to say that the prospect is one of imperial rivalry, in which a number of relatively autonomous states, which we have called 'imperialist metropolises', are in conflict with each other as they try to support their respective capitals. Whether these metropolises will consist of certain of today's nation states or of wider units will depend on a number of political and other factors, most of which have not been discussed. There are strong forces pushing European states into closer and closer alliance with each other, but whether this alliance will become sufficiently close to constitute a single true metropolis is not yet clear. Unless they can find allies, certain nation states, of which Britain is the leading example, will become, or perhaps already are, relatively subordinate. In contrast to the imperialist metropolises they might be called 'imperialist satellites'.

The reason these countries are or will be satellites is not necessarily to be found in the weakness of their capital, but in some cases may be in a lack of correspondence between the needs of this capital and the state power available to it. Where big capital operates internationally on a large scale and the state is relatively powerless, one of its prime needs is to keep on good terms with powerful foreign states. Thus, in economic affairs it will oppose the policies necessary for an indigenous solution to economic crises, for such policies may lead to foreign retaliation, and in foreign affairs it will not want the state to antagonize those states upon whose good will it depends.

Although these conclusions have important implications for the future of the imperialist system, we shall not discuss them here. One point is, however, worth making. The problems and prospects facing the working class and revolutionary movements in advanced capitalist countries will depend partly on the extent to which big capital is prepared to support an indigenous path of economic development in times of crisis, i.e. on the extent to which it acts as a nationalist force, where the term 'nationalist' must be interpreted widely to include such phenomena as Common Market or European 'nationalism'. In a metropolis where this is the case, the danger exists of a new kind of 'social imperialism', whereby – in return for the benefits of an indigenous development – the working class accepts the capitalist system and supports or at least acquiesces in imperialist policies. 'Benefits' need not, of course, mean an actual increase in the standard of living of the working class. On the contrary, in a severe world crisis, the main benefit of an indigenous development would be to cushion the shock rather than actually to improve the workers' position. In a satellite, by contrast, where big capital is not prepared to support an indigenous development and acts, therefore, as a cosmopolitan force, the state's room for manoeuvre is greatly reduced and at times of crisis it is correspondingly more difficult to provide any benefits for the working class. Indeed, within the constraints imposed by the international needs of big capital, the state may be compelled to tackle the crisis by making a frontal attack on working-class living standards.

APPENDIX: PRODUCTIVITY AND COMPETITIVENESS

Ernest Mandel in his article 'Where is America Going?' says: 'If the concentration of European and Japanese industry starts to create units which operate on the same scale as American units, with the same dimensions as American corporations, then American industry will ultimately find itself in an impossible position. It will then have to pay three times higher wages, with the same productivity as the Europeans or the Japanese. That would be an absolutely untenable situation, and it would be the beginning of a huge structural crisis for American industry.'[8]

This argument depends on two assumptions, neither of which is necessarily correct: 1. productivity increases in Europe and Japan will not be matched by corresponding increases in real wages and, as result, the rate of exploitation in these countries will rise; 2. a rise in the rate of exploitation in Europe or Japan would make the exports of these countries cheaper, and, therefore, more competitive in American markets. Let us examine these assumptions.

The rate of exploitation reflects the balance of class forces. An increase in productivity will cause this rate to rise, therefore, only if the working class is too weak to gain a corresponding increase in real wages. Thus Mandel's argument, that real wage increases in Europe and Japan will not match productivity increases brought about by mergers and accumulation, rests on the tacit assumption that the working classes of these countries are weak. This assumption is inconsistent with the views expressed elsewhere in his writing, where he stresses correctly their growing strength and militancy.

A rise in the rate of exploitation makes exports more competitive in American markets only if it causes costs of production in the exporting country measured in *dollars* to fall relative to costs of production in America measured in *dollars*. Costs of production in the exporting country, measured in dollars, are determined by costs of production measured in *local currency*, and by the exchange rate. Thus, to know how a rise in the rate of exploitation affects competitiveness we need to know 1. how it affects costs of production, measured in local currency, and 2. how the exchange rate responds to changes in these costs. Let us examine these two questions – referring, for convenience, to costs of production measured in local currency as *money costs* and to costs of production measured in dollars as *dollar costs*.

The answer to the first question is simple. There is no necessary connection between changes in the rate of exploitation and changes in money costs. A rise in the rate of exploitation may be accompanied by a fall, a rise, or no change at all in money costs. Which of these occurs depends on the extent to which the working class can force employers to increase their money wages as productivity increases, and the extent to which employers can respond by increasing the prices of goods consumed by workers. Consider, for example, the typical case of a working class which is strong enough at an economic level to force money wages up by a considerable amount, but too weak at a political level to influence prices. If employers raise prices sufficiently the result will be inflationary growth in which productivity rises faster than real wages, and both money costs and prices rise. As a numerical example of such a situation consider the following case.

Productivity rises by 15 per cent, money wages rise by 20 per cent and all prices rise by 10 per cent. Since the increase in real wages is equal to the increase in money wages *minus* the increase in prices, real wages must rise by 20 per cent − 10 per cent = 10 per cent. This is less than the rise of 15 per cent in productivity and the rate of exploitation, therefore, rises. Assuming labour is the only cost of production, the increase in money costs equals the increase in money wages *minus* the increase in productivity.

Thus, money costs rise by 20 per cent— 15 per cent = 5 per cent. In this example, therefore, money costs rise even though the rate of exploitation rises.

The reason that both things can happen together is simply that the value of labour-power is not determined by the wage bargain alone, which fixes money wages, but also by the ability of employers to determine prices. In the example just given, workers were strong enough to cause inflation by forcing up money wages, but capitalists were strong enough to raise the rate of exploitation by increasing prices.

If money costs rise rapidly and the exchange rate remains constant, a higher rate of exploitation may cause dollar costs to rise rapidly with the result that exports become less rather than more competitive. Now the exchange rate is determined by many factors, such as the ability of the country concerned to borrow overseas, or the state of the current balance of payments. There is no infallible mechanism by which changes in relative money costs in different countries are offset by changes in exchange rates. Rising money costs may not, therefore, be offset by devaluation and dollar costs may, as a result, rise.

It is clear from this discussion that the effect of increased productivity on the competitiveness of European and Japanese exports depends both on the militancy and strength of the

TABLE 5

Productivity, Wages and Wage Costs per Unit of Output

percentage increase in manufacturing

	Output per man-hour	Earnings per man-hour	Wage costs per unit of output
	1956–1968		
USA	53	55	2
West Germany	92	147	30
Japan	147	209	25
	1960–1968		
USA	29	33	4
West Germany	58	84	17
Japan	111	151	20

Source: National Institute Economic Review.

working classes of these countries and on the flexibility of exchange rates. If exchange rates remain as inflexible as they have been in the past and their working classes become more militant, as they appear to be doing, European and Japanese exports may become less rather than more competitive.

A simpler way of seeing that a faster growth of productivity need not imply a lowering of relative money costs is to examine the experience of the last decade and a half. Table 5 shows the percentage increase in output per man-hour (productivity) in the United States, Germany and Japan between 1956 and 1968. Productivity rose by 147 per cent in Japan, 92 per cent in Germany and a mere 53 per cent in the US. Money wages per man-hour, on the other hand, rose by 209 per cent, 147 per cent and 55 per cent respectively.

The combined effect of these two sets of increases was a rise of 2 per cent in wage costs per unit of output in the US, 30 per cent in Germany and 25 per cent in Japan. Thus, although productivity rose more in both Germany and Japan than in the United States, money costs also rose more.

NOTES

1. Articles by Robin Murray in NLR 67 and Bill Warren in NLR 68 have analysed the relationship between capital and the nation state. Although this is not the place to discuss these articles at length, one particular aspect of them is directly relevant to the present paper. Broadly speaking, with many qualifications, Robin Murray takes the view that the inter-nationalization of capital is leading to the weakening of the nation state vis-à-vis large firms. For this he is criticized by Bill Warren, who says that in many ways states have *strengthened* their power over large firms and that the formation of the EEC will shift the balance still further in favour of the state. Unfortunately, although correct, Bill Warren's criticism does not take us very far, for he is largely concerned with the *independent* power of the large firm vis-à-vis the individual nation state considered in *isolation*. As I have tried to show in this paper, however, the central questions arise when we consider situations in which more than one nation state is involved. In particular:

a. How does the state best serve the capital whose general interests it is defending? What policies should it adopt when dominant sections of this capital are operating in economic or territorial spaces where they are subject to the power of foreign states? These questions arise even where the state has absolutely dictatorial power over individual capitals.

b. How far does the ability of certain firms to call upon the support of foreign states place them effectively beyond the control of the domestic state? In other words, how far does the power of foreign states serve to offset the increasing power of the domestic state so rightly stressed by Bill Warren?

2. H. Magdoff, *The Age of Imperialism*, Monthly Review, 1969; P. Sweezy and H. Magdoff 'The Multinational Corporation', *Monthly Review*, October and November 1969, P. Jalée *L'Impérialisme en 1970*, Paris, 1969; M. Nicolaus 'The Universal Contradiction', NLR 59. In a subsequent article, Paul Sweezey seems to have changed his position and now admits the ability of European and Japanese firms to mount some kind of challenge and resistance to American firms (see *Monthly Review* June 1971). On an economic level he recognizes the existence of a genuine and growing rivalry between the big firms of various capitalist countries. He does not, however, seem to believe that this has any significant implication for the political relations between capitalist states, or for the class struggle *within* the advanced capitalist world. Indeed, he reiterates his long-held view that 'since the Second World War, it has become increasingly clear that the principal contradiction in the system, at least in the present historical period, is not *within* the developed part but *between* the developed and underdeveloped parts'. In the 1950s this was a plausible view. In the 1970s it is not, for it ignores both the increasing intensity of class struggle in almost every advanced capitalist country and the growing imperial rivalry between these countries. This does not mean, of course, that the national liberation struggles in underdeveloped countries have become unimportant. On the contrary, they will continue to play a crucial role in determining the future of the imperialist system. So too, however, will contradictions within the developed capitalist world. To elevate either kind to the level of a permanent principal contradiction would be both dangerous and misleading.

3. E. Mandel, *Europe versus America?*, NLB 1970; 'Where is America Going?', NLR 54; 'The Laws of Unequal Development', NLR 59; M. Kidron, *Western Capitalism Since the War*, London, 1968.

4. Y. Varga, 'The Problem of Inter-Imperialist Contradictions and War', *Politico-Economic Problems of Capitalism*, Moscow, 1968.

5. *Imperialism, The Highest Stage of Capitalism*, in *Selected Works*, Moscow, 1967, Vol. 1, p. 723.

6. Theodore R. Gates and Fabian Linden, *Costs and Competition*, New York, The National Industrial Conference Board, 1961, pp. 14–15.

7. Ernest Mandel, *Europe versus America?* p. 63.

8. NLR 54, p. 13.

3

Britain and the World Economy*

1. Introduction

Any attempt to plan the economy and implement progressive social policies must come to terms with the realities of Britain's international position. She derives certain material benefits from her role as a major imperial power and yet at the same time her close links with the world capitalist economy restrict internal policies in a variety of ways. Britain is in the paradoxical situation of being both an imperial power and a dependent economy. Labour governments have always accepted this situation, regarding it as either inevitable or desirable, and have framed their policies accordingly, sacrificing the interests of the working class under the pressures of the world market and the demands of foreign creditors. In this article we examine the consequences of rejecting such a path and making a determined attempt to break the hold of imperialism and world capitalism on the British economy. We assume a specific scenario in which the rest of the Western World remains capitalist.

There is a view on the left that the power of world capitalism over the British economy is now so great that it is no longer possible on a national basis to gain any freedom of action to pursue progressive policies, and that change is only possible within the framework of a world or European revolution. According to this view, whilst the rest of the Western World remains capitalist, a detailed examination of the problems of creating socialism in Britain is pointless, diverts attention away from the basic task of establishing world socialism and may also fuel dangerous chauvinistic sentiments already so prevalent in this country.

There are, however, a number of problems with this cavalier approach. Firstly, it is based on a rather strange view of the dynamics of class struggle which are seen only on an

* First published in *Britain's Economic Crisis* (Cambridge Political Economy Group, 1974), and republished in *Marxism Today*, August 1974.

international plane, completely ignoring their national dimension. One of the most effective ways of politically destabilising the world capitalist system would be a serious attempt to detach one of the main western countries from this system. Such an attempt will never be made if the left restricts itself to defensive trade union struggles, however militant, and to the building of an international movement. The left must take seriously Marx's words in the *Communist Manifesto*:

> Though not in substance, yet in form, the struggle of the proletariat with the bourgeoisie is at first a national struggle. The proletariat of each country must, of course, first of all settle matters with its own bourgeoisie.

To do this requires a strategic perspective appropriate to the country concerned, which in turn requires a detailed understanding of its links with the world economy and the problems these pose.

Secondly, starry-eyed internationalism has served the left ill in the past. The Bolsheviks, for example, dreaming of a simultaneous world revolution, awoke to find themselves in power, surrounded by formidable enemies and quite unprepared for the real material and political problems facing them. Even if one believes that European or World socialism is an imminent reality, prudence would suggest taking seriously the possibility that this is not the case and that the left may take power in Britain before it does elsewhere. And finally, those who talk of European or world revolution never get beyond the realm of abstract slogans which, valid as they may be, provide no theoretical perspective beyond the need to create an international working class movement, something which all on the left support, even those such as ourselves who believe that the problems of socialism in Britain must be taken seriously.

The fact that we consider a particular scenario in which other western countries remain capitalist does not imply that we believe this to be the only possibility. A shift to the left in Britain, for example, could well be part of a general European movement as a result of which it became possible to plan the socialist development of Europe as a whole. Clearly, the left must retain sufficient flexibility to respond to such developments as they arise and lend them every possible support. It must also avoid the chauvinistic excesses and little

Englandism that have characterized much of the campaign against the Common Market.

The national struggle in Britain against the forces of world capitalism is in fact international in two senses. Its success depends on the support of working class movements in other countries to prevent a trade boycott of the UK and to force their governments to adopt a co-operative stance towards a socialist Britain. And it is firmly internationalist in its attack on the roots of British imperialism.

2. Freedom of Action

Britain is deeply enmeshed in the world capitalist system. Its economy is highly international, both financially and industrially. The City of London is the world's leading financial centre; key industries are dominated by multinational firms, many of which are foreign controlled, and Britain relies heavily on other economies both to supply her needs and to purchase her goods. Much of the activity in these various economic spheres is conducted by capitalists operating in a virtually uncontrolled fashion. If these capitalists do not like what the government is doing or are unhappy about domestic economic prospects, they can shift their money abroad and precipitate a financial crisis in which the British government is faced with bankruptcy.

Particularly powerful in this respect are the multinational firms, which engage in currency speculation on an enormous scale. In addition they can undermine the balance of payments by importing what could have been produced in Britain and producing overseas what could have been exported. In these and many other ways the present situation subjects Britain to the discipline of the world capitalist system. Any government which tries to introduce radical changes in such areas as the distribution of income or the ownership of property will find itself facing bankruptcy as money pours out through the foreign exchanges and multinational firms boycott the economy, shifting their activities elsewhere. Sometimes this flight of capital may be politically motivated, an act of deliberate sabotage. More often it will merely be the natural response of suspicious investors, worried for the safety or profitability of their assets.

Under these circumstances the government has a number of choices. It can abandon its programme in a desperate bid to regain capitalist 'confidence'. Alternatively, it can finance the flight of capital by borrowing from foreign governments, but these loans will usually be given only on condition that the British government abandons its radical aims and behaves 'responsibly'. Or, finally, it can stick to its aims and fight the power of international capital. To succeed in such a struggle it will need to be both determined and resourceful, using every stratagem at its disposal to divide and out-manoeuvre its opponents. It will need a strategic perspective to guide its day to day struggle, and most important, it will need to mobilize popular support at home and solidarity abroad both from the socialist countries and the working class movements of Europe and elsewhere.

3. What Can be Done?

Measures

Faced with the massive array of capitalist power we have just described, what can a left government do to ensure that its programme is not wrecked by the actions of hostile foreign and domestic investors? To begin with, at the first sign of trouble or preferably before, it can take emergency measures to prevent a flight of capital. Dealings on foreign exchange markets and the stock exchange can be suspended and foreign money banked or invested in Britain can be temporarily frozen. None of these measures is particularly revolutionary, having been used by right-wing nationalist governments such as those of Gaullist France or even in an earlier period by British governments. But, by their nature, they are stop-gap measures which must be replaced by a more flexible and comprehensive system of controls on capital movements, both short- and long-term, together with controls on the behaviour of multinational firms covering their production, investment and foreign trade policies, the transfer prices they charge and so on. Naturally, these controls would have to be chosen in accordance with the general priorities of the government as laid down in some kind of national plan.

But to believe that the process can stop here, that it is merely enough to impose controls on international capital, would be a mistake. Controls may not be effective and they may be resisted. Capitalists have at their disposal a number of means by which they can evade or completely sabotage controls. Capitalist institutions may prove obstructive, either by disobeying instructions or withholding vital information. Firms may reschedule overseas payments and receipts and the consequent 'leads and lags' may cause the loss of hundreds of millions of pounds worth of foreign exchange. Or they may undercharge for exports or overpay for imports, thereby evading restrictions on the export of capital. In this respect multinational firms may prove the most troublesome, being the best placed both to evade regulations and withhold information.

Without the active co-operation of other states it would never be possible to develop a foolproof or even adequate system of controls on the operations of international capital. Since a left government is unlikely to receive such co-operation it would sooner or later, and probably sooner, be driven to more radical measures. Much of the international business of the City would have to be run-down and most of the rest taken over and administered directly by the Government. Equally, many international firms would have to be taken over, either completely or with majority government participation. Exactly which institutions or firms should be taken over or run-down, and when and how this should be done, depends of course on the exact circumstances of the time and upon detailed conditions which are beyond the scope of this article to discuss. Even so it is realistic to expect that the reaction of international capital would dictate a rapid and extensive transfer of ownership embracing the bulk of the City and many big multinational firms, both foreign and domestically controlled.

The need to run down parts of the City and take over foreign controlled multinationals would be reinforced by the reaction of foreign investors and their parent states. Faced with the inevitable uncertainties surrounding any left government in its initial years, together with extensive controls on capital movement and business operations, many foreign investors would want to wind up their operations fairly quickly and withdraw their funds. This would confront the government with a number of possible choices. It could simply refuse to allow liquidation and risk retaliation in the form of trade boycotts or worse. Or it could confiscate the property of foreign controlled firms and repudiate Britain's financial debts. The risks of retaliation then would be even greater than if assets concerned were merely frozen. Or, finally, it could allow some liquidation, paying off short-term debts and nationalising with compensation foreign owned subsidiaries. This would reduce, although not eliminate, the risk of foreign retaliation. The feasibility of such a path is discussed below. What matters for the moment, however, is simply that foreign capitalists and their parent states may not tolerate a policy of freezing the flow of funds into and out of the country and controlling the operations of foreign owned firms. Consequently, the government may then be compelled to wind-up much of the City's international activity and take over many foreign owned firms.

4. Breaking the Chains

Thus, in order to exercise effective power over the economy and because of foreign pressure for liquidation, a left government would be compelled to nationalize wide sections of the City and industry and to wind-up much of the City's international business. Furthermore, in the absence of sympathetic regimes in what are now the advanced capitalist countries, it would in many cases be necessary to honour Britain's debts and offer compensation for foreign property nationalized.

This is not a question of abstract morality but of politics. In any particular case the choice between compensation and confiscation must be guided by general political criteria – which of these best contributes to the long-run survival of socialism in Britain; whether the assets concerned belong to poor countries which have long been exploited or to rich imperialist countries, and so on. In most cases, provided the money can be found, compensation is likely to be the more advisable course, for widespread confiscations, especially of European-owned property might lead to a crippling trade-boycott which seriously damaged the regime's chances of survival or drive it in the direction of greater authoritarianism as its popular base was eroded.

The obvious question at this point is could the money be found? If the answer is no, then a serious left government might be driven into a confrontation with one or several of the major capitalist powers, as were Chile and Cuba who had little choice but to take over foreign property without compensation. For each of them the costs of confrontation were high and had they been able to pay compensation their relations with the United States might have developed differently, although given the threat their existence posed to US interests throughout Latin America, this is not certain. Even so, the confiscation of American property provided the US Administration with the excuse that it needed to act against the regimes concerned. Had they offered genuine compensation it would have been more difficult for the US Administration to justify its policies to the American people.

Fortunately Britain is not a simple neo-colony as were Cuba and Chile. British capitalists own enormous assets overseas and, if these were requisitioned by the government, they would in theory be sufficient to repay all of Britain's debts, buy out foreign subsidiaries in this country, thereby weakening British capitalists by depriving them of foreign support. In practice, of course, things would not be so simple, for many of Britain's assets overseas such as industrial subsidiaries would be difficult to sell quickly, except at knock-down prices, and there might be serious political problems in actually requisitioning them. Even so, the existence of these enormous assets provides opportunities for a determined British government not available to its counterparts in Cuba or Chile.

British Assets

Table 1 based upon data published by the Bank of England gives a breakdown of Britain's external assets and liabilities at the end of 1973.

In almost all spheres the private sector is a massive net creditor. British industrial firms own production facilities overseas worth £12,000 million which is nearly twice as much as the holdings of foreign industrial firms in Britain. Even if British holdings in underdeveloped countries are excluded from the picture, Britain remains a net creditor, owning far more industrial assets in the advanced capitalist countries than they own here.

Similarly, the City is a net creditor. Britain's huge 'portfolio' holdings of stocks and shares in America, Europe, Australia,

TABLE 1

UK External Assets and Liabilities End 1973 (£ millions)

	Assets	Liabilities	Net Assets
Private Sector			
Industrial			
1. Non-oil	9,725	4,655	+ 5,070
2. Oil	2,350	1,900	+ 450
3. Total industrial	12,075	6,555	+ 5,520
Financial (The City, etc.)			
4. Eurodollar banking	35,719	39,017*	− 3,298
5. Sterling banking	3,665	3,271	+ 394
6. Portfolio	7,150	2,925	+ 4,225
7. Other financial	2,439	2,548	− 109
8. Total financial	48,975	47,760	+ 1,215
9. Total Private	61,050	54,315	+ 6,735
Public Sector			
10. Long-term loans etc.	1,790	1,545	+ 245
11. UK official securities		2,651	− 2,651
12. UK short-term borrowing		1,091	− 1,091
13. UK official reserves	2,235		+ 2,235
14. Total Public	4,025	5,285	− 1,260
15. Grand Total	65,075	59,600	+ 5,475

Source: Bank of England Quarterly Bulletin, June 1974.
Notes: Totals are rounded to the nearest five, following Bank of England practice.
* Includes £890 millions borrowed abroad by UK banks on behalf of public bodies.

South Africa and elsewhere are more than enough to offset comparatively small deficits in the Euro-dollar Market. Overall the City owns assets worth about £1,200 millions more than its liabilities. If the City could be eliminated by trading off Britain's financial assets against its financial liabilities, this is the surplus that would remain.

By contrast with the private sector, the public sector is an international pauper. Part of the overseas expansion of British capital has been financed by official borrowing, with the result that the Government now owes a considerable amount overseas. Even so the overall position is still favourable to Britain, with private sector credits greatly exceeding public sector debts. If all UK private holdings overseas were taken over by the Government, it would be possible to reduce dramatically the hold of international capitalism over the British economy. In some cases foreign firms could be bought out and financial creditors repaid. British holdings of US securities, for example, could be sold and the money used as compensation for American firms taken over, or where appropriate to purchase a majority holding in such firms.

British holdings in underdeveloped countries would have to be treated rather differently from those in the developed world. The simplest, and probably the best solution, from our own point of view, would be to hand over British investments free of charge to the countries concerned, offering to provide any technical assistance necessary for their continued operation. This would open the way for genuinely co-operative and mutually beneficial trade agreements between Britain and the countries concerned.

Their remains one important problem. Would it be possible to requisition British assets held overseas? There are certainly precedents. In both world wars the Government requisitioned British assets abroad and sold them to pay for the war effort. Legally there is no reason why this should not be done again. In the final analysis, of course, it would not be international law but politics which decided the issue. The capitalist world would only accept such a programme if it was faced with a determined Government, willing to mobilize popular support at home and working class solidarity abroad.

Costs

The balance of payments would be effected in a number of ways by the above programme of requisitioning British assets overseas and reducing substantially the role of the City, the activities of British companies abroad and those of foreign companies in this country. Many of the overseas earnings of the City would be lost, for its business would contract as foreign capitalists moved their funds to safer havens. British property income in the form of interest, profits and dividends from abroad would decline, as would payments of property income to foreign capitalists with investments in this country. Table 2 gives a pessimistic estimate of how some of these changes might affect the balance of payments.

These calculations assume that the bulk of service income received by the City would be lost as would all net UK property income from abroad. Given these assumptions we estimate that the annual service income of the City would drop by about £380 millions, and net UK property income by about £500 millions, giving a total of £880 millions. This would be a big loss but it would not cripple the economy. It is just a little larger than British exports earn every fortnight. It is also equal to about $1\frac{1}{4}$ per cent of gross domestic product. If unemployment could be reduced by about 400,000 and the additional output sold abroad, the entire loss would be made up.

Great efforts have been made to convince the British people that their well-being depends on the continued activity and expansion of the City and the overseas investment of British firms. 'Invisibles', we are told, provide a large and indispensable part of Britain's foreign exchange earnings. And so they do. But we are rarely told that the bulk of these earnings have nothing whatsoever to do with the City or overseas investment, but consist of such items as shipping and civil aviation. The City itself accounts for only one tenth of all invisible exports and less than 4 per cent of total exports. Its receipts are little larger than those of civil aviation alone and only a quarter of those of British shipping. Banking, the most troublesome of the City's activities, earned a mere £77 millions of foreign exchange in 1972.

One item often mentioned in this context is the export of capital. It is widely believed to be one of the main components of Britain's balance of payments deficit. Savings of £1,500 millions are sometimes quoted as the immediate benefits of banning the export of capital. This is in our opinion incorrect. In the first place, Britain's massive deficits are on *current* account which excludes all capital transactions. A ban on capital export would have no direct affect on such deficits. In the second place, the export of capital has recently been matched by corresponding imports in in the form of foreign long-term investment in Britain and borrowing overseas by UK companies and banks acting on their behalf. A radical programme of disengagement from the capitalist world system would lead to a drastic fall in this inflow, sufficient to offset any saving in the export of capital. Britain cannot expect to have its cake and eat it.

There remains one more cost to be mentioned which is impossible to quantify but could prove important. A substantial part of Britain's trade takes place within multinational firms; components produced in one country are shipped to a subsidiary of the same firm in another country. Ford motor cars, for example, are produced on a European-wide basis. If a foreign subsidiary in this country were nationalized its parent company might refuse to supply necessary components or purchase its output, causing a significant if temporary dislocation. But this weapon cuts both ways, for the parent company itself often depends on its British subsidiary. Given an appropriate combination of threats and blandishments a determined British Government could in the short-run take over many foreign subsidiaries and continue trading as before, but in the longer run it would be wise to diversify and lessen dependence on the former parent companies. Even so, the multinational companies pose difficult problems for any British government attempting to disengage from the world capitalist system.

5. Military Alliances and the EEC

Britain has signed treaties which would inhibit any left government attempting to transform the social and economic structure of this country, both directly through their military and political provisions and indirectly through their economic costs.

Under NATO agreements American troops are stationed in Britain and British troops in Germany. The former would provide valuable allies for reactionary forces in Britain, should they attempt to overthrow our democratic institutions, whilst the latter although safely out of harm's way, are very expensive to maintain. This reactionary alliance should be wound up. One immediate benefit of such a step would be a reduction in the level of overseas military expenditure currently running at around £400 millions a year. Further savings could be made by withdrawing from imperial outposts in the Far East and elsewhere. Some of the expenditure is used to purchase exports from Britain so the actual savings of foreign exchange would be less than the full figure. At the very least, however, £200 millions per annum could be saved.

The Rome Treaty binding Britain to the EEC also inhibits our freedom of action significantly by imposing conditions on the way the economy is run. Effective planning is prevented by: free trade within the Market; movements towards the greater mobility of capital; competitive requirements for nationalized industries and so on. In the longer run, if it survives, the Common Market may reduce national sovereignty even more and Britain may be administered as part of a unified and capitalist West European bloc. Under present circumstances this would make a radical shift to the Left impossible in Britain. Naturally if continental Europe went to the Left the situation would change and it would be correct for our working class to support integration. But, as things stand, this is not likely and for the foreseeable future the Common Market will be an alliance serving to consolidate and extend capitalist power in Western Europe. To oppose it is not chauvinism but class interest.

Until now the foreign exchange costs of Common Market membership have been less than anticipated, as world food prices have risen dramatically. Quite soon, however, world prices will be paying large amounts under the Common Agricultural Policy. It will also be importing very expensive food from the Common Market instead of cheaper, although still expensive food from elsewhere. On the most conservative calculations, the direct foreign exchange costs of Common Market membership will soon be at least £400 million per annum. This is in fact the official Treasury estimate of Britain's annual net contribution to the EEC budget by 1980.

6. Direct Effects on the Balance of Payments

Table 2 brings together some of the balance of payments effects of the above forms of disengagement. Drastically cutting Britain's role in international investment and finance would produce a *maximum* loss of £880 million in the form of service

TABLE 2

Estimated Direct Effects on Balance of Payments
(£ millions 1974 prices)

Losses:		
City Service Income:		
Insurance		235
Banking		90
Merchanting		20
Brokerage		35
Total City		380
2. UK Property Income (net)		500
	Total losses	880
Gains:		
3. Overseas Military Expenditure (net)		200
4. Common Market		400
	Total gains	600

Net loss=£280 millions p.a.

and property income foregone. Against this must be set the savings from pulling out of the EEC and bringing the troops home. Between them these would mean a *minimum* saving of £600 millions per annum. Overall the net loss would be at most £280 million. This is a mere 1·5 per cent of Britain's total exports of goods and services, and is equivalent to the output of 100,000 workers – one-sixth of the registered long-term unemployed in 1973. A small price to pay for the freedom of action a left government would gain as a result of disengagement.

In addition to this figure there are of course the losses caused by changes in the pattern of international trade following attempts to control the activities of multinational firms or the nationalization of their subsidiaries in this country. As we have seen above, however, no quantitative estimate can be made of these and they might be small or large depending on the exact course of events.

7. Foreign Trade

Recent predictions suggest a current account deficit of well over £3,000 millions in 1974 and a cumulative deficit by 1977 of nearly four times as much. With a higher growth rate the deficit would be worse, and any determined attempt to break with the world capitalist sytem might impose further costs on the balance of payments. In the present situation a socialist goverment would have no practical alternative but to take vigorous steps to reduce this deficit. Not to do so would saddle Britain with huge debts to foreign bankers and governments and give the capitalist world a veto over our economic and social policies. But it would also be wrong to adopt the orthodox solutions of devaluation or deflation, for the former by itself is hopelessly inadequate (though it might be useful as one component in a total strategy), while the latter involves unacceptable costs in terms of unemployment and waste.

Immediate action to hold down imports and raise exports would be essential, involving a crash programme to produce exports and import substitutes; direct controls to hold down imports; and negotiations to expand exports, especially by developing new markets with socialist third world countries. The main aim of such a crash programme would be to eliminate completely the non-oil deficit and to permit a fast and sustained growth of domestic output unconstrained by balance of payments problems. In practice, a socialist government might have to go further and attempt to eliminate the oil deficit itself, should the Arab countries refuse to finance oil inflows until North and Celtic Sea fields reach full production. Though Britain could reduce its oil deficit by switching from suppliers such as Kuwait and Saudi Arabia which cannot absorb a large quantity of British exports, in favour of such countries as Nigeria, Iraq, Iran and the Soviet Union, which may be prepared to exchange oil for British goods.

In the longer term trade can be planned in a variety of ways – direct controls in the form of import and export licences; State trading so that goods are bought and sold overseas by Government agencies on behalf of private or official clients; and domestic nationalization so that the import and export decisions of firms are directly determined in conjunction with the central planning authorities. If British trade was planned in this way it would be much less difficult to combine sustained economic growth with national solvency. The National Plan of the last Labour Government foundered, not because of union militancy or a failure to devalue, but because no serious attempt was made to plan and control foreign trade.

Long-term trading plans would have to recognize the need to establish alternative patterns of trade, especially with the third world and the socialist countries. This would imply certain planned shifts of production, for example existing capacity in the motor industry could be used to produce trucks and tractors for the third world. There could also be a planned expansion of trade with capitalist countries either on the basis of a negotiated realignment of currencies or in the last resort by bilateral deals. At the moment, the benefits of much trade are only marginal, for instance we just exchange different brands of car with other European countries. But certain imports are essential and we must be able to produce and sell the exports to pay for them, therefore it is fundamental to the development of the economy that trade is organised effectively.

8. Retaliation

If all of Western Europe and North America united to boycott the British economy the effect would be crippling. Together they account for two-thirds of all Britain's imports and exports. The loss of these is the spectre always raised by the defenders of free trade whenever planned trade is mentioned. But is such a widespread boycott likely? The answer depends, of course, on Government tactics and strategy. Outright confiscation of all foreign property in this country, combined with random and senseless cuts in imports might provoke fairly wide retaliation.

On the other hand, if Britain offered compensation for property taken over and proposed reasonable trade deals, most capitalist countries would have strong reasons for co-operating. The alternative would be a protracted trade war which few of them can afford, together with the possible loss of their property without the compensation originally offered. In the case of Europe, with its progressive Labour movements, it would also be possible to mobilize working-class solidarity against a boycott. There is, therefore, every reason to believe that a determined but reasonable Government could negotiate a new system of planned trade with Western Europe and most of the rest of the world.

One problem arises in this context. The US might institute a single handed boycott of the British economy in an attempt to bring down the Government. Against this Britain would have a powerful weapon. It could threaten to nationalize without compensation all US property here. Equally important in deterring an American Administration would be the knowledge that Britain is not so very dependent on America, which accounted for only one tenth of our trade in 1973. The most important items were tobacco and wheat. The former would have to be replaced by other, less familiar types and the latter could be purchased on the world market. Indeed, more wheat could be grown at home. Increased trade with the socialist countries would also help cushion the impact of an American boycott. Given Britain's alternative sources of supply and markets, a boycott might easily boomerang, causing insufficient dislocation to bring the Government down, whilst being widely resented as an interference in our internal affairs. For this reason the US administration might decide that a boycott would do more harm than good.

NOTE

1. In 1972 – a record year for capital export – UK private investment overseas was £1,479 millions. Against this can be set the following imports of capital: direct borrowing overseas by UK companies and institutions £252 millions, foreign currency borrowing (net by UK banks to finance UK investment overseas £733 millions), and £721 millions provided by foreign direct and portfolio investment in the UK.

4

'Late Capitalism'*

Three years after its publication in Germany, Ernest Mandel's *Late Capitalism* has now appeared in a revised and updated English edition.[1] Whatever one's criticisms, it is a major contribution to the revival of Marxist economics now occurring in Britain and some other Western countries. Indeed it is probably one of the two most important works of Marxist political economy to have appeared in English during the past decade, the other being Harry Braverman's *Labour and Monopoly Capital*. Mandel, like Braverman, takes as his starting-point capitalist production, rather than income distribution and demand, which for many years have dominated socialist and radical thought in Britain. Naturally, he considers demand and distribution; however, these are seen, not as independent entities, but as conditioned by and dependent on what happens in the sphere of production. This approach represents a return to the concerns of classical Marxism; at the same time, potentially, such an approach could herald a new era in the development of Marxism in Britain, where until recently it has existed under the shadow of left Keynesianism, lacking any genuine theoretical basis of its own. *Late Capitalism* is not an easy book to read; its subject matter is extremely complex, its approach is often eclectic and its arguments are at times confused or unnecessarily abstruse. None the less, to anyone patient enough to master its contents, it contains a wealth of ideas and empirical material and is a work of truly creative Marxism. In the space of a single review it is impossible to do justice to a book whose coverage is so vast, so I shall consider only those aspects which I have found particularly interesting.

Method

Mandel begins with a chapter on method entitled 'The Laws of Motion and the History of Capital' in which he makes a forceful

* First published in *New Left Review*, July–August 1976.

plea for the reintegration of theory and history. He then asks, 'Why is it that the integration of theory and history which Marx applied with such mastery in the *Grundrisse* and *Capital* has never since been repeated successfully, to explain . . . successive stages of the capitalist mode of production? Why is there still no satisfactory history of capitalism as a function of the inner laws of capital . . . and still less a satisfactory explanation of the new stage in the history of capitalism which clearly began after the Second World War?' His answer is as follows. In part he blames the social pressures of Stalinism, which discouraged a creative approach to political economy and replaced theory by apologetics. More fundamentally, however, he points to a problem in the realm of theory itself, arguing that twentieth-century Marxism has developed according to a certain inner logic which has seriously inhibited its ability to formulate adequate theories and explain concrete events. He identifies two specific aspects of this logic as primarily responsible: 1. the use of Marx's reproduction schemas for purposes for which they were never intended; 2. the monocausal nature of twentieth-century Marxism, whose practitioners have tried to explain the whole of capitalist development in terms of a single key factor, such as the anarchy of production or the difficulty of realizing surplus-value.

The reproduction schemas, claims Mandel, were designed for one purpose only, to explain 'why and how an economic system based on "pure" market anarchy in which economic life seems to be determined by millions of unrelated decisions to buy and sell does not lead to continuous chaos and constant interruptions of the social and economic processes of reproduction, but instead on the whole functions normally . . .' and thus 'to prove that it is possible for the capitalist mode of production to exist at all'. I agree that this was one of the purposes for which the reproduction schemas were designed, but surely there were others? For example, Marx used the schemas to analyse what Keynesians nowadays call the 'circular flow of income' and it is fair to say that he anticipated modern national income accounting by many decades. He drew his inspiration from the Physiocrats and used the schemas with great effect in criticizing Adam Smith's analysis of national income. On the other hand, Mandel is correct in saying that the schemas were primarily designed for the analysis of equilibrium and that later Marxists often used them inappropriately to analyse disquilibrium situations. He makes too much of this point, however, and his criticism of Hilferding is unconvincing.

Mandel is more impressive when dealing with the second aspect of twentieth-century Marxism – its monocausal nature. He argues forcefully that 'any single factor assumption is clearly opposed to the notion of the capitalist mode of production as a dynamic totality in which the interplay of *all* the basis laws of development is necessary in order to produce any particular outcome. This notion means that up to a certain point *all* the basic variables of this mode of production can partially and periodically perform the role of autonomous variables – naturally not to the point of complete independence, but in interplay constantly articulated through the laws of development of the whole capitalist mode of production.' He then criticizes a number of famous Marxists for their exclusive concern with one single factor – Rosa Luxemburg for her obsession with the realization of surplus-value, Henryk Grossman for his mechanical breakdown theory, and so on.

Mandel's criticism of monocausal theories is, of course, correct. Marxism has undoubtedly been held back by its failure to develop more elaborate theories and by its futile search for the universal answer, the unique factor whose operation determines the entire course of history. On the other hand, having correctly criticized earlier Marxists and specified what must be done, Mandel rather under-estimates the complexity of this task and certainly does not live up to his own promises. Although he discusses at length many different aspects of capitalism, he fails to produce a convincing picture of how they interconnect in either the long or the short term. His basic analysis is of the classical falling-rate-of-profit type and depends almost exclusively on movements in the rate of surplus-value and the organic composition of capital. Problems of realization and interdepartmental proportions are discussed, but they are never properly integrated with the basic theory, and the result is sometimes confusing. It is never clear, for example, whether Mandel considers capitalism has an inherent tendency towards overproduction which periodically *expresses* itself in a falling rate of profit, or whether overproduction itself is *caused* by a falling rate of profit. As a result, his repeated references to demand and realization exist in something of a vacuum, and one is left wondering what, if any, is their connection with his basic theory of development.

This is most evident in Chapter 9, which deals with the role of armaments. After reading this several times, I still do not understand how military expenditure is supposed to have functioned in the post-war period. In places the author here sounds like Baran and Sweezy, arguing that armaments have absorbed surplus-value for which there was no investment outlet, and thereby maintained demand and prevented a realization crisis. Yet elsewhere in the same chapter he argues that military expenditure has been accompanied by an equivalent reduction in workers' consumption, in which case it does not help avert a realization crisis; all that happens is that one kind of demand and investment outlet (military) replaces another (civil), and the overall realization of surplus-value is in no way affected. These two theories are obviously incompatible. They imply quite different views of the post-war period, one suggesting there was a latent realization crisis or shortage of demand throughout the entire period which was only staved off by spending a vast amount on armaments, the other denying this. Yet Mandel does not choose between these alternatives, nor does he specify very clearly how either might be integrated with his basic long-wave theory of development.

Long Waves

The most profound aspect of *Late Capitalism* is its attempt to identify, characterize and explain 'long waves' in capitalist development, and to locate the post-war boom and recent crisis within this framework. Mandel argues that the 7–10 year industrial cycle is superimposed on and conditioned by a more fundamental movement which determines the general character of a whole era as one of relatively fast or slow accumulation. As Mandel himself admits, this is not a new idea; but it became unfashionable for economists to study long waves during the nineteen-fifties and sixties, so he has performed an important service in raising the issue once again. Moreover, his approach is more systematic than that of most earlier writers and he makes an original attempt to explain long waves, using the tools of classical Marxism. In his own words, 'the specific contribution of our own analysis of the problem of "long-waves" has been to relate the diverse combinations of factors that may influence the rate of profit (such as a radical fall in the cost of raw materials; a sudden expansion of the world market or of new fields of investment for capital; a rapid increase or decline in the rate of surplus-value; wars and revolutions) to the inner logic of the process of long-term accumulation and valorization of capital, based upon spurts of radical renewal or reproduction of fundamental productive technology. It explains these movements by the inner logic of the process of accumulation and self-expansion of capital itself'.[2]

In essence, Mandel's basic theory is rather simple. Accumulation depends on the rate of profit, and anything which raises the latter stimulates accumulation. The expansionary phase of a long wave occurs when the rate of profit is lifted radically upwards by what he calls 'triggering factors', which lower the organic composition of capital or raise the rate of surplus-value. It draws to a close when the effect of these triggering factors begins to wear off, as their potential is exhausted and the rate of profit begins to fall because of unfavourable changes in the organic composition of capital or the rate of surplus-value. A new expansionary phase occurs when the rate of profit is once again lifted radically upwards by some new combination of factors. Thus, capitalism develops in a series of spurts, each initiated by an external shock whose effect is gradually dissipated by the process of accumulation itself.

Among the triggering factors which provide such a shock, Mandel mentions specifically the following: '1. A sudden fall in the average organic composition of capital, for example, as a result of the massive penetration of capital into spheres (or countries) with a very low organic composition. 2. A sudden increase in the rate of surplus-value, due to a radical defeat or atomization of the working class . . . 3. A sudden fall in the price of elements of constant capital, especially of raw materials . . . or a sudden fall in the price of fixed capital due to a revolutionary advance in the productivity of labour in Department I. 4. A sudden abbreviation of the turn-over time of circulating capital due to perfection of new systems of transport and communications, improved methods of distribution, accelerated rotation of stock, and so on.'[3] Mandel argues that if these factors operate to a limited degree, then the upswing will be short-lived, the initially high rate of profit will quickly decline and accumulation will tail off. If, on the other hand, 'several factors are simultaneously and cumulatively contributing to a rise in the long-run rate of profit', then accumulation will continue for a long time and there will be a 'revolution in technology' and a 'fundamental renewal of productive technology' which induces a qualitative change in the productivity of labour.

The above approach to capitalist development is very fruitful. It provides a conceptual framework within which to consider the effect of a wide variety of technological, economic and political factors; yet, at the same time, it maintains a close connection with classical Marxism by focusing on the internal dynamics of the long wave itself and emphasizing the inherent tendency of accumulation to undermine the foundations of its own success. On the other hand, Mandel's own particular version of this approach suffers from a number of theoretical and empirical weaknesses. First, the influence of economic factors on technology is at times obscure, and it is not clear how far the author believes a 'technological revolution' is an ongoing process of discovery and how far it rests upon the exploitation of discoveries which had already been made when the 'revolution' began. Yet this is a crucial question, for if the ongoing aspect of discovery is predominant, then there is no real reason to assume that the organic composition of capital will rise and we must look elsewhere for an explanation of why expansion peters out. If, on the other hand, ongoing discovery is of secondary importance, then expansion will peter out as the pool of previous discoveries is exhausted and it becomes more difficult to raise productivity.

Secondly, Mandel says that the shift which gives rise to a phase of expansion must be *sudden*, whereas in fact its speed of occurrence is irrelevant; what matters is that it be *radical*. For example, to subordinate the working class and lay the foundations for post-war expansion took about 20 years, from 1929 to the late forties. During this time depression, fascism, war-time integration and the Cold War all contributed, in their own way, to the creation of an effective mechanism for containing working-class demands and making possible a sustained and profitable accumulation. In his search for a *sudden* shift in the balance of power, Mandel assigns almost exclusive responsibility to fascism which, at one blow, smashed the workers' movements in Germany, Japan and certain other countries. This leads to an exaggerated emphasis on the purely repressive aspects of capitalist power, and an under-emphasis on more subtle mechanisms of control which, at one level, rest on consent rather than coercion and incorporate trade unions as junior partners in capitalist society. Such mechanisms, by their nature, are built slowly; yet they play a central role in making possible a sustained accumulation of capital.

Thirdly, Mandel has a peculiar notion of how the expansionary phase of a long wave is financed. During an expansionary phase, there is a very high level of investment which, Mandel says, is financed out of reserve funds *already in existence* when expansion begins; these funds, he argues, were built up in the course of several industrial cycles, during the preceding non-expansionary phase of the long wave. In the non-expansionary phase, capitalists have an excess of capital which they place in reserve funds; later, when expansion begins, they use these funds to finance a large-scale investment programme. This argument is mistaken. Once expansion gets under way, it is self-supporting; profits are high and provide a sufficient flow of money to finance investment on the required scale; capitalists then have no need for the 'historical reserve fund of capital' on which Mandel lays so much stress. The only time when such a reserve might be necessary is in the initial stages of expansion, before profits have started to flow on a large enough scale to finance investment. But, even then, there is an alternative source of finance, namely bank credit. When expansion begins economic prospects are good, anticipated profits are high and banks are prepared to lend, confident their loans are secure. Thus, firms can finance their initial investment by borrowing from the banks. Later, as profits start to flow, they can use their own internally generated funds. Now the key point about bank credit is that it can increase *total* purchasing power in the economy. Banks are not merely a funnel through which other people's savings are channelled. They can actually create *new* purchasing power by means of the overdraft system, and, in this way, can provide investment finance in excess of what has *already* been saved by capitalists or anyone else.[4] When they do this, banks are not lending reserve funds built up in the previous non-expansionary phase of the long wave. They creating genuinely new purchasing power! Mandel has fallen victim to a well-known fallacy, that no one can lend what they, or someone else, has not already saved. The peculiar characteristic of banks is that they can do just this. Like the State, they can create new purchasing power. The State does it by issuing money, and the banks do it by extending overdraft facilities.

So much for the theoretical weaknesses in Mandel's long-wave theory. Quite apart from these, however, there are a number of weaknesses in his use of the theory to characterize and explain the actual history of capitalist development.

The Organic Composition of Capital

Movements in the organic composition of capital play a central role in Mandel's analysis of capitalist development from 1793 to the present. Yet he provides very little empirical evidence to support his various claims; his general approach is impressionistic and his treatment of fixed capital unsatisfactory. Now conventional statistics are not always well suited for the testing of Marxist hypotheses, because they rest on a different conceptual basis. However, in the case of fixed capital there exists a reasonably good measure, namely, the capital-output ratio. Although not perfect, this does give us some idea what has been happening to the fixed capital part of the organic composition, which Mandel calls C_f.

The main sources of information on the historical behaviour of the capital-output ratio are the various publications of Simon Kuznets. Mandel himself cites some of these works, yet he never makes any use of the data they contain on average and incremental capital-output ratios. This is a pity, as they confirm much of what he has to say about the general pattern of capitalist development: as industrial methods of production have spread from industry to other sectors, there has indeed been a convergence of capital-output ratios, so organic compositions have become much more uniform across such diverse sectors as public utilities, manufacturing and agriculture; waves of technological innovation have indeed been accompanied by huge shifts in the organic composition of capital, clearly of great importance in the accumulation process;

and organic compositions were indeed much lower after the Second World War than before it.

On the other hand, Kuznets's data do not confirm all of Mandel's ideas. For example, although he never states it explicitly, Mandel seems to believe that there is at work a very long-run tendency which is causing the organic composition to rise *permanently*. This is not confirmed by empirical evidence, which shows clearly that, over the past hundred years, there has been no general rise in the organic composition – rises in some sectors have been offset by falls in others. This does not, of course, disprove the existence of a long-run upward tendency; but it does show that such a tendency has not yet manifested itself in reality, and its existence is therefore rather speculative. Table 1 gives data for the US economy over the period 1880 to 1948. Between 1880 and 1922 the capital-output ratio rose dramatically in agriculture, mining and manufacturing, but this was more than offset by an enormous fall in public utilities (transport, electricity, etc.), so that overall the ratio remained fairly stable. Between 1922 and 1948, however, the ratio fell in all four sectors, so that by 1948 the fixed capital part C_f of the organic composition was much lower than it had been some seventy years before in 1880.

TABLE 1

Ratio of Capital Stock to Net Product

	Agriculture	Mining	Manufacturing	Public Utilities	Total
1 June 1880	1·74	1·68	0·78	23·60	2·98
1 June 1900	1·51	2·21	1·26	10·04	2·65
31 December 1922	2·28	3·29	1·58	5·65	2·73
31 December 1948	2·02	1·47	0·98	2·50	1·57

Source: S. Kuznets, *Capital in the American Economy*, Princeton, 1961, p. 199.

Kuznets does not give much data on the post-war period and for this we must look elsewhere. Table 2 is drawn from the *UN Economic Survey of Europe in 1971, Part 2*. In 8 out of 11 countries for which data is given, the incremental capital-output ratio was lower in the nineteen-sixties than in the nineteen-fifties, often by a substantial amount. This suggests that C_f may actually have

TABLE 2

Incremental Capital-Output Ratios in Manufacturing

	1950–59	1960–69
Belgium	3·8	3·3
Denmark	2·0	1·8
West Germany	1·8	3·0
Finland	3·6	3·4
France	3·6	3·7
Italy	2·8	2·3
Netherlands	3·3	3·2
Norway	5·0	3·5
Sweden	4·4	2·5
UK	3·9	3·8
USA	5·4	2·2

Source: See text.

fallen during this period. Now these figures should be treated with caution as they reflect cyclical as well as structural influences; and they are based on so-called 'constant prices' and do not therefore allow for a change in the relative price of fixed capital and manufacturing output. Even so, they are sufficient to disprove what Mandel says about fixed capital during the post-war period. He is wrong when he says that C_f has been rising since the Second World War.[5] It is true that the physical *quantity* of equipment per worker has been rising, but, because of the greater productivity of labour, this equipment has become cheaper and its *value* has fallen. Over the nineteen-fifties and sixties this cheapening of fixed capital was enough to offset its greater quantity, so that the overall *value* of fixed capital per worker did not rise. In other words, the greater quantity of fixed capital did not lead to a rise in the organic composition of capital.

This brings us to the most recent period of history. Since the mid-sixties, there has been a fairly widespread tendency for the rate of profit (net of tax) to fall.[6] Mandel argues that the decline has been caused primarily by a rise in the organic composition of capital. Yet numerous studies, including some cited by Mandel himself, have shown this is not the case. They have proved conclusively that the rate of profit has fallen because, properly measured, profits per worker are less than they were in the mid-sixties. In other words, because the share of profits in output has fallen, and not because the organic composition has risen. For the United States, Nordhaus shows this quite clearly in an article aptly entitled 'The Falling Share of Profits'.[7] Mandel himself cites this article and it is strange that he did not take the hint contained in its title. Indeed, his use of evidence in this context is altogether rather dubious. He begins one passage with the following sentence: 'Predictably, the rise in the organic composition of capital, combined with the stagnation in the rate of surplus-value since the sixties, has led to a decline in the average rate of profit.' Then, just six lines later, he continues with the statement: 'In the USA two enquiries have yielded similar results, independently of each other. Nell has estimated a fall in the rate of surplus-value from 22·9 per cent in 1965 to 17·5 per cent in 1970 (i.e. the share of profit and interest in net value added of non-financial share companies).' Now how can a fall in the rate of surplus-value from 22·9 per cent to 17·5 per cent conceivably be described as stagnation? It accounts for the *entire* reduction in US profitability between 1965 and 1970, and establishes quite clearly that the rate of profit did not fall because the organic composition rose, but because the share of output going to profits fell.

Mandel displays a similar perversity in his reference to the well-know study of the profits squeeze in Britain by Glyn and Sutcliffe.[8] Like Nell and Nordhaus, they identify the reduced *share* of profits as the factor responsible for a lower profit rate. Yet once again Mandel cites them as confirming his thesis that a higher organic composition is responsible. Now these three references – Glyn and Sutcliffe, Nell, and Nordhaus – comprise the bulk of Mandel's statistical evidence in support of his position; yet in each case we find that he has drawn conclusions which are unjustified and contrary to the explicit opinions of the authors. Such an obstinate refusal to face facts is not, however, surprising. If Mandel were to change his position on the organic composition and admit that it has not yet risen significantly, he would need to modify substantially his explanation of the present crisis. He would need to consider in depth why and how profits have been squeezed; and, if he continued to believe the organic composition of capital is an important variable, he would need to argue why it will rise in the future, even though it has remained fairly stable for the past 25 years. To do this would not be easy, but I am sure it is possible, using the various elements of Mandel's own theory. He does not need to jettison this theory – it provides an extremely useful general framework – but he does need to reassess his application of it to the post-war period.

End of an Era?

Mandel's views on the present crisis are not always clear or consistent, but his main argument seems to be as follows. World capitalism has reached the end of an era. The expansionary phase of the post-war long wave is over and we are entering an indefinite period of stagnation; industrial cycles will continue to occur, but booms will be shorter and slumps longer than they were in the fifties and sixties. Post-war expansion was based on a 'third technological revolution', which enabled the industrial capitalist countries to improve their production techniques with comparative ease. During this period, industrial techniques spread to all branches of economic life and the 'real cost' or value of raw materials, food and manufactures fell substantially. By the mid-sixties, however, the immediate potentialities of this revolution were approaching exhaustion and easy gains were no longer possible. More investment was needed to raise productivity by a given amount and the organic composition of capital began to rise quite quickly. To maintain the old rate of profit under these conditions required the extraction of more surplus-value from the working class. But workers were not prepared to provide this additional surplus-value and they resisted capitalist attempts to make them. As a result, the rate of profit began to fall and the expansionary phase of the long wave was brought to a close.

This raises an obvious quesion: why was the working class able to resist so effectively and prevent the rate of surplus-value rising? Mandel's answer is as follows. By the mid-sixties, labour was in short supply throughout the advanced capitalist world and workers were in a strong bargaining position. Several decades of sustained accumulation had virtually exhausted the huge post-war reserves of unemployment and cheap rural labour. Although employers imported foreign workers, they were never able to do so on a sufficient scale to eliminate the shortages. Thus Mandel identifies two factors as primarily responsible for the new phase of capitalist development: 1. the disappearance of easy productivity gains, once the immediate potentialities of the third industrial revolution had been exploited; 2. a stronger working-class movement, because labour was in short supply and the reserve army of labour had been greatly depleted. The first of these is reflected in a higher organic composition of capital, the second in a relatively low rate of surplus-value.

The above is, of course, a classic analysis based directly on Marx's *Capital*. Mandel extends it by considering the role of inflation which, he says, 'is the mechanism specific to late capitalism for braking a rapid downturn in the rate of surplus-value and of profit under conjunctural conditions of relatively rapid capital accumulation and relatively high levels of employment'.[9] However, Mandel considers that inflation is inadequate as a means of maintaining the rate of profit and sustaining accumulation. It impedes but does not prevent a rise in real wages and, despite rising prices, the rate of profit continues to fall. Moreover, inflation is ultimately self-defeating, for it has an inherent tendency to accelerate and, if it is allowed to continue unchecked, prices eventually rise so fast that accumulation becomes impossible. Thus inflation can delay the crisis but cannot prevent it indefinitely. The rate of profit continues to fall and prices rise ever faster; accumulation slows down, and it is only a matter of time before a full-scale crisis occurs.

Mandel's prognostication for the future of the capitalist economies is gloomy. It will become steadily more difficult to raise productivity and to 'devalorize' constant capital; investment will not be matched by a corresponding cheapening of constant capital, so the organic composition of capital will continue to rise. Particular problems will be experienced with primary commodities, whose production has been revolutionized since the war and is now fully 'industrialized'. They will become relatively more expensive and the circulating part C_c of the organic composition will rise even faster than its fixed part C_f. To maintain the average rate of profit when the organic composition of capital is rising quickly requires a substantial increase in the rate of surplus-value. This is 'to be accomplished by the reconstruction of the industrial reserve army, and the cancellation of the democratic freedoms of the workers' movement (among other things, state repression of strikes and the right to strike). The struggle over the rate of surplus-value moves into the centre of the dynamic of economy and society, as it did in the period from the turn of the 20th century to the thirties.'[10]

However, under existing technological conditions, it is becoming more expensive to replace living labour by fixed capital, and thus more difficult to reconstitute the reserve army. Capitalism is in a double bind. On the one hand, it can 'deepen' capital stock by investing heavily in labour-saving equipment; but this way of reconstituting the reserve army would cause the organic composition of capital to rise very sharply. On the other hand, it can 'widen' capital stock, by not bothering so much with expensive labour-saving methods; but heavy investment of this kind would create a huge demand for labour, and would soon exhaust the reserve army. Thus, if carried out on a large scale, 'deepening' is unprofitable because it drives up the organic composition of capital, and 'widening' is unprofitable because it exhausts the reserve army of labour and makes the extraction of surplus-value more difficult. Given that heavy investment of either kind – 'deepening' or 'widening' – is unprofitable, the only alternative is to invest less; and to contain accumulation within the limits set by reduced technological possibilities and an incipient labour shortage. Only in this way can the organic composition be kept within reasonable bounds and the reserve army preserved. In practice, this means an indefinite period of stagnation, characterized by short booms and long recessions. The reserve army will be preserved, not through the dynamic replacement of labour by machines, but by a process of repeated slumps which hold down the long-term rate of accumulation.

The above exposition of Mandel's views on the present situation is by no means complete, and may not be entirely accurate. He nowhere gives an adequate summary of his ideas and to identify them in his vast and sprawling text is not always easy. Even so, I think I have captured the main thrust of his argument, although I may have expressed it in rather different language. Much of what Mandel says is certainly correct. The industrial reserve army is, indeed, capitalism's own specific means of labour discipline. Its depletion by the nineteen-sixties was partly responsible for ending the expansionary phase of the long wave. Sustained accumulation will be very difficult unless this reserve can be reconstituted in some way. Mandel is also right to emphasize technology and the need to 'devalorize' capital, so as to keep down the organic composition. The need for this has been ignored by one school of Marxists who have focused almost exclusively on income distribution. Moreover, as he says, it will in future be more difficult to raise productivity, especially in the raw materials sector which is now largely industrialized. This will make it more difficult to devalorize constant capital and the result may, indeed, be a rising organic composition.[11] For this reason, I think he is right to claim that capitalism is in for a period of stagnation, caused by the difficulty of reconstituting the reserve army without at the same time raising the organic composition of rapital. Finally, I agree that inflation has been used to maintain the rate of profit and prolong expansion, and that it has proved inadequate to this task.

On the other hand, there are a number of points where Mandel is incorrect or his approach is inadequate. I have already argued that his analysis of the recent past is wrong in one important respect: the rate of profit fell from the mid-sixties onwards, not because the organic composition of capital rose, as he claims, but because the amount of surplus-value going to industrial capital fell or, to put it differently, because profits were squeezed. Naturally, Mandel does not specifically discuss the profits squeeze, for the simple reason that he does not recognize its existence. Secondly, he never convincingly explains why inflation failed to maintain the rate of profit and prolong the boom indefinitely. Finally, his discussion of technology and its application, although correct at the most general level, ignores certain specific features of the third technological revolution which have already been important and could become even more so in the future. Let us examine in some detail these main areas of contention: the profits squeeze, inflation, and technology.

The Profits Squeeze

For more than a decade the share of post-tax profits in output has declined throughout the advanced capitalist world. The immediate causes of this decline are as follows: rising state expenditures, often under the impact of popular pressure for better social services and benefits; worsening terms of trade with primary producers during 1972–4, in part because of a shortage of primary commodities and in part because of the organized power of the OPEC cartel; and finally, the existence of a strong working-class movement demanding higher real wages and unwilling to restrain its consumption and free resources for use by the state and transfer to primary producers. Given the competing claims of workers, the State and primary producers, the amount left for profits was greatly reduced. Industrial capital attempted to shield itself from the full effects of this reduction by shifting part of the burden onto small savers, thereby redividing total profits at their expense. In this it was helped by inflation, which enabled firms to repay their debts with depreciated currency. Even so, despite a redivision of total profits in its favour, industrial capital still received a smaller quantity of surplus-value than before and its share of output fell. This was reflected in a lower rate of profit on 'shareholders' equity'. Thus there were three main factors which accounted for the profit squeeze: 1. state expenditure; 2. the terms of trade with primary producers; 3. working-class power. Let us examine each of these briefly.

State Expenditure

In most capitalist countries the share of GDP absorbed by the state was fairly stable during the nineteen-fifties. This stability was the result of two opposing tendencies: State expenditure on civil items (such as administration, education or social benefits) was increasing its share of GDP; but the share of military expenditure was falling rapidly, because of partial demobilization following the armistice in Korea and disengagement from former colonial empires. These two tendencies – a higher civil and a lower military share – partially offset each other and the overall share of state expenditure did not change very much. In the sixties, however, things were rather different. The pace of demobilization slowed down, and in West Germany and the USA there was even a phase of rearmament, so that the share of military expenditure remained fairly stable, yet the civil share continued to rise as fast or even faster than before. The result was a marked increase during the sixties of the proportion of GDP absorbed by the state. As can be seen from Tables 3 and 4, this wave of expansion reached its peak in 1963–8, when the state share of GDP rose by 2·8 per cent

TABLE 3

Share of Government Expenditure in GDP (%)

	1953	1958	1963	1968	1973
USA:					
Military	13·2	10·2	8·8	9·2	5·9
Civil	14·3	18·9	20·4	22·8	26·8
Total	27·5	29·1	29·2	32·0	32·7
UK:					
Military	9·0	6·4	6·1	5·6	4·7
Civil	26·6	25·9	28·2	33·2	35·7
Total	35·6	32·3	34·3	38·8	40·4
JAPAN:					
Military	n.a.	n.a.	n.a.	n.a.	n.a.
Civil	n.a.	n.a.	n.a.	n.a.	n.a.
Total*	15·7	15·0	13·9	14·4	15·7
FRANCE:					
Military	7·8	5·6	4·5	3·8	n.a.
Civil	25·1	27·6	31·1	34·3	n.a.
Total	32·9	33·2	35·6	38·1	37·2†
GERMANY:					
Military	4·3	2·6	4·6	3·2	2·9
Civil	26·6	30·2	29·9	33·4	35·5
Total	30·9	32·8	34·5	36·6	38·4
ITALY:					
Military	3·0	2·6	2·5	2·2	2·1
Civil	22·9	26·2	27·9	32·4	38·1
Total	25·9	28·8	30·4	34·6	40·2

Sources: OECD National Accounts 1950–68, 1962–73.
Notes and Definitions: Gross Domestic Products (GDP) at current market prices. Government expenditure includes all current expenditure (goods and services; transfers, subsidies, interest on debt, etc.) plus gross fixed capital formation by the government, but excludes expenditure by public corporations.

* Figures for Japan exclude gross fixed capital formation.
† The 1973 figure for France is not comparable with earlier figures.

TABLE 4

Changes in the percentage Share of Government Expenditure in GDP

	1953–8	1958–63	1963–8	1968–73
Total government expenditure				
USA	+ 1·6	+ 0·1	+ 2·8	+ 0·7
UK	− 3·3	+ 2·0	+ 4·5	+ 0·7
Japan*	− 0·7	− 1·1	+ 0·5	+ 1·3
France	+ 0·3	+ 2·4	+ 2·5	− 0·9†
Germany	+ 1·9	+ 1·7	+ 2·1	+ 1·8
Italy	+ 2·9	+ 1·6	+ 4·2	+ 5·6
Average	+ 0·5	+ 1·1	+ 2·8	+ 1·7
Military expenditure				
USA	− 3·0	− 1·4	+ 0·4	− 3·3
UK	− 2·6	− 0·3	− 0·5	− 0·9
Japan	n.a.	n.a.	n.a.	n.a.
France	− 2·2	− 1·1	− 0·7	n.a.
Germany	− 1·7	+ 2·0	− 1·4	− 0·3
Italy	− 0·4	− 0·1	− 0·3	− 0·1
Average	− 2·0	− 0·2	− 0·5	− 1·1
Civil expenditure				
USA	+ 4·6	+ 1·5	+ 2·4	+ 4·0
UK	− 0·7	+ 2·3	+ 5·0	+ 2·5
Japan	n.a.	n.a.	n.a.	n.a.
France	+ 2·5	+ 3·5	+ 3·2	n.a.
Germany	+ 3·6	− 0·3	+ 3·5	+ 2·1
Italy	+ 3·3	+ 1·7	+ 4·5	+ 5·7
Average	+ 2·7	+ 1·7	+ 3·7	+ 3·6

Source: Table 3.
Note: Averages are unweighted.
* Figure for Japan excludes gross capital formation.
† For 1968–73 the figure for France is not reliable.

in the USA, 4·5 per cent in the UK, 2·5 per cent in France, 2·1 per cent in Germany and 4·2 per cent in Italy. Japan was an exception and her state share rose by a mere 0·5 per cent. After this peak, expansion tailed off somewhat, particularly in the United States, where the military budget stagnated once the Vietnam build-up was complete. Even so, the state share was in general considerably higher in 1973 than in 1968.

Thus, following a period of comparative stability in the fifties, the share of GDP absorbed by the state rose considerably. The changes in any given year were small, but cumulatively they were often very big. Clearly, if workers were unwilling to finance such an expansion of state expenditure, the resulting pressure on profits must have been considerable, and it is reasonable to assume that growing state expenditure was a major factor behind the profits squeeze.

The civil part of state expenditure has grown rapidly for a number of reasons, of which the following are particularly important: popular pressure for better social services and benefits; a relatively slow growth of productivity in service activities organized by the state (administration, health, education); and a growing need for economic infrastructure to underpin capitalist development (roads, research and development, skilled manpower, etc.). Among the popular forces demanding more social expenditures has, of course, been the trade-union movement, so the growth of state expenditure is itself partly a reflection of greater working-class power. This seems very obvious and is a commonplace among social-democratic writers, yet it is never seriously discussed by Mandel who, apart from scattered reference to 'indirect wages' and 'horizontal redistribution', makes no attempt to assess its significance. He never confronts the possibility that state expenditure may be partly financed out of profits, rather than wages, in which case it will reduce the rate of profit.

The Terms of Trade

During the nineteen-fifties and early sixties, primary products became steadily cheaper in relation to manufactures, a phenomenon which Mandel considers to be an example of 'unequal exchange'. Whether or not one agrees with this characterization, the phenomenon itself is genuine enough, and the industrial countries benefited greatly from their better terms of trade with primary producers (see Table 5). In the late sixties, however, these terms of trade stabilized and the relative price of primary products stopped falling. Finally, in the commodity boom of 1972–4, primary product prices rose rapidly and the terms of trade shifted strongly against the industrial countries. In 1974, primary products were on average 65 per cent more expensive relative to manufactures than they had been two years earlier. The oil price rise alone was equivalent to around 4 per cent of GDP in Italy, Japan and the UK. Thus in the late sixties the industrial countries ceased to benefit from improving terms of trade, and then in 1972–4 there was a huge transfer of resources from them to the primary producing countries.

TABLE 5

Terms of Trade for Primary Products

1951	1954	1958	1963	1966	1967	1968	1969	1970	1971	1972	1973	1974
119	108	93	87	85	82	81	82	81	81	84	105	139

Source: *UN Yearbook of International Trade*, various years.

Definition: Terms of Trade $= \dfrac{\text{Price of primary products}}{\text{Price of manufactures}}$

Mandel explains this last shift in the terms of trade as follows: 'since 1972 a new rise in primary commodity prices has occurred – determined in part by short-term speculation and the inflationary boom of 1972–3, but also partly reflecting real relative scarcities, caused by the slower rate of capital investment in the primary producing sectors than in the manufacturing sector during the previous long-term period. This new upswing in prices will not be entirely cancelled by the 1974–5 world recession; it will enable the semi-colonial bourgeoisies to ameliorate their position as junior partners of imperialism, not only politically but also financially and economically'.[12] This explanation is correct as far as it goes, but it ignores two factors: adverse weather conditions which caused a world shortage of wheat, and the new-found power of the oil-exporting countries which formed a cartel to force up the price of oil. Apart from this qualification, however, I find Mandel's analysis of movements in the terms of trade convincing.

What is less convincing, however, is his discussion of its

implications for the industrial countries. He considers only its effect on the organic composition of capital, and ignores completely its effects on the rate of surplus-value and the share of profits.[13] Yet the falling relative price of primary products may have played a part in keeping up the share of profits during the fifties and early sixties. Ever cheaper imports of primary products helped raise real wages at no cost to industrial capital, and without therefore impinging on profits. When the terms of trade stabilized in the late sixties, this source of easy wage increases dried up.

True, primary products were still cheap, but they were not getting any cheaper, and it was accordingly more difficult than before to raise real wages. Finally, when commodity prices exploded in 1972–4, there was a huge transfer of resources to primary producers, especially those of the Third World. This transfer made it extremely difficult to maintain the pace of real wage increases which workers of the metropolitan countries expected, and these could be granted only at the expense of profits.

Working-class Power

Higher state expenditure and worse terms of trade do not in themselves lead to lower profits, *provided* the personal consumption of workers can be reduced by an equivalent amount below what it would otherwise have been. Indeed, many governments based their policies on exactly this argument, seeking to restrain working-class consumption and free resources for use by the state and for the purchase of primary products.

They were not, however, very successful and there was a definite fall in the share of profits. This suggests that workers were unwilling to make the required sacrifices and were often strong enough to resist attempts to force them to do so. What are the origins of this power? Mandel points to the reserve army of labour, arguing that by the mid-sixties it had been severely depleted and could no longer perform its disciplinary role properly. This is surely correct, and the author's discussion of the reserve army is one of the best parts of his book. He insists on the primacy of class struggle, arguing that the reserve army does not function primarily through supply and demand in the labour market, but through its effect on working-class bargaining power: a large reserve of unemployed or cheap labour demoralizes the working-class movement and undermines its organizational strength. He criticizes the 'Phillip's curve' for its mechanical and automatic approach to wages and unemployment, arguing correctly that the relationship is mediated by trade unions and other working-class organizations, and that unemployment can influence wages only by undermining the strength and combativity of these organizations.

Unfortunately, this is as far as Mandel goes. He does not discuss in detail the influence of other factors which might have affected working-class strength and combativity during the nineteen-fifties, such as the Cold War and religious conflicts, both of which set worker against worker and legitimized right-wing leaders. This is a pity, because these factors were important; their declining influence in the sixties must have contributed to the re-emergence of a powerful and combative working-class movement. In both France and Italy, for example, the Cold War division between Catholic and non-Catholic workers seriously weakened the working-class movement during the fifties. The healing of this split was an important factor behind the militancy which erupted in the May Events in France and the Hot Autumn in Italy, both of which resulted in massive wage increases and placed considerable pressure on profits.

This discussion may be summarized as follows. Three main factors were responsible for the profits squeeze which began around the mid-sixties. First, state expenditures were increasing rapidly and absorbing an ever-growing share of national income. Secondly, the terms of trade with primary producers were no longer improving, and in 1972–4 deteriorated sharply, causing a huge transfer of resources from industrial countries to primary producers. Finally, the working class was much stronger and more combative than it had been in the fifties. Workers expected substantial wage increases and were not prepared to shoulder the burden of greater state expenditures or, in 1972–4, of worse terms of trade. They resisted attempts to make them shoulder this burden and, when taxes and prices were raised, they demanded wage increases in compensation. In this way they were able to shift most or even all of the burden back onto profits, and this is the main reason why the share of profits fell. Mandel examines each of the above factors separately, but never combines them to form a coherent analysis of why profits were squeezed.

Inflation

The above explanation of the profits squeeze raises an interesting question. Inflation, as Mandel says, was used to defend profits in the face of higher costs (including taxes paid by capitalists). By raising prices, capitalists sought to shift on to consumers, and ultimately on to the working class, the burden of higher wages, more expensive materials and higher taxes. Yet, as the profits squeeze shows, they were not entirely successful, and inflation proved inadequate as a device for defending profits. Why was this? Why was it not possible to raise prices so that they always remained one jump ahead of costs? Clearly, there must have been factors which prevented prices from rising fast enough. What were these factors?

Mandel answers this question in a chapter entitled 'The Industrial Cycle in Late Capitalism', where he identifies two main factors, both of them associated with the existence of independent nation states. Firstly, inflation can undermine the competitive position of a country in world markets by making its products too expensive; this in turn may lead to a loss of home and overseas markets to foreign competitors, and to an unsustainable balance of payments deficit. The need to remain internationally competitive thus imposes definite constraints on the freedom of individual governments to pursue a policy of domestic inflation. Secondly, to support world inflation may require the creation of an ever larger and more unstable system of international credit, whose existence poses a dangerous threat to the whole financial structure of world capitalism. This imposes a severe constraint, not just on individual countries, but on the collectivity of major capitalist powers who must take responsibility for the world financial system; they must collectively contain the expansion of credit, even though this slows down the pace of inflation, stops them from protecting profits and ultimately provokes a recession.

Thus Mandel identifies two main factors which limit the use of inflation as a device for protecting profits: 1. the need of individual countries to remain competitive on world markets; 2.

the collective need to prevent an over-extension and ultimate collapse of the world credit system. The first factor has, he argues, been in operation throughout the entire post-war period, for individual countries have always been faced with the problems of international competitiveness and national solvency. The second factor has, however, become really important only in the nineteen-seventies, with the decline of US hegemony and the collapse of the Bretton Woods system. The United States can no longer perform its role as co-ordinator of world capitalism, nor can it underpin the tottering world credit system. Indeed, Mandel ascribes the present recession primarily to this second factor, arguing that it was caused primarily by a 'collective need to put a brake on any further expansion of the menacing debt pyramid'. To stabilize the world financial system, the major capitalist powers imposed simultaneous credit restrictions and refused to provide the finance necessary to fuel inflation and keep prices rising ahead of costs. This in turn caused the rate of profit to fall and led to a 'generalized world recession'.

Thus, in Mandel's view, the main factors limiting the use of inflation were both associated with the existence of independent nation states or, if you like, with international contradictions. In the fifties and sixties, these contradictions expressed themselves primarily at a national level, with first one country and then another taking action to safeguard its competitive position, while America held the ring and looked after the interests of capitalism as a whole. By the seventies, however, the United States could no longer perform these tasks, and contradictions expressed themselves, not just as a problem for the individual country, but as a threat to the entire world financial system. It was a question not simply of mushrooming debt, but of the absence of a dominant state which would underpin this debt and ensure that the whole structure did not collapse.

Mandel's general argument is clearly an impressive and subtle attempt to combine two levels of analysis. He uses his long-wave theory to expose the underlying forces which were exerting pressure on the rate of profit, and his theory of international contradictions to explain why inflation failed to relieve this pressure. We have already seen what is wrong (and what is right) with his analysis of the forces pressing on the rate of profit – his mistaken emphasis on the organic composition of capital and neglect of the pressure on profits exerted by higher state expenditures and, in 1972–4, worse terms of trade. Are there also defects in his analysis of inflation? Was its use limited primarily by international contradictions, as he claims, or were there other, equally important factors at work?

To answer this question one need only consider the political content in which money and credit policy is formulated and the decision whether or not to permit a given rate of inflation is made. Governments cannot simply consider the immediate interests of big capital; they must also take into account the wishes of other classes and strata. If they do not do so, they risk losing their electoral support and may find themselves engaged in a trial of strength which threatens to destabilize the whole structure of bourgeois society. These are not considerations which apply only under extreme conditions, when prices are rising at a fast and accelerating rate. Even when prices are rising quite slowly, as in Germany or the USA during the fifties or early sixties, inflation may be very unpopular. In some cases, such as Germany, this partly reflects a collective memory of hyper-inflation and its real or alleged consequences (ruin of the middle classes, fascism, etc.). In other cases, however, more prosaic factors are at work. Trade unionists want prices restrained so as to reap the full benefit of any wage increases they have received. They may express their wishes directly through the ballot box, or indirectly by threatening economic disruption if prices are not restrained. This latter threat raises the spectre of a cumulative, and perhaps explosive, wage-price spiral in which capitalists, with tacit state support, attempt to keep prices always one step ahead of wages. The desire to avoid such a spiral has clearly been an important consideration of those governments which have adopted a firm anti-inflationary stance. In addition to trade unionists, there are many others who oppose inflation and, although they may lack economic power, their political support is still important. Among these are small savers who may not be able to protect themselves against its effects; and people, such as pensioners, whose incomes may not be fully adjusted to match rising prices. Taken together these various, and sometimes overlapping, categories – workers, small savers, pensioners, etc. – may constitute a formidable anti-inflationary coalition and severely limit the use of inflation as a device for maintaining profits.

Thus even creeping inflation may meet with strong domestic opposition and not be feasible on the scale required. Moreover, such considerations are even more important once inflation gets under way and looks like getting out of hand. The political consequences of accelerating inflation are well known. It undermines the legitimacy of capitalism by rewarding the speculator; it destroys faith in the market by rewarding the strong at the expense of the weak; and it leads the previously unorganized to organize themselves in defensive associations. In this way it destroys the moral basis of capitalism and leads to a widening circle of conflict, as ever more sections of society are drawn into battle. If this process continues, the result is hyper-inflation, and ultimately the collapse of bourgeois democracy – to be replaced, depending on the balance of class forces, either by socialism or by some form of right-wing authoritarian regime, such as fascism or military dictatorship. Clearly a primary objective of state policy in modern bourgeois democracies is to prevent such a degeneration.

Mandel himself recognizes that international contradictions may not be the only factors limiting the use of inflation, but he believes these other factors operate only during the accelerating phase when it looks as though 'galloping' inflation is a real possibility. Moreover, he considers the problem in narrowly economic terms arguing that galloping inflation must be prevented because it interferes with the accumulation of productive capital. Accumulation, he says, requires a certain degree of price stability, without which capitalists refuse to invest, instead hoarding their capital in some non-productive form. Now this argument does have some validity, for explosive inflation can interfere with the accumulation of capital. However, except in extreme hyper-inflationary situations, the political consequences of inflation are usually far more important than its narrowly economic impact on capital accumulation. Inflation threatens the political stability of capitalism long before it seriously disrupts its economic mechanism. In my opinion, the capitalist powers did not provoke the crisis of 1974 primarily because they were frightened of a collapse of the world financial system – the bank failures to which Mandel refers were more of a consequence than a cause of the crisis. Nor did they do it primarily because they were frightened that galloping inflation would disrupt the accumulation of capital. They did it primarily for political reasons, because inflation was extremely unpopular and, if allowed to continue, might lead to a collapse of bourgeois democracy and perhaps even to the suppression of capitalism itself. Thus although I agree that international contradictions have limited the use of inflation, I think Mandel has over-emphasized them to the exclusion of other factors. Moreover, what few comments he does make concerning these other factors are narrowly economic; he virtually ignores the political dimensions of inflation, which have been extremely important.

Technology

Mandel talks at some length about a third technological revolution based on the 'reserve of unapplied technical discoveries or potential technological innovations' built up during the interwar period and the Second World War, and 'culminating in the release of nuclear energy, cybernetics and automation'. He says that this potential was exploited during the post-war period, and the result was a very rapid rise in productivity whose effect was to cheapen or 'devalorize' constant capital, thereby retarding the organic composition's tendency to rise. He then says that, as this potential was exhausted, it became more difficult to raise productivity and the organic composition began to rise quite rapidly. I have already argued that this is factually incorrect, although I do think the organic composition may rise in future. Let me now make some comments on Mandel's view of technical progress itself. While agreeing with his general stress on the importance of modern technology, I think his argument suffers from three weaknesses: 1. he gives too little weight to the phenomenon of 'catching up' which has allowed Europe and Japan to make huge productivity gains by adapting more advanced American technology; 2. he lays too much stress on technology as such and not enough on the institutional factors which govern its application and development; 3. his treatment of the service sector is inadequate, and he does not recognize that productivity advance in this sector is one of the central problems of modern capitalism.

Catching Up

The spectacular rise in productivity since the Second World War
contains a substantial amount of catching up by Europe and
Japan. Nothing like the same progress has been recorded by the
US economy which, as world leader in 1945, had no one else to
catch up on. Indeed, American productivity has not grown so
much faster since the war than it did before, and the accelera-
tion of innovation, to which Mandel refers, is less evident in
America than elsewhere. This suggests that productivity growth
will slow down as other countries approach the American level
and the scope for catching up diminishes. Some are likely to
overtake the United States, but none is likely to sustain its earlier
spectacular performance.

The phenomenon of catching up is, of course, an aspect of
uneven development. On a world level there remain enormous
differences between one country and another: many
underdeveloped countries have not yet gone through their
second, or even first, industrial revolution, yet alone their third.
Given appropriate political conditions – stability and a strong
modernizing state – there is every reason to believe that catching
up will spread to much, although by no means all, of the Third
World. In part this depends on internal conditions in the
countries concerned, but in part it reflects the growing problems
of technical advance in the developed countries. As it becomes
more difficult to raise productivity in Europe and Japan, their
big firms will increasingly look towards the Third World.
During the next phase of capitalist development, dynamism will
shift from the present advanced countries towards the underdeveloped countries. Naturally, this process will be uneven;
many countries, including the giant India, will remain
backward. Even so, industrialization of the Third World will
occur on a larger scale than Mandel seems to believe, and will
represent a significant extension of the capitalist mode of
production into hitherto unconquered areas.

Institutional Factors

Technological potential can only be realized within a certain
institutional framework. Firms must be big enough to operate
processes on an efficient scale, resources must be placed in the
hands of firms willing and able to use them creatively, workers
must be persuaded or compelled to co-operate in the

introduction and development of new processes, and so on. In creating this framework the state plays a central role, undertaking certain tasks itself, channelling resources in the right direction, and ensuring 'industrial relations' conducive to change. Now Mandel recognizes all this, but seems to consider it less important than technology *per se*. Yet there is a counter-argument which runs as follows. There remains enormous technological potential which is not exploited for *structural* reasons; what is needed is a major shake-up which will centralize existing capitals into larger units, weed out inefficient producers and force the adoption of more advanced techniques. To bring about these changes requires a combination of crises, to weaken resistance to change, combined with vigorous state intervention to promote the necessary restructuring. Given such a shake-up, expansion can be sustained for many years on the basis of existing technological potential. Moreover, techno-logical progress is itself dependent on institutional factors, and active state encouragement of research and development would lead to many new discoveries. Thus, with appropriate state policies for restructuring and technology, there is no reason for the present expansionary phase to run out of steam in the near future.

Now the above argument is exaggerated, both because it neglects the catching up element in European and Japanese performance, and because it neglects the problem of raising productivity in the service sector, a problem which I discuss below. Even so, it has some force and one should not underestimate the advances which active state intervention can achieve. Indeed, it is the very potential for such advance which will create the battleground for future struggle. From a capitalist point of view, state intervention can be a two-edged weapon, whose immediate and often substantial economic benefits may be outweighed by its potential political dangers. We saw this very clearly in Britain with Benn's programme for moderniza-tion, which involved widespread state intervention and the nationalization of a number of profitable firms. This was bitterly resisted by the Right and the Confederation of British Industries, who argued that it would open the floodgates to socialism. To forestall such an ultimate disaster, they were prepared to sacrifice the immediate benefits the programme offered. Now these fears were exaggerated, but they did have a certain basis in reality. The implementation of Benn's programme would have given confidence to militants and would have established the Left as a real force in British politics – something it has not been since the nineteen-forties. In perceiving this danger, the Right showed themselves to be better dialecticians than many on the Marxist Left, who took a rather negative attitude to the whole affair on the grounds that Benn's programme was little more than 'an attempt to shore up British capitalism'.

Thus, by emphasizing the narrowly technological aspects of the third technological revolution, Mandel has underestimated the importance of institutional factors and state intervention. In doing so he has neglected questions of crucial political significance, namely the battle to determine how and where the state will intervene, which firms it will nationalize, and so on. Mandel may consider this a reformist perspective, but these are the questions which will confront the entire Left during the coming years, whether we like it or not.

Services

Mandel devotes an entire chapter to the service sector. Unfortunately, despite some interesting insights, this chapter is unsatisfactory. It fails to come to grips with the central problem posed by the service sector, namely the relatively stagnant nature of its techniques and a consequent slow growth of productivity. Instead of discussing this properly, he devotes most of his energies to a confusing and unconvincing attempt to distinguish between 'productive' and 'unproductive' services. Now the purpose of making such a distinction is not to determine in some quasi-theological manner whether or not these activities 'produce' value or surplus-value, but to help determine their laws of motion and how they relate to the rest of the economy. Most discussions, including that of Mandel, never really do this, and hence their quasi-theological and often moralistic tone.

The relevant facts about the service sector are as follows. Employment has been growing fast ever since the Second World War, mainly because 'productivity' has risen slowly at a time of expanding demand and output. This rise in employment is primarily due to the continued backwardness of techniques in the service sector. With a few exceptions, there has been no technological revolution comparable to that which has transformed industry and agriculture. Mandel is wrong when he says 'late capitalism . . . appears as a period in which all branches of the economy are fully industrialized for the first time'. A casual visit to the average garage, retail shop, restaurant, school, or government department should dispel that illusion. Of course, there have been advances and modern equipment is used, but there has rarely been anything like the wholesale transformation which has occurred in other sectors.

The technological lag in services has had two consequences. 1. They are becoming more expensive in comparison with industrial products, so that they account for a growing share of national expenditure, *even though their output is growing relatively slowly*. This is most clear in the state sector, whose output includes many services like health, education and administration, and whose costs are rising rapidly as service productivity lags behind real wages. The 'fiscal crisis of the state' is in large measure due to the continued technological backwardness of services *in general*, of which those run by the state are a particular example. 2. Services are beginning to compete with industry for labour. In the fifties there was a huge pool of agricultural and unemployed labour in most advanced capitalist countries, which provided ample workers for both services and industry. With the disappearance of this pool, however, labour is no longer so plentiful. A new round of accumulation would soon lead to a situation in which the services could only expand by drawing labour from the industrial sector. Thus services are becoming more expensive and are potentially in competition for scarce labour with the industrial sector. For those reasons the service sector, in its present state, constitutes a serious obstacle to sustained accumulation. A continuation of the long upswing depends in large measure on the ability of advanced capitalist countries to tackle the service sector and revolutionize its production methods.

The difficulties in raising productivity in the services are twofold: institutional and technical. In the private sector many services are supplied by small inefficient producers who display an amazing capacity for survival, or by monopolists who have no incentive to change because they are protected by trade or professional organizations. Many public sector services are not subject to external competition – there is no 'law of value' forcing them to revolutionize their techniques – and are often highly resistant to change, both because of their organizational structure and because of employee resistance to changes which may cost them their jobs or alter the character of their work. However, even where institutional factors are favourable to change, productivity is often difficult to raise for the simple reason that the required techniques do not exist in usable form, are extremely expensive or have not even been invented.[14] Taking account of both institutional and technical factors, it is clear that the service sector will not be easy to modernize.

To produce a revolution in services, comparable to that which has occurred in industry and agriculture, will require a concerted attack on the institutions and mode of operation of this sector, together with the development of a whole range of new techniques. To bring about these changes will require vigorous action by the state. Indeed, we have already seen the first signs of such action during the present crisis in Britain. Public expenditure cuts are primarily aimed at saving money by reducing the quantity or quality of public services, but they are also being used to undermine established work practices and to pave the way for the introduction of new techniques and methods of operation.

This latter aspect of official policy will become more important in future years as the state becomes increasingly concerned about the lagging service sector, both public and private. It is clear, from the hints contained in Mandel's chapter on the service sector and the general approach of his book, that he could have analysed very well the problems I have just mentioned. Unfortunately, like most Marxists who have written on the service sector, he has allowed himself to be sidetracked and his analysis has suffered accordingly.

Conclusions

Rather than summarize what I have said in this review, let me conclude by listing some of the crucial questions which are raised by *Late Capitalism*. What is the role of the state in promoting technical advance and in restructuring industry? How extensive will state intervention be in the coming decades, and what forms will it take? What are the political implications of such intervention? What is the role of the service sector in modern capitalism, and does it constitute a serious obstacle to continued accumulation? What is the significance of increased state expenditure? Is it merely a once-and-for-all structural shift, caused by a now largely satisfied need for better social services and benefits, or will the share of state expenditure continue rising into the indefinite future? If the latter is true, what are its implications for capitalist development? What is the role of the reserve army of labour in modern capitalism? Is it the only practical means of containing the working class, or can it be replaced by some other mechanism in a new corporate state? If the reserve army is in fact necessary, how can capitalism reconstitute this reserve on a permanent basis in the advanced countries? How will relations with primary producers, especially those of the Third World, affect economic development in the advanced capitalist world? Some of these questions are now being debated by Marxists, but none has yet received a very satisfactory answer.

NOTES

1. Ernest Mandel, *Late Capitalism*, NLB, London, and Humanities Press, Atlantic Highlands, N.J., 1975.
2. ibid., p. 145.
3. ibid., p. 115.
4. I have used the term 'purchasing power' to avoid what, in the present context, is a sterile debate on whether or not bank deposits are 'money'.
5. *Late Capitalism*, pp. 131–2.
6. The precise timing of this decline varies from country to country, and the long-term trend has often been disguised by short-term cyclical variations. Even so, there is no doubt that the underlying trend in profits has been downward since the mid-sixties.
7. William Nordhaus, 'The Falling Share of Profits', in A. Okun and L. Perry (eds), *Brooking Papers on Economic Activity*, No. 1, 1974.
8. Andrew Glyn and Bob Sutcliffe, *British Capitalism, Workers and the Profit Squeeze*, Harmondsworth, 1972.
9. *Late Capitalism*, p. 422.
10. ibid., pp. 472–3.
11. It is clear that I agree with Mandel when he says that capitalism is entering a new phase in which it will be more difficult to raise productivity. State intervention may ease the difficulty by restructuring capital and promoting research and development, but it is unlikely to produce spectacular advances of the kind we have witnessed since World War Two. To achieve a given increase in productivity will thus be more difficult than previously and the organic composition may consequently rise. I say may

rise, rather than will rise, because what happens to the organic composition does not just depend on technical progress; it also depends on the rate of accumulation. When the stream of newly available techniques is very rapid, as it has been since the Second World War, capital is devalorized quickly and a high rate of accumulation can be sustained without causing the organic composition to rise. Conversely, when this stream of newly available techniques is slow, capital is devalorized slowly and a high rate of accumulation causes the organic composition to rise. To prevent the organic composition from rising, therefore, requires a reduction in the rate of accumulation in line with the reduced stream of newly available techniques. Thus movements in the organic composition are determined by the *relationship* between two factors: 1. the rate of accumulation; 2. the flow of newly available techniques. The organic composition rises when accumulation outstrips the flow of new techniques, and falls when the reverse is true. (The two factors are not of course, independent of each other. Accumulation stimulates invention and thereby increases the flow of newly available techniques. In principle, this stimulating effect could lead to a rapid devalorization of capital and allow a high rate of accumulation to be sustained indefinitely, without causing the organic composition of capital to rise. The argument in the text assumes that in the coming period this will not occur, and that a high rate of accumulation really would outstrip the flow of newly available techniques.) Any statement about future movements in the organic composition is therefore conditional upon what happens to accumulation. The stream of newly available techniques is almost certainly becoming weaker, but this will only lead to a big rise in the organic composition if accumulation is maintained at a high rate. If, however, there is a long period of stagnation, in which the rate of accumulation is drastically reduced, then the organic composition may not rise, for the reduced flow of newly available techniques may be matched by a corresponding reduction in the rate of accumulation. The extreme possibilities are: 1. a high rate of accumulation and a fast rising organic composition of capital; 2. a very low rate of accumulation and a stable (or even falling) organic composition. The most likely outcome is somewhere in between – a moderate rate of accumulation, combined with a moderate rise in the organic composition.

12. ibid., p. 371.

13. Primary products enter directly and indirectly into workers' consumption. Changes in their cost can thus affect the value of labour power and thereby the rate of surplus-value and the share of profits. With a given real wage, the more expensive are primary commodities, the lower, other things being equal, will be the share of profits and the rate of profit.

14. To say that it is extremely expensive to raise productivity in the service sector means that substantially greater productivity requires the use of techniques with a very high organic composition of capital. A new wave of technological discovery could overcome this problem 1. by cheapening constant capital, thereby reducing the cost of equipment used to replace labour; 2. by finding ways of saving service labour which do not require the use of large amounts of equipment.

5

*Inflation and Crisis**

Inflation is a subject which has caused deep divisions of opinion within the left, both in Britain and elsewhere. There is little agreement about either its causes or cures, and the debate between rival schools of thought has been intense and at times bitter, which is not really suprising as the issues at stake are important, and the theoretical and practical questions involved are difficult. The complexity of the subject and the extent of disagreement are clearly visible in the *Marxism Today* debate on inflation which was originally sparked off by Pat Devine's article of March 1974.[1] It is not, however, my intention to describe or criticize the various positions taken in this debate, for many of the views expressed are correct in their own way and the problem is not to decide in favour of one side or another, but rather to find a wider framework within which their positive insights can be encompassed.

A start has already been made in this direction by Laurence Harris in his recent article in *Marxism Today* and by John Grahl and others in their joint contribution to the Party *Economic Bulletin*.[2] They argue that, in the advanced capitalist world, inflation is closely connected with the process of capital accumulation and with attempts by the state to regulate this process, and in consequence any adequate analysis of inflation must base itself on the more general theory of accumulation and crisis. This approach is in my opinion correct and it will be the main theme of the present article. The plan of the article is as follows. Part One describes the basic analysis of accumulation and crisis which is contained in the writings of Karl Marx. Part Two examines how this analysis must be modified to take account of the modern state which plays a far more active role than Marx assumed and seeks to control both the pace and direction of capitalist expansion. In the course of this discussion it argues that the state may deliberately foster inflation as a convenient way of handling problems which it is unable or

* First published in *Marxism Today*, November 1977.

unwilling to tackle in a more fundamental way. Part Three considers the practical implications of this view, and argues that the wages struggle must not be seen and must not be fought in isolation from the wider political struggle for an alternative economic policy which would make possible the satisfaction of working-class demands.

I THE SELF-REGULATING ECONOMY

Marx states in a preface to *Capital* that his aim is to 'lay bare the economic law of motion of modern society'. To this end he identified two basic features of a capitalist economy which differentiates it from other kinds of economy. Firstly, there is a division of labour in which individual producers specialize in producing particular goods and services which they exchange in return for money. The activities of these various producers are not consciously co-ordinated by a central planning agency, as under socialism, but are blindly controlled by the market. Producers base their decisions on how they think the market will behave: how much they will pay for what they purchase, and how much they will receive for what they sell. What happens to the economy as a whole is not consciously decided by anyone, but is the result of independent decisions by countless individuals whose only links with each other are through the market. Secondly, a capitalist economy is divided into antagonistic classes: capitalists who organise production and workers who work under their control. Workers are not legally compelled to accept this subordinate position but in practice they have no choice. Capitalists own the factories, materials and other means of production without which it is impossible to produce, so workers cannot survive on their own and are forced to earn their living by working for others, or as Marx put it 'by selling their labour-power'.

Thus, Marx characterized capitalism as an unplanned economy divided into antagonistic classes, whose motion is determined by the interaction of countless individual producers and consumers, buyers and sellers, workers and capitalists, all of whom are legally free to pursue their own self-interest. At first sight it might appear that such an economy would be a complete mess without any coherent pattern, but Marx, like the classical economists before him, argued that this is not the case, that the economy obeys definite laws, and that out of the apparent chaos there emerges spontaneously a certain order. The interplay of supply and demand automatically co-ordinates the different parts of the economy and makes it function coherently. For example, when there is too much of a particular commodity its price falls and firms produce less, when there is too little its price rises and firms produce more, and in this way production is brought into line with social requirements. Thus, market forces automatically control the division of labour and the economy is able to regulate itself without external intervention. Now, Marx knew very well that no actual economy is allowed to function in quite such as automatic fashion and he mentions a number of ways in which the state may intervene in its operation. But his observations on the state are of secondary importance in comparison with his main theme which is concerned with capitalism's ability to regulate itself without state intervention and to generate spontaneously a particular form of economic development. For the most part, he keeps the state firmly in the background and assigns to it a minimal role; nowhere in his writing does the state intervene in a systematic way to control the rhythm and direction of economic expansion.

Crises

Bourgeois apologists always portray the process of self-regulation as a harmonious affair, in which supply and demand operate smoothly and painlessly to co-ordinate the various parts of the economy. Marx's picture is very different. Capitalist development is extremely irregular, and is characterized by wild bursts of accumulation interspersed with periods of crisis and depression, by a violent alternation of boom and slump. During the expansionary phase imbalances arise which eventually become unsustainable. The rate of profit falls sharply, expansion grinds to a standstill, and there is a crisis in which factories cut back production and workers are laid off. But this crisis does not last forever and, after a time, investment becomes once more profitable, the economy begins to expand, and the whole cycle starts once again. Now, to those who suffer their effects, crises appear like a terrible nightmare, a horrific accident, but within the brutal logic of capitalism they have a function. They are the means by which the economy spontaneously regulates itself and eliminates obstacles which have arisen during the course of expansion. In the crisis weaker firms are driven out of business, production is reorganized, the working class is disciplined, and the conditions for profitable expansion are re-established. In this way the path is cleared for a new burst of accumulation. As Marx says: 'From time to time the conflict of antagonistic agencies finds vent in crises. The crises are always but momentary and forcible solutions of the existing contradictions. They are violent eruptions which for a time restore the general equilibrium.'

There are many different kinds of imbalance which may interfere with the smooth accumulation of capital, and Marx himself mentions quite a few, although he gives prominence to just two of them: a rising organic composition of capital and rising wages, each of which may lead to a fall in the average rate of profit. Now, Marxists have argued interminably about which is the primary factor behind economic crises, but there is really no general answer, for any kind of imbalance or contradiction, if severe enough, can cause a crisis. Indeed most actual crises are the result of a combination of different factors, none of which is by itself sufficient to cause a crisis, but which collectively are able to do so by forcing the rate of profit down to the point where capitalists refuse to accumulate.

Wages

As an example of capitalism's ability to regulate itself, let us consider the question of wages. Marx's writing on this subject is not very consistent and he oscillates between a variety of different views. In *Capital*, for example, when he is dealing with accumulation and crisis, he implies that wages are determined purely by supply and demand, they rise *automatically* when labour is scarce because capitalists are forced to compete amongst themselves for new workers and to keep their existing workforce, and when labour is plentiful wages fall *automatically* because workers compete for the few jobs available. This view is most clearly stated in the following passage where Marx is discussing the effect of the 'reserve' army of unemployed and semi-employed labour on wages:

> Taking them as a whole, the general movements of wages are *exclusively regulated* by the expansion and contraction of the

industrial reserve army, and these again correspond to the periodic changes of the industrial cycle[2] (my italics).

In other words, wages rise automatically in booms and fall automatically in slumps. This is a very extreme position, of course, and elsewhere, in his pamphlet *Wages, Price and Profit*, Marx replaces the rigid expression 'exclusively regulated' by the more flexible term 'depends upon'. He says:

'the value of labour . . . always depends upon supply and demand, I mean the demand for labour on the part of capital, and supply of labour by the working men'.

This formulation allows for the influence of factors other than supply and demand. Indeed, the entire pamplet was intended as a rebuttal of Citizen Weston's view that trade unions cannot either raise wages or prevent wage reductions. Marx replies that, provided they are well organized, trade unions can do both of these things. In fact, he says that the actual level of wages is determined by the struggle between capital and labour, and that the 'matter resolves itself into a question of the respective power of the combatants'. Clearly, this struggle does not take place in a vacuum, and both the fighting strength of trade unions and the room for advance depend on economic circumstances. When times are good the balance of power is favourable to labour, and workers can achieve better results than when times are bad, but even so the outcome is not just a passive reflection of economic circumstances, and a well-organized trade-union movement may operate quite effectively in the face of substantial unemployment.

No matter how strongly organized the trade-union movement, however, there are inherent limits to the effectiveness of purely economic struggle.[3] Capitalists control production and they will not invest unless they receive a certain 'normal' rate of profit. If wages rise too rapidly, either because of extreme labour shortage or because of militant trade unionism, the rate of profit falls below its 'normal' level, capitalists refuse to invest, expansion grinds to a standstill and there is a crisis. This crisis has two effects. Firstly, it brings about changes in the sphere of production so that weaker capitals are weeded out and there is a general improvement in production techniques. In consequence, when the economy eventually recovers, less labour is needed than previously and productivity rises sharply as the potential of these new techniques is exploited. Secondly, the crisis leads to a sharp increase in unemployment, which brings home to workers the precariousness of their position and forces them to moderate their demands or even to accept a reduction in wages. So the crisis restores profitability by affecting both wages and production. By terrorizing the working class it holds their demands in check, and by forcing a reorganization in production it increases the ability of capitalism to meet these demands.[4] In this way the crisis spontaneously regulates the relationship between capital and labour, and re-establishes the conditions for profitable accumulation. Naturally, this is not a permanent solution, and there will eventually be another crisis, caused either by the tendency for wages to outstrip productivity, or by some other factor or combination of factors.

To sum up. In the course of a boom the demand for labour may rise so quickly that the reserve army of unemployed and underemployed labour is reduced in size. This strengthens the bargaining position of workers and helps them force up wages. If wages rise so much that the rate of profit is forced below its 'normal' level, capitalists refuse to invest and the result is a crisis. During this crisis changes occur which make investment once more profitable, after a time the economy will begin to expand once again. A strong and militant trade-union movement may force up wages and resist wage cuts even in the face of high unemployment. In a boom situation this may squeeze profits and bring expansion to a premature end, whilst there is still a large surplus of labour; and in a depression it may delay recovery by reducing profitability. This may sound like a condemnation of the trade union movement, but it is not. It is simply stating the obvious fact that, so long as capitalists control production, they hold the whip hand, and workers cannot afford to be too successful in the wages struggle. If they are, capitalists respond by refusing to invest, and the result is a premature or longer crisis. To escape from this dilemma workers must go beyond purely economic struggle and must fight at the political level to exert control over production itself.

Prices

Crises occur when the rate of profit falls so low that capitalists refuse to invest. Now, if capitalists could fix prices at any level they chose, a crisis could never occur, because any tendency for the rate of profit to fall could be offset by an increase in prices. Higher prices would insulate the rate of profit from forces which might otherwise cause it to fall, such as higher wages or taxes, or a rise in the organic composition of capital. This would, of course, have serious consequences for Marx's analysis of capitalist development which relies on a falling rate of profit to explain crises. In preventing crises it would remove one of the basic mechanisms by which capitalism regulates itself and eliminates the imbalances which arise in the course of expansion. So clearly, if Marx's analysis is to remain valid, there must be something which prevents capitalists from raising prices and passing on higher costs (or taxes) to the consumer. And, indeed, there is. Capitalists are subject to a monetary discipline which prevents them from arbitrarily raising the overall level of prices. This works as follows. National currency is linked to gold at a fixed parity, so that its purchasing power rises or falls with that of gold. To ensure that the national currency behaves in this way is the responsibility of the Central Bank, and Marx considers several ways in which it might achieve this objective. However, the details do not concern us here, for what really matters is that national currency is linked to gold and is, for practical purposes, interchangeable with gold. Marx argued that this would impose a discipline on prices, because gold has an intrinsic value of its own which regulates its purchasing power and thereby regulates the purchasing power of national currency.

Thus, the discipline of gold prevents capitalists from raising prices so as to maintain the rate of profit, and Marx's basic analysis is saved; when serious imbalances arise in the course of expansion the rate of profit begins to fall, capitalists cannot protect themselves by raising prices because they are prevented from doing so by the discipline of gold, and in consequence there is eventually a crisis. Later, we shall see how governments seek to avoid crises by relaxing the discipline of gold and allowing firms to raise their prices. Indeed, we shall argue that modern inflation is a means by which governments seek to raise the rate of profit so as to foster the accumulation of capital, and avoid or ameliorate crises. In this way they seek to block one of the internal mechanisms by which capitalism spontaneously regulates itself and eliminates obstacles to profitable expansion. Marx, however, was not primarily concerned with conscious attempts to control economic development, but with the automatic mechanisms by which capitalism controls itself, and for this reason he ignored the question of inflation and made assumptions which would ensure that prices remained fairly stable.

II THE MODERN STATE

We have seen how Marx rather neglected the state in order to concentrate on the automatic mechanisms of self-regulation which he considered to be so characteristic of capitalist economies. Let us now examine how the modern state seeks to obstruct, complement or replace these mechanisms so as to exert conscious control over the economy. We have already mentioned inflation in this context but, before dealing with the question of rising prices, let us consider other methods of control. Broadly speaking, these other methods seek to achieve one or both of the following objectives: (1) reduce pressures on the rate of profit by cutting costs or taxes, or (2) reduce the 'normal' rate of profit so that the economy functions with lower profits than was previously the case. Each of these aims may be achieved in a variety of different ways and, although there is no space to discuss them in detail, some deserve explicit mention. Costs may be reduced in a conservative or revolutionary way. The conservative way is to reduce the standard of living of the working class or some other section of society like the peasantry, either by reducing their income or making them work harder. This may be done directly through, for example, an incomes policy, or indirectly through redistributive taxation. The revolutionary way is to produce more efficiently by re-organising production and adopting more advanced techniques. This may require a systematic policy which includes such measures as the compulsory merger or nationalization of certain existing firms, state support for research and development, the education of a skilled labour force, and so on. Instead of reducing costs the state may simply cut taxes levied on profits, and either shift the tax burden on to some other section of the population or reduce its own expenditure. These are some of the ways in which the rate of profit can be increased. An alternative policy is to accept a lower rate of profit as inevitable or desirable, and take steps to ensure that investment and expansion continue unhindered.[5] Short of nationalizing most of the big firms or directly instructing them what to do, the scope for such a policy is, of course, rather limited. Even so, by a combination of investment incentives, direct controls, and negotiated agreements, it may be possible to produce some reduction in the 'normal' rate of profit which is required for expansion.

The Limits of State Intervention

If state intervention of the above kind were always successful, there would be neither crises nor inflation, and expansion could be sustained indefinitely without any rise in the general price level. But such a scenario assumes that the state has unlimited power and that it exercises this power without any political constraints. In reality, the state apparatus is an historical creation which, at any particular moment, is only able to perform certain tasks, and to modify it may require time, and may be resisted by forces inside and outside of the apparatus itself. Moreover, the actual use of state power is a political question, for what is beneficial to some may be harmful to others, and particular forms of intervention may have far-reaching strategic consequences. And, finally, individual countries exist in a world economy over which many of them exert very little influence, and are often forced to adapt themselves to world events beyond their control.

The history of post-war capitalism contains all these features. In the liberal environment of the fifties and sixties, capitalist states failed to develop the machinery required for a concerted intervention in the private sector, and in some cases even dismantled part of the machinery already in existence. Both the development and use of the state apparatus has been inhibited by the open or latent hostility of rival classes. Capitalists and workers have resisted changes which would have harmed them materially, or those long-term political consequences they found objectionable. For example, Tony Benn's proposals for modernizing British industry made good sense, but they were seen as the thin end of the socialist wedge, and were bitterly opposed despite their potential benefit to many British firms. Indeed, the whole of post-war British history illustrates how class conflict may result in a stalemate: neither left nor right has been strong enough to impose its own definitive solution and create a state apparatus which is able to tackle the underlying problems of the British economy. And, finally, on an international plane, the problems of economic control have become greater with the decline of the United States as a world power and the collapse of the colonial empires. Here is an example. Just after the Second World War the United States provided assistance in the form of Marshall Aid to the old imperial powers such as Britain and France. In return they agreed to foster the exploitation of minerals and raw materials in their imperial territories. This ensured a cheap and plentiful supply of primary products during the 1950s and 60s. Such an agreement would be impossible today; there is no country able to control the development of primary products, and in consequence their future supply is very uncertain.

A Dilemma

Suppose the state is unable or unwilling to intervene on a scale sufficient to ensure both a sustained expansion and stable prices. Then it is in a dilemma and must abandon one or both of these objectives. It may decide to bring expansion to an end and provoke a crisis, in the hope that this will (a) spontaneously solve some of the underlying problems of the economy in the ways we have described above, and (b) make possible new forms of state intervention which were not feasible during the preceding boom, such as a draconian incomes policy or drastic industrial restructuring. Now, for obvious reasons, a crisis is not exactly an attractive proposition to either workers or capitalists, and the state may be tempted to choose the other alternative, and accept rising prices as the inevitable cost of economic growth. It will therefore create the conditions under which firms can raise prices, pass on higher costs and taxes to the consumer, and thereby maintain the rate of profit at a level which they regard as satisfactory. This is the inflationary way of fostering economic expansion.

During the post-war period most governments have used inflation as a deliberate instrument of policy. They have been unable or unwilling to intervene on a scale sufficient to resolve the basic contradictions of capitalist development, and yet they have been unwilling to face the consequences of a potentially very serious crisis. Where imbalances have arisen which threaten to squeeze profits and provoke a crisis, governments have used their control over expenditure to maintain demand. This has created relatively buoyant demand conditions and allowed firms to raise prices, and thereby maintain or even increase the rate of profit. In consequence the role of gold has changed, so that it no longer acts as a discipline on prices as Marx assumed it would.

As a rule, demand has not been maintained specifically to allow firms to increase their prices, but in response to some other pressure, such as the need to maintain full employment or provide cheap finance for industry. On the other hand, when firms have made use of favourable demand conditions in order to raise their prices, governments have not usually prevented them from doing so. Price controls, even where they have been imposed, have usually been applied in a half-hearted fashion, and firms have been allowed to pass on all or a part of any higher costs or taxes. So, it has clearly been government policy to allow higher prices, and to this extent we can say that inflation is a *deliberate* policy designed to foster the accumulation of capital by maintaining or even raising the rate of profit.[6]

No Solution

Keynesians used to argue that a little inflation is a good thing because it keeps up profits by reducing the real purchasing power of wages. As events have shown, however, this argument contains a serious flaw, for it ignores the inherently unstable nature of the inflationary process. At first, when prices rise, people are caught unawares and can do very little to protect themselves. After a time, however, they realize what is happening and take steps to defend themselves. Workers seek compensation for past losses and may even seek additional wage increases to offset the effect of *future* price increases; the interval between wage settlements becomes smaller, and in extreme conditions wage rates may be adjusted every week or even every day; the unorganized begin to organize in an attempt to protect themselves; interest rates rise to offset the effects of a depreciating currency; speculators begin to hoard materials or purchase property in the expectation of future price increases. In this way inflation gets built into the system and to maintain a given rate of profit requires ever larger price increases. The result is an accelerating spiral of rising prices, taxes and costs.

No country can withstand such a process indefinitely, for if unchecked it will eventually destroy confidence in the national currency and cause severe economic disruption. Moreover, well before this point is reached, popular discontent begins to manifest itself and the state comes under growing pressure to stabilize prices. At a certain stage, inflation ceases to be a practical way of fostering economic expansion and evading the problems which expansion creates. These problems must be resolved, and the state faces a choice. Either it tackles these problems directly, by intervening in the private sector to produce the required changes, or else it must provoke a crisis in the hope that this will help set things right. There are various ways of provoking a crisis, but all of them have one thing in common. They all involve some restriction on the ability of capitalists to raise prices and keep up their profits. A deflationary budget does this by reducing the level of demand and creating a more competitive market environment in which firms are frightened to raise their prices for fear of losing their markets; direct controls achieve the same result by making it illegal for firms to raise prices by more than a specified amount. Whichever method the state chooses the result is the same. Profits are squeezed, firms refuse to invest and there is a crisis.

So inflation provides a temporary respite but it does not remove the basic dilemma. Capitalism's spontaneous way of regulating itself is by means of periodic crises, and the only long-term alternative is to replace this self-regulating mechanism so that crises become unnecessary. Indeed, inflation may actually make things worse in the long-run, for it allows the situation to drift and provides an excuse for doing nothing, so that when a decision must eventually be made the problem is even more difficult to handle, and requires either more intervention or a deeper crisis than would have originally been necessary.

Summary

We may summarize this discussion as follows. Inflation is a device for regulating the rhythm of economic expansion: it is designed to raise profits at the expense of other incomes and to foster the accumulation of capital. It is an alternative to other methods of control which involve direct intervention in the workings of the economy, either to reduce costs so that profitability is increased, or to alter the way in which decisions are taken so the economy can function with a lower rate of profit. Governments resort to inflation because they are (1) unable or unwilling to tackle the basic problems which arise in the course of economic development, and (2) are unwilling to face a crisis of sufficient magnitude to resolve these problems. But inflation deals with symptoms and not causes, and the economy adapts to take account of rising prices, so that ever larger doses of inflation are required to keep the patient healthy. Eventually, this approach becomes impractical and the state is faced with the choice it originally tried to avoid. Either it must intervene to tackle the basic problems, or it must provoke a crisis in the hope that this will cure the patient. In reality, of course, governments usually take an intermediate position and opt for a combination of intervention and crisis. Indeed, intervention and crisis are not simple alternatives, for the crisis itself makes possible new forms of intervention which were not previously feasible.

Thus, crisis, intervention and inflation are all associated with the general problems of economic expansion, and are all, in some way or other, methods of regulating this expansion: crisis acts as a purge which periodically clears away obstacles to further expansion, state intervention is a form of surgery which removes these obstacles directly, and inflation is a palliative which provides temporary relief and allows the economy to tolerate these obstacles for a time. The modern state relies on all of these methods, and the exact combination in use at any moment depends on the nature of the economic problems, the character and effectiveness of the state apparatus, and the political situation.

III   WORKERS AND CAPITALIST DEVELOPMENT

It should be obvious from what has been said, that the working class is always a factor in the situation. Slogans like 'Their crisis, not ours', or 'Wages do not cause inflation' express the determination of workers to resist capitalist blackmail and may help in mobilizing mass resistance. But, by themselves, they are inadequate and may even be counter-productive if they prevent a correct understanding of the role of the working class in modern capitalism, and its ability to influence events.

The most elementary way in which workers can influence events is by defending themselves, and resisting measures designed to solve the problems of capitalism at their expense. For example, if prices are raised or new taxes are levied on them, workers may seek higher wages in compensation; or if capitalists try to make them work more intensively, workers may refuse. Quite apart from its obvious and immediate economic effects, such resistance has important political effects. Suppose the government is pursuing a strategy whose success depends on a reduction in working class living standards. A determined defence of these living standards may make the whole strategy impractical and thereby provoke a political crisis. The outcome of this crisis depends, of course, on the actual circumstances under which it occurs, and may be either favourable or unfavourable to the working class.

Economic Offensive

At a more advanced level, workers may go beyond purely defensive struggles and launch an economic offensive designed to win them higher wages (or better conditions). As we have seen earlier, there are a variety of ways in which the state can respond to such an offensive.

(1) The state may create the conditions under which firms can raise prices and take back some of what they have conceded in the wages bargain. However, if workers are determined, this is not a permanent solution because it leads to even greater wage claims and ultimately to an explosive inflation.

(2) The state may prevent price increases so that capitalists cannot pass on their higher costs to the consumer. This will have the immediate effect of squeezing profits, and capitalists may

respond in several ways. They may reorganize production and adopt more advanced techniques so that costs are reduced and the rate of profit is restored to its old level. Thus, pressure for higher wages may act as a stimulus which forces capitalists to modernize the economy. But, clearly there are limits to this process, and, beyond a point, higher wages lead to a reduction in profits. At first this may be accepted by capitalists and cause no real problem, but, if profits are severely squeezed, capitalists refuse to invest and the result is a crisis. So clearly, after a certain point, higher real wages result in crisis rather than growth.

(3) The state may decide that a more positive policy is required, and may take concrete steps to satisfy working class aspirations. This may involve a re-allocation of existing resources, away from such items as arms expenditure and upper-class consumption in favour of wages or social services. Or, at a more fundamental level, it may involve a whole new strategy of intervention in the private sector to promote faster economic growth.

Thus, depending on the response of capitalists and the state, the outcome of a wages offensive may be inflation, crisis, or a faster rate of economic growth.

Britain's Decline

As an example of the significance of economic struggle consider Britain during the 1950s and 60s. During most of this period British governments gave a rather low priority to domestic economic development, and devoted both resources and energies to the creation of a world role for British capitalism. This involved rebuilding the City of London as a world financial centre, facilitating overseas investment by big industrial firms and supporting a huge military establishment. It absorbed resources which could have been used productively at home, and was accompanied by a laissez-faire economic policy of non-intervention in the private sector. As a result, British industry failed to keep up with its rivals and economic development was relatively slow. Clearly, such a process of relative decline must eventually lead to severe problems and, indeed in the late 1960s Britain entered a prolonged period of crisis. Now the crisis itself is no surprise, but what is strange is that it took so long to manifest itself, and that for fifteen years our ruling class was able to follow a strategy which is now widely agreed to have been suicidal. Why was this? Part of the answer lies in the behaviour of the working class. British workers, despite propaganda to the contrary, were not very militant in this period and put up with a rather modest increase in their living standards. Wages rose fairly slowly and the state responded by allowing prices to go up at a moderate pace. In consequence, profits remained fairly high and the whole system remained viable. So, the suicidal strategy of our ruling class was made possible by the quiescence of British workers.

Suppose workers had been really militant and demanded a much faster rise in their living standards. What would have happened? At first, the state might have responded by increasing the rate of inflation so as to protect capitalist profits in the face of rising wages; or it might have simply provoked a crisis to 'teach the workers a lesson'. However, if workers had persisted in their demands, neither inflation nor crisis would have been an adequate answer and the state would have been forced to do something more positive. It would have been forced to abandon its pretentious strategy for overseas expansion, and given priority to the domestic economy. Thus, a more militant stance by workers would have forced the government to step in and modernize the economy. So we reach the paradoxical conclusion that British capitalism declined, not because workers were too militant, as many people say, but because they were not militant enough and were willing to foot the bill for a suicidal strategy which put overseas expansion before domestic development.

The Alternative Policy

The preceding example of post-war Britain may suggest that blind economic struggle, provided it is militant enough, will in the long run always succeed, and that really the working class has no need for politics. Nothing could be further from the truth. In the first place it is difficult to unify the working class in a prolonged economic struggle unless this is linked to a broader political perspective which gives workers some idea of how their demands can be met. Without such a perspective, workers are, like anyone else, easy victims for bourgeois propaganda which preaches that there is no alternative to the present situation and that, instead of battering their heads against a brick wall, they should reconcile themselves to the inevitable and submit to the dictates of capital. Thus to sustain an effective movement for economic advance or resistance, the left must of necessity adopt a political approach. This does not mean simply preaching socialism in the abstract; it also means putting forward a concrete set of proposals for dealing with immediate economic problems – the so-called 'Left Alternative'. Under present conditions in the advanced capitalist countries such a left alternative would not be a revolutionary programme, but rather a set of reforms which, if implemented, would bring certain material benefits to the working class and, by challenging the undisputed authority of capital, would destabilize the political situation and lead to demands for further change.

Quite apart from its use in mobilizing workers in the economic struggle, an alternative policy has several other benefits. It helps create a *political* movement in the working class by raising wider questions of political power and making clear the actual limitations of economic struggle. It also helps organized workers escape from their isolation and forge links with other elements of society, such as unorganized workers, pensioners, students or the 'middle' strata. To the extent that workers fight a purely economic struggle, they often appear to these other elements of society as a purely sectional group whose interests are not necessarily those of the population as a whole. The existence of such a division between organized workers and the rest of society both weakens the internal cohesion of the trade-union movement, and prevents the emergence of the broad popular alliance which is required to establish socialism. An alternative policy can help overcome this division by placing the economic demands of workers in a wider context – and linking their economic struggle to the more general battle for political change. The proposals contained in the alternative policy would not just benefit organized workers; they would also benefit other sections of society. If these other sections can be convinced that the alternative policy is in their interest, their attitude towards organized workers will change and they may become valuable allies, rather than the actual or potential enemies which many of them are at present.

Thus, an alternative economic policy is beneficial in at least three ways. It helps mobilize and sustain workers in economic struggle; it raises their political consciousness; and it helps build an alliance between organized workers and other sections of society.

The Wages Struggle

The above discussion has important implications for how the wages struggle should be fought. The trade-union movement contains many diverse elements and there is a strong temptation to avoid or play down political questions so as to avoid controversy and unify the movement. This approach, however, has major limitations and in the long run is disastrous for the left. In the first place, as we have already mentioned, sustained working class unity in the economic struggle is only possible if politics is placed firmly in command. Unless this is done, the sought-after unity will either never materialize or will soon disintegrate. In the second place, if politics is pushed into the background, the left is forced to appeal to purely sectional interests within the working class. This is not only divisive within the movement, but it stores up trouble for the future by creating traditions of struggle which make the transition to socialism more difficult.

These failings have been seen in the recent campaign against the social contract. There has been a widespread, although by no means universal, tendency for the left to submerge its politics altogether and appeal to purely sectional interests, or else to put forward political positions in an abstract way without linking them properly to the economic struggle. The demand for higher money wages and for a return to 'free collective bargaining' have often been made as though they were simply ends in themselves, unrelated to questions of political change and an alternative economic policy. As a result, instead of achieving victory based on maximum unity, as it hoped, the left has suffered a setback and the working-class movement is deeply divided. This is, in my opinion, the inevitable result of the left's failure to link economics and politics in a coherent way. The 'Left Alternative' is not merely something to be tacked onto the end of a string of economic demands, it is the essential framework upon which economic demands should be based and within which economic struggle should be fought.

NOTES

1. For clear summary of this debate up until the end of 1976 see James Harvey, 'Theories of Inflation', *Marxism Today*, January 1977.
2. Laurence Harris, 'Economic Policy and Marxist Theory', *Marxism Today*, April 1977; John Grahl, David Curry, Sam Aaronovitch, *Economic Bulletin*, Autumn 1977.
3. The argument contained in the following paragraph is never stated by Marx in so many words, and is a synthesis of his discussion of crises in *Capital*, and of trade unions in *Wages, Price and Profit*.
4. Through its effect on wages (and the intensity and length of the working day) the crisis helps restore profitability by increasing the amount of 'absolute surplus value', and through .ts effect on productivity it works by increasing the amount of 'relative surplus value'.
5. The 'surplus' of a nationalized firm has a different economic significance from the 'profit' received by a private firm. In the text, however, this difference is ignored, and the terms 'profit' and 'rate of profit' refer to both private and public enterprises without distinction.
6. This does not mean that inflation is a simple conspiracy against the working class, for there are times when it is in the interest of workers to support higher prices. For example, during the transition to socialism under a left government there will still be private firms in existence whose operations must be profitable if they are to survive, and the best way of ensuring that may be to let them raise their prices.

6

Conflict, Inflation and Money*

Conflict is endemic in the capitalist system and concerns all aspects of economic life: the techniques of production to be used, the length and intensity of the working day, and the distribution of income. Naturally, these are all interconnected and what happens in one sphere influences what happens in the rest, and all in some way affect the behaviour of wages and prices. So much is obvious, but, in view of the complexity of the inflationary process, the present article focuses on just one particular area, namely how conflict over the distribution of income affects the general level of prices in advanced capitalist economies. A formal model is constructed in which the following factors are combined in a coherent fashion: taxes, the terms of trade, expectations and money. In writing this article I have drawn on a wide variety of past writing on the subject of inflation, although usually without explicit acknowledgment. Amongst the works which influenced me most were: Marx's writing on the reserve army of labour, Keynes's *How to Pay for the War*, Maynard's *Economic Development and the Price Level*, Philips's famous article on unemployment and wages, Wilkinson's contribution to *Do Trade Unions Cause Inflation?* and, finally, monetarist writing on expectations.[1]

The Basic Model

In a capitalist economy inflation may increase profits by reducing the real purchasing power of other kinds of income. It can only do this, of course, if some of the other parties involved are unable to protect themselves against its effects. We must

*First published in *Cambridge Journal of Economics*, no. 1, 1977. I should like to thank the following people who have commented on various drafts of this article: Frank Hahn, Michael Kennedy, Gernot Mueller, David Purdy, Brian Van Arkadie and Erico Wolleb. I am also particularly grateful to David Vines and the editors of the *Cambridge Journal of Economics* for their many valuable criticisms and suggestions.

begin by distinguishing between two concepts which are often confused but which are really quite distinct: expectation and anticipation. The former refers to a state of mind, whereas the latter refers to actual behaviour. To *expect* something means simply to believe with greater or less confidence that it will occur, whereas to *anticipate* something means both to expect it and to act upon this expectation. So inflation has no redistributive effect if it is fully anticipated by all concerned, for then everyone takes advance measures to allow for or anticipate future price increases. To redistribute income, inflation must therefore be *unanticipated*. With this in mind, we shall now construct a simple model in which unanticipated inflation transfers real income from workers to capitalists within the same country. The model also contains a state sector and a foreign sector, but these are fully protected against inflation, so that their real incomes are unaffected by domestic price changes. Thus, capitalists cannot raise their profits at the expense of the state or foreigners, and any redistribution caused by price changes is always at the expense of workers.

Let us make the following assumptions. The economy is divided into two parts: a state sector and a private sector, and the only sources of finance for the state are taxation and borrowing (which includes the creation of money).[2] The private sector contains two classes – capitalists and workers; goods and services are produced in this sector and output per worker is constant. The private sector also purchases goods and services from foreign suppliers; these are not sold directly to private consumers but are used as inputs in the production of further goods and services for sale at home and abroad. The volume of imports required to produce a unit of private sector output is a given constant which does not vary in response to changes in the terms of trade.

The Aspiration Gap

In the above economy the gross income of the private sector is subject to four major claims and must be divided amongst the following parties: (1) the state (taxes), (2) foreign suppliers (import costs), (3) workers in the private sector (post-tax wages), and (4) domestic capitalists (post-tax profits). Let T denote the share of private sector income absorbed by taxes levied on workers and capitalists in this sector, and F the share of import costs, and assume that both of these shares are exogenously determined.[3] This means that a proportion $T + F$ of income is pre-empted by taxes and import costs, leaving $1 - T - F$ available for distribution to workers and capitalists in the private sector. Now, unless wage and price decisions are centrally co-ordinated, there is no automatic mechanism which ensures that this amount is exactly sufficient to meet the rival claims made upon it. On a firm by firm basis workers may negotiate increases designed to give them a certain standard of living, and individual capitalists, having agreed on these wage payments, may then set prices so as to achieve a certain target rate of profit. For any individual capitalist this need not imply a deliberate attempt to alter the level of real wages and vitiate what has been agreed in the wage bargain. Yet aggregating over the whole economy this may be the objective consequence of their individual and uncoordinated decisions. So the rival claims on income – those negotiated by workers in the wage bargain and those pursued by capitalists in their pricing policy – may exceed or fall short of what is available after the payment of taxes and import costs. In this case there is a conflict between capitalist pricing policy and what has been agreed in wage negotiations.

Suppose wage settlements make a notional allowance for future inflation, and on this basis the two sides agree on a certain money wage. If prices rise as anticipated, this money wage will provide workers with a certain after-tax real income, and moreover, since productivity is constant, will give the working class as a whole a certain *share*, say W^n, of private sector income. Since taxes and import costs absorb a further amount $T + F$, it follows that capitalists will be left with the residual share Π^n given by

$$\Pi^n = 1 - T - F - W^n. \tag{1}$$

Let us call W^n the *negotiated wage share* and Π^n the *negotiated profit share*. These are what workers and capitalists actually receive if prices rise as anticipated in the wage bargain. Next, suppose that, having fixed wages, capitalists follow a pricing policy which is designed to give them a certain *target share* Π^* of private sector income. Then we have two potentially different profit shares, one negotiated in the wage bargain on the assumption that the price level will change a given amount, and another which capitalists seek to achieve through their pricing policy. If these shares are identical there is no conflict between the two levels of decision-making, but if they are different there *is* a conflict and capitalist pricing policy is inconsistent with what has been agreed in the wage bargain. The extent of this conflict can be measured by the quantity $\Pi^* - \Pi^n$ which we shall denote by the symbol A. Thus,

$$A = \Pi^* - \Pi^n \qquad (2)$$

which can also be written,

$$A = \Pi^* + W^n + T + F - 1. \qquad (3)$$

We shall call this quantity the *aspiration gap* because it indicates how far the aims of capitalist pricing policy are inconsistent with other claims on private sector income. Note that A may be positive or negative.

The price equation.   To derive an equation for the behaviour of prices let us make the following assumptions. Wages are fixed simultaneously throughout the economy in bargains which take place at discrete intervals, say y times per year, and once settled do not change until the next general round of bargaining. When negotiations take place, the share $T + F$, absorbed by taxes and import costs, is already known, and the following mechanisms ensure that it is unaffected by domestic inflation: international trade is conducted in foreign currency at world market prices which are fixed in advance of the wage bargain, and the exchange rate is continuously adjusted to compensate for differential rates of inflation at home and abroad; government revenue is raised by means of a uniform proportional tax, announced in advance of the wage bargain and levied on all incomes in the private sector. Under these assumptions tax payments rise in line with the value of private sector output, and so too do import costs.[4] Thus, capitalists cannot change the share going to the state and foreign suppliers, and any redistribution in their favour must be at the expense of workers.

When defining the aspiration gap, we assumed that wage settlements make an allowance for future inflation, and on this basis workers negotiate for themselves a certain share W^n of private sector income. To specify this more exactly, suppose that settlements are based on the assumption that prices will rise by Θ^a during the coming period. Then, if prices do actually rise by this amount, workers will receive their negotiated share W^n and capitalists will be left with the residual Π^n which is, of course, equal to $1-T-F-W^n$. Now, we also assumed that capitalist pricing policy aims at a certain target share Π^* for profits, so to derive the required price equation, all that remains is to specify the speed with which capitalists respond to cost and tax changes.

Let us assume that the amount Θ by which they adjust prices immediately after any particular bargain is given by the following rule,

$$\Theta = \beta(\Pi^* - \Pi^n) + \Theta^a \qquad (4)$$

where β is a positive constant.[5]

This rule means that capitalists raise prices by more or less than the anticipated amount, depending on whether their target share is greater or less than what they have achieved in the wage bargain, and they raise prices by exactly the anticipated amount if the wage bargain gives them exactly what they seek.

Since there are γ bargains per year, the annual rate of inflation is given approximately by

$$p = \gamma \Theta \qquad (5)$$

and price rises anticipated in the wage bargain are equivalent to an annual rate of inflation given by

$$p^a = \gamma \Theta^a. \qquad (6)$$

Substituting in (4) we get

$$p = \gamma\beta(\Pi^* - \Pi^n) + p^a \qquad (7)$$

which can be written as follows:

$$p = \lambda A + p^a \qquad (8)$$

where $\lambda = \gamma\beta$.

Since unanticipated inflation is the difference between price rises which actually occur and those anticipated in the wage bargain, the annual rate of *unanticipated* inflation is given by

$$p^u = p - p^a. \qquad (9)$$

Substituting in (8) we get

$$p^u = \lambda A. \qquad (10)$$

This equation tells us that the rate of unanticipated inflation depends: (1) on the degree to which capitalist pricing policy is in conflict with what has been agreed in wage negotiations, and (2) on the speed with which wage and price adjustments take place. The former is indicated by A and the latter by λ. Since $\lambda > 0$ it follows that *unanticipated* inflation is positive when capitalists seek more than they have negotiated in the wage bargain $(A > 0)$ and negative when they seek less $(A < 0)$.

Demand and Burden Effects

Let us now consider how the aspiration gap is determined. As in any conflict model, the answer is simple enough: it is determined by the market power of workers and capitalists, and by their willingness to use this power. Thus anything which affects the extent or use of power will affect the aspiration gap and, through it, the rate of inflation. For example, a well organized and militant working class may win very big wage increases and place considerable pressure on profits. If, at the same time, product markets are dominated by a few giant firms or cartels, then capitalists may pursue an aggressive pricing policy designed to obtain a high share of income for themselves. Thus, on the one hand workers are strong in the labour market, whilst on the other capitalists are strong in the product market, and as a result there is a major inconsistency between the two levels of decision-making: workers use their power to obtain big wage increases, whilst capitalists respond with price increases. The aspiration gap is in consequence very large and there is a high rate of unanticipated inflation. Or, to take another example, consider the effect of an 'incomes policy' which seeks by force or persuasion to co-ordinate wage and price decisions. If successful, such a policy fixes wages at some predetermined level, consistent with a 'reasonable' rate of profit, and capitalists do not use prices to take back what has been 'conceded' on the wage front. In such a world, wage and price decisions are always perfectly consistent, the aspiration gap is zero, and there is no unanticipated inflation.

Amongst the many different factors of an economic, political or ideological nature which influence the extent of market power and its use by workers and capitalists, one factor is of particular importance, namely *demand*. Demand acts as a regulator of conflict, imposing a *discipline* on the private sector, and making it easier or more difficult for workers to raise wages and capitalists to raise prices.

When there is a large surplus of labour, either visibly unemployed or hidden in rural or other labour reserves, the bargaining position of trade unions is relatively weak, and their members may be demoralized or quiescent. However, as reserves are progressively exhausted or unemployment reduced, their bargaining position becomes stronger and workers become more confident and aggressive. This can be expressed formally by making the negotiated wage share W^n an increasing function of some index D^l of the demand for labour,

$$W^n = W^n(D^l). \tag{11}$$

This tells us that, as demand rises, workers use their greater power to extract higher wages from their employers.

Similar considerations apply to capitalist pricing behaviour. When there is a large surplus of capacity, firms may pursue a cautious pricing policy for fear that other firms, which also have excess capacity, will invade their markets. Conversely, when capacity is more fully utilized, firms can raise their prices more freely, secure in the knowledge that other firms are in a similar position to themselves and unable to launch a major invasion of their markets. So, as the discipline of demand is relaxed, firms become stronger and use their power to force up prices. This can be expressed formally by making the target profit share Π^* and increasing function of some index, D^c, of capacity utilization,

$$\Pi^* = \Pi^*(D^c). \tag{12}$$

This tells us that, as demand rises, firms seek higher profits and set their prices accordingly.

Note that, although D^l and D^c move together cyclically, they may diverge over longer periods of time, and a high D^l may coexist with a low D^c and vice versa. In Germany during the 1950s, for example, there was a large surplus of labour and yet capacity was fully utilized because of Germany's export-led boom. Labour's 'pretensions' were held in check by the reserve army of labour, whilst capitalists both expected and obtained high profits under favourable demand conditions in the product market.

Taxes and the terms of trade   When taxes or real import costs rise, they reduce the share of income available for post-tax wages and profits, thus imposing a certain burden on the private sector. Now, since workers and capitalists possess a degree of market power, they may try to resist this burden, seeking higher wages or prices to compensate for part or all of the reduction in their real disposable incomes, and the more they resist, the greater is the conflict over distribution and the higher is the rate of unanticipated inflation. Before attempting to formalize this notion within the present framework of analysis, let us consider briefly why anyone should resist the burden of higher taxes or real import costs. This is obvious enough in the case of higher real import costs, because they mean an unrequited transfer from the private sector to foreign suppliers, as more domestic products must be exchanged for a given quantity of imports. In the case of higher taxes, however, the situation is less straightforward, as these are often accompanied by higher government expenditure, the benefits of which may partially compensate for the loss of disposable income caused by higher taxes. But this does not mean that these taxes will be passively accepted by workers or capitalists in the private sector. Government expenditure may be used for a variety of purposes, such as the armed forces, the social services and welfare payments to the aged, the sick, and the poor; and the willingness of capitalists and workers to support this kind of expenditure depends upon their evaluation of its social usefulness. A left-wing worker, for example, is less willing to finance colonial wars than is his right-wing counterpart, and is therefore likely to resist any burdens placed upon him. But, even if government expenditure is regarded as desirable, there may be nobody prepared to pay for it. For example, everyone may think that more hospitals or higher pensions are a good thing, and yet simultaneously believe that someone else should pay for them. The capitalist argues that workers, as the main beneficiaries, should pay, whilst workers may argue that they see state expenditure as a redistributive device which provides them with benefits at the expense of profits. Thus, the capitalist argues that a higher 'social wage' should be matched by a lower 'individual wage', whereas the worker may see it as an additional benefit. The 'social contract' and the propaganda surrounding it spring from just such a conflict – workers are told they must make sacrifices to pay for the welfare state. Or, to take another example, everyone may argue that state research centres are a good thing, but once again, no one may be willing to pay for them. Workers may argue that they help capitalist industry and should therefore be financed out of profits, whilst capitalists may argue that they cannot afford to pay higher taxes, for they need profits to finance dividend payments and future investments.

So workers and capitalists may be unwilling to accept the burden of higher taxes or import costs and may use their market power to resist this burden and obtain compensatory wage and price increases. We can allow for such resistance within the present model by making the shares W^n and Π^* depend on the variables T and F. Taking account also of the influence of demand on market power, we can write

$$W^n = W^n(D^l, T, F) \text{ and } \Pi^* = \Pi^*(D^c, T, F). \tag{13}$$

Differentiating, we obtain the following *acceptance coefficients*,

$$a_T^l = -\frac{\partial W^n}{\partial T}, \, a_T^c = -\frac{\partial \Pi^*}{\partial T},$$
$$a_F^l = -\frac{\partial W^n}{\partial F}, \, a_F^c = -\frac{\partial \Pi^*}{\partial F}. \tag{14}$$

These tell us how, under given demand conditions, wage and price setting are affected by higher taxes and import costs: how far the two sides are forced or agree to accept the additional burden without receiving a compensatory increase in their money incomes.

Inflation   From equations (3) and (14) the aspiration gap can be written as follows:

$$A = \Pi^*(D^c, T, F) + W^n(D^l, T, F) + T + F - 1 \tag{15}$$

and hence the rate of unanticipated inflation can be written as a function of the four variables D^c, D^l, T and F:

$$p^u = \lambda A(D^c, D^l, T, F). \tag{16}$$

Any increment in A or p^u can be decomposed into two parts: *demand effects* associated with changes in the demand variables D^c and D^l, and *burden effects* associated with changes in the burden variables T and F.[6] Thus,

ΔA = demand effects + burden effects

$$= \left[\frac{\partial A}{\partial D^c}\Delta D^c + \frac{\partial A}{\partial D^\ell}\Delta D^\ell\right] + \left[\frac{\partial A}{\partial T}\Delta T + \frac{\partial A}{\partial F}\Delta F\right] \tag{17}$$

$$= \left[\frac{\partial \Pi^*}{\partial D^c}\Delta D^c + \frac{\partial W^n}{\partial D^\ell}\Delta D^\ell\right] + \left[(1 - a_T^c - a_T^\ell)\Delta T + (1 - a_F^c - a_F^\ell)\Delta F\right]$$

and, since $\Delta p^u = \lambda \Delta A$,

Δp^u = demand effects + burden effects

$$\tag{18}$$

$$= \lambda \left[\frac{\partial \Pi^*}{\partial D^c}\Delta D^c + \frac{\partial W^n}{\partial D^\ell}\Delta D\right] + \left[\lambda(1 - a_T^c - a_T^\ell)\Delta T + (1 - a_F^c - a_F^\ell)\Delta F\right].$$

Burden effects have received relatively little attention in the academic literature, so, in order to isolate these effects and consider them in more detail, assume that demand, and therefore the power of the rival parties, remains constant. Then $\Delta D^c = \Delta D^l = 0$ and burden effects are given as follows:

$$\Delta A = (1 - a_T)\Delta T + (1 - a_F)\Delta F$$

and

$$\Delta p^u = \lambda[(1 - a_T)\Delta T + (1 - a_F)\Delta F] \tag{19}$$

where

$$a_T = a_T^c + a_T^\ell \text{ and } a_F = a_F^c + a_F^\ell.$$

The meaning of equation (19) is very simple. The parameter λ is determined by the mechanism of 'buck-passing' and tells us how quickly each side can pass an unacceptable burden on to the other, and a_T and a_F tell us what proportion of any extra burden the two sides accept without receiving compensatory wage or price increases. When $a_T = 1$ and $a_F = 1$ the burden effect is zero, for the burden is fully accepted by one side or the other and the rate of inflation is unaffected by higher taxes or real import costs. At the other extreme, when $a_T = 0$ and $a_F = 0$, the burden effect is at its maximum, neither side will accept any reduction in its real disposable income, and there may be a fierce inflationary struggle as each side seeks to shift the entire burden on to the other: workers win wage increases designed to compensate them fully for any losses they have suffered, but then, having agreed to these increases, capitalists raise prices by more than the anticipated amount, so that in the event the compensation recovered by the workers turns out to be insufficient. And this process may continue indefinitely, with workers repeatedly demanding and obtaining compensatory wage increases, only to find that part of these are taken back again by unanticipated price increases. (So an unaccepted burden leads to greater conflict over income distribution and a permanent rise in the rate of *unanticipated* inflation.)

Demand effects may be isolated by assuming that the shares T and F taken by taxes and import costs remain constant. To clarify the discussion, let us consider a special case. Suppose there is a close correlation between conditions in the labour market and in the product market, so that labour becomes less plentiful when capacity utilization rises, and vice versa. Under these circumstances, the level of unemployment U may provide a good indication of conditions in both markets and may thus be taken as an adequate proxy for both of the variables D^c and D^l. In this case we can write

$$W^n = W^n(U,T,F) \text{ and } \Pi^* = \Pi^*(U,T,F). \qquad (20)$$

In general these will be decreasing functions of U, indicating that capitalists and workers become weaker and moderate their claims when demand is reduced. The aspiration gap can be written as

$$A = \Pi^*(U,T,F) + W^n(U,T,F) + T + F - 1 \qquad (21)$$

and the rate of unanticipated inflation as

$$p^u = \lambda A(U,T,F). \qquad (22)$$

Taking $\Delta T = \Delta F = 0$, we get demand effects given by

$$\Delta A = \left[\frac{\partial \Pi^*}{\partial U} + \frac{\partial W^n}{\partial U} \right] \Delta U,$$

$$\Delta p^u = \lambda \left[\frac{\partial \Pi^*}{\partial U} + \frac{\partial W^n}{\partial U} \right] \Delta U. \qquad (23)$$

With T and F constant, equation (22) gives us a 'Phillips curve' relating p to U.[7] The curve cuts the horizontal axis at a point U^0. With this level of unemployment the aspiration gap is zero, the total claims on private sector income are just compatible with what is available to meet them and the rate of unanticipated inflation is zero (see Fig 1). As unemployment falls, the level of demand rises in both markets (labour and product), both wages

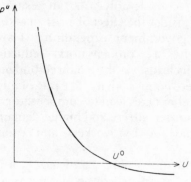

Fig. 1.

and profits make a greater claim on real income, conflict intensifies, and unanticipated price rises begin to occur. Conversely, when unemployment rises above U^0, wages and profits claim less than the quantity available to meet them and prices rise less than anticipated, or even fall.

The position of the Phillips curve is determined by the level of taxes and import costs. When T or F is raised the curve is shifted upwards by an amount which depends on how far the burden is 'accepted' by the private sector, and how far each side obtains a compensatory increase in money income. Demand effects are thus associated with changes in U [equation (23)] and burden effects with changes in T and F [equation (19)]. The former correspond to movements along the Phillips curve, and the latter to shifts in the curve itself. Various possibilities are illustrated in Fig. 2. In the combination NOP, positive demand and burden effects reinforce each other, so that the rate of

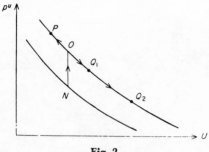

Fig. 2.

inflation rises considerably. As an example of such a combination consider the effect of a rise in taxes matched by an equal rise in government expenditure. Provided it is not counteracted by a compensatory reduction in private expenditure, this leads, via the balanced budget multiplier, to a higher level of economic activity. The rate of inflation is affected in two ways: higher taxes lead to compensatory wage and price rises (positive burden effect), and higher demand leads to more aggressive behaviour by workers and capitalists (positive demand effect).

In the combinations NOQ_1 and NOQ_2 a positive burden effect is partly or completely offset by a negative demand effect. As an example, consider the effect of a rise in taxes unaccompanied by any change in government expenditure. This influences the rate of inflation in two ways. It imposes a new burden on the private sector and it reduces the level of economic activity. In the normal course of events, workers and capitalists might resist this new burden and seek compensatory wage and price increases (positive burden effect). Their capacity to do so, however, is weakened by the adverse market conditions they face as a result of economic contraction (negative demand effect). The final outcome of higher taxes thus depends on which of these effects is the more powerful. The rate of unanticipated inflation may be higher, at Q_1, or lower, at Q_2.

To conclude this discussion let us consider an example drawn from the realm of foreign trade. Suppose that, as a result of an export boom, there is an improvement in the balance of trade. If no offsetting action is taken by the government, the economy may move along the Phillips curve so that inflation accelerates. This is illustrated in Fig. 3 by the movement OP. Suppose the

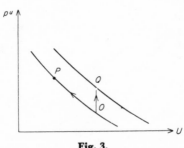

Fig. 3.

government now decides to offset this expansion by raising taxes so that demand returns to its old level. If these taxes are accepted by the private sector, the Phillips curve is unaffected and the economy ends up back in its original position O, so that the inflationary impact of the export boom is completely neutralized. If, however, they are not accepted, there is a spiral of compensatory wage and price increases in the private sector as each side seeks to shift the burden onto the other, and the rate of inflation does not return to its old level. The Phillips curve is shifted upwards and the economy ends up at the point Q. Higher taxes have eliminated the demand effect, but only to replace it by a burden effect!

Distribution and Inflation

In the present model the distribution of income is determined by conflict between the two sides in the private sector. The working class can shift distribution in its favour by fighting more vigorously for higher wages, although the cost of such militancy is a faster rate of inflation, as capitalists try, with only partial success, to protect themselves by raising prices. Likewise, capitalists can shift distribution in their favour by pursuing a more aggressive profits policy, but workers fight back, so that once again the rate of inflation rises. Thus wage militancy and an aggressive profits policy are both inflationary, but their effects on distribution are different. The former shifts distribution in favour of wages and the latter in favour of profits.

Demand can affect distribution through its influence on the extent and exercise of market power. When labour is scarce workers seek and obtain bigger wage increases which, as we have just seen, lead to a faster rate of unanticipated inflation and a larger share of wages in private sector income. Similar changes occur when capacity is more fully utilized. The target share of capitalists rises and, once again, the result is faster inflation, although in this case distribution shifts in favour of capital and the share of wages falls. Thus, the two kinds of demand have similar effects on inflation but opposite effects on distribution. As we have already mentioned, the ideal position from a capitalist point of view is a combination of surplus labour and fully utilized capacity, which enables them to combine high profits with stable prices.

In the present model the share of taxes and import costs is

exogenously determined, so that the private sector as a whole must always shoulder the given burden, and compensatory wage or price increases cannot protect both workers and capitalists, for one of them must in the end pay. Acceptance coefficients do not therefore determimine how much of the given burden is borne by the private sector as a whole, but rather how this burden is shared between workers and capitalists, and what impact it has on prices. The ultimate incidence of taxes and import costs is settled dynamically by an inflationary conflict in which each side seeks to shift part or all of the burden on to the other.

Adaptation

Inflation performs a redistributive function only to the extent that it has not already been anticipated in the wage bargain. To achieve a given redistribution in favour of profits, prices must always keep a certain distance ahead of their anticipated value, which under certain conditions may be possible only at the expense of an explosive and ultimately unsustainable rate of inflation. So there are inherent limits to the effectiveness of inflation as a redistributive device. In this section we shall examine the nature of these limits and how they affect the present analysis. It is important at this stage of the argument to recall the distinction made above between expectation and anticipation. The former, it will be remembered, refers to a state of mind, whereas the latter refers to actual behaviour. For example, workers may expect prices to rise but, for a variety of reasons, may do nothing about it – they may have little faith in their own predictions, or may consider it easier to seek compensation in the future, if and when prices actually do rise. In this case the wage bargain makes no allowance for future price rises, even though they are expected to occur. Such a divorce between expectations and behaviour is most likely when prices are rising slowly, for under these conditions neither side may think it worthwhile to make specific allowance for the small price changes which are expected. Moreover, in any real situation, prices do not rise steadily, and an era of slow inflation is likely to contain short spells in which prices are stable or even falling, so that at any time no one can be very sure that prices are going to rise in the immediate future. Thus, in an era of slow inflation, expectations about future price changes may not be held with any great certainty and, even if they are, it is not particularly important to act on them. By contrast, in an era of fast inflation, the cost of inactivity may be high and workers must do something to protect themselves against the effects of future price changes. Moreover, even though there may be uncertainty about exactly how much prices will rise, everyone can be sure they will rise by a considerable amount. Under these circumstances, wage settlements are likely to contain some provision against future inflation. In practice, this can take a variety of forms, such as tying wages to the cost of living or shortening the period covered by the wage contract, but in line with our original model we shall continue to assume that the only provision against inflation is an advance payment to workers in anticipation of future price increases.

The transition from one kind of behaviour to another may be rather abrupt. At low rates of inflation there may be little or no anticipatory behaviour, but then suddenly, when inflation passes a certain critical point, qualitative changes may occur in the whole mechanism of wage bargaining and it may become a standard practice to make provision against future price rises. Moreover, this transition may be irreversible, so that anticipatory behaviour continues even when the rate of inflation falls again, but we shall ignore this possibility and assume that the transition is reversible.

Suppose there is a threshold p^{th} below which expected inflation is ignored completely, and above which it is fully taken into account by all concerned. Then the *anticipated* rate of inflation p^a is related to the *expected* rate of inflation p^e as follows,

$$p^a = 0 \qquad \text{for } p^e < p^{th}$$

and

$$p^a = p^e \qquad \text{for } p^e \geqq p^{th}. \qquad (24)$$

This is, of course, an extremely crude formalization of a rather subtle relationship, and its faults are only too obvious: it makes no allowance for the certainty with which expectations are held, the transition from one kind of behaviour to another is too abrupt and is assumed to be reversible, and no allowance is made for anticipatory behaviour when prices are falling. None the less, equation (24) captures the essence of the problem.

Since $p = \lambda A + p^a$, we obtain the following relationship between expectations and inflation,

and

$$p = \lambda A \qquad \text{for } p^e < p^{th}$$

$$p = \lambda A + p^e \qquad \text{for } p^e \geqq p^{th}. \tag{25}$$

This still leaves open the question of how expectations are formed. The simplest assumption is that they adapt in the light of past experience, although with a certain lag. To formalize this let us use the conventional schema,

$$p^e_t - p^e_{t-1/\gamma} = \delta[p_{t-1/\gamma} - p^e_{t-1/\gamma}]. \tag{26}$$

Remember that wages and prices are adjusted γ times per year, so the above schema means that expectations change by an amount which depends upon how wrong they were on the previous occasion. Equation (26) ensures that expectations follow price movements with a lag and that, provided inflation is non-explosive, expectations are on average fulfilled. In particular, if the rate of inflation stabilizes at a certain value (or fluctuates around it) then the expected rate of inflation will also stabilize at this value (or fluctuate around it).

Steady State

Provided the behaviour of A is known, then, beginning from an arbitrary starting point, equations (25) and (26) determine the behaviour of prices through time. Assume now that A is constant and let us see what happens to prices. Various possibilities are shown in Fig. 4, whose horizontal axis measures

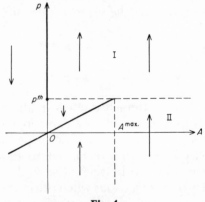

Fig. 4.

the aspiration gap, and whose vertical axis measures the actual rate of inflation. The economy can remain indefinitely anywhere on the heavily drawn curve where actual and expected inflation coincide. Below the threshold, along the lower, sloping part of this curve, expectations exert no influence on behaviour, so that inflation, although expected, is unanticipated, and wage bargaining does not adapt to take account of rising prices. For this reason inflation is able to redistribute income in favour of profits. However, along the vertical part of the curve, above the threshold, expectations do influence behaviour and the adaptive mechansim ensures that inflation is fully taken into account in the wage bargain. As a result, inflation is fully anticipated and exercises no redistributive effect. This only occurs, of course, where the various claims on private sector income are mutually consistent, and the aspiration gap is zero.

The diagram also shows what happens when the economy begins from an arbitrary starting point. If it begins in region I, above the expectations threshold, then a positive aspiration gap, however small, leads via the adaptive mechanism to an explosive inflation; and if it begins in region II, with an initially low rate of inflation but with an intense conflict over distribution, then inflation will accelerate, and the economy will cross the threshold into region I, where the adaptive mechanism comes into play and prices explode. And, finally, if it begins outside these two regions, the economy will eventually converge to a stable rate of inflation on the sloping part of the curve. Now, no economy can withstand an explosive inflation indefinitely, so we can summarize the above discussion as follows. Inflation can only *permanently* raise profits at the expense of wages if (a) the conflict is not very great $(A < A^{max})$, and (b) the economy begins below the expectations threshold $(p < p^{th})$. If either of these conditions is not satisfied prices eventually get completely out of control and hyperinflation sets in.

The Special Case

To illustrate how anticipatory behaviour can affect the relationship between inflation and demand, let us consider the special case in which unemployment U is a proxy for demand in general, in which case the aspiration gap A is a function of the form $A(U,T,F)$. With given T and F, only certain combinations of unemployment and inflation can be permanently sustained, and

these are shown in Fig. 5 by the heavily drawn 'long-term
Phillips curve'. Mathematically they are given by

$$\lambda A(U,T,F) = p \qquad \text{for } p < p^{th}$$

and   (27)

$$A(U,T,F) = 0 \qquad \text{for } p \geqq p^{th}.$$

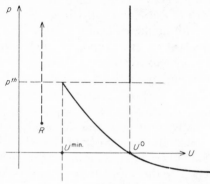

Fig. 5.

Along the lower section of the curve expectations are fulfilled
($p^e = p$), but the wage bargain takes no account of future rises in
the general price level ($p^a = 0$), so that inflation is expected but
not anticipated. Over the range concerned, inflation acts as a
redistributive device and there is a trade-off between inflation
and unemployment. Along the vertical section of the curve
expectations are again fulfilled, but this time wage bargains take
full account of future price rises ($p^a = p$), so inflation is both
expected and anticipated. The aspiration gap is zero, inflation
performs no redistributive function, and there is no trade-off
between unemployment and inflation. Note that the vertical
section of the curve lies directly above the point where the lower
section cuts the axis, and unemployment is equal to U^0. This is,
of course, just the amount of unemployment required to
reconcile the various claims on income and ensure that capitalist
pricing policy is consistent with what has been agreed in the
wage bargain.

The diagram illustrates clearly the way in which adaptive
behaviour may impose severe constraints on economic policy.
With given T and F it is impossible to maintain a level of
unemployment less than some minimum value U^{min}. Any

attempt to do so will lead to intense conflict over the distribution of income, and will eventually push the economy over the expectations threshold and initiate an explosive inflation, in which each side seeks to protect itself against future price changes. Such a situation is illustrated by the dotted line starting at the point *R* in Fig. 5. To stabilize the rate of inflation once the economy has passed the threshold may be very difficult, and the economy may eventually end up on the vertical section of the curve with both faster inflation and more unemployment than it had originally.

To see how the burden effect operates in a threshold model, consider what happens when there is an increase in the burden of taxes or real import costs. If the private sector does not 'accept' this additional burden the long-run Phillips curve is shifted bodily to the right, with *BC* going to *B'C'* and *DE* going to *D'E'* in Fig. 6. This shift may have quite dramatic affects on

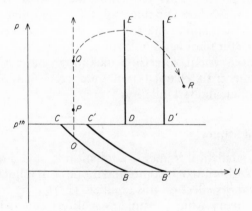

Fig. 6.

inflation and unemployment. Suppose the economy is initially below the expectations threshold at the point *O* in Fig. 6, where prices are rising steadily. When the curve shifts to the right, inflation accelerates and the economy moves to the point *P*. If this new position is below the threshold, the economy can remain there indefinitely, for prices are not rising fast enough to cause any fundamental change in decision-making and expectations still exert no influence on actual wages or prices. On the other hand, if *P* is above the threshold, expectations begin to influence wages and prices, and decision-making is radically altered. When the economy reaches P it does not stop, inflation continues to accelerate and the economy moves upward along the dotted line. But this cannot go on for ever and eventually, spontaneously or by design, the economy moves into crisis, demand falls and unemployment rises until inflation is brought under control again. The economy follows a path illustrated in Fig. 6 by the broken line QR and ends up with both faster inflation and more unemployment than it had originally. In this example, a greater burden of taxes and import costs leads to a severe economic crisis because it pushes the economy over the expectations threshold and alters the way in which decisions are made. Something of the kind seems to have occurred in the advanced capitalist world during the years 1964–76. Over this period, higher taxes and, later, worse terms of trade led to a big reduction in the share of private sector output available for wages and profits. This reduction was widely resisted by capitalists and workers and the result was faster inflation as each side tried to maintain its share. Countries were pushed over the expectations threshold and inflationary expectations were built into the whole system of decision-making. Eventually there was an economic crisis characterized by a combination of high unemployment and fast inflation.[8]

The Role of Money

Within our analytical framework inflation is caused by conflict over the distribution of income, and money can influence prices only through its effect on this conflict. There is no room for a monetary theory which postulates a direct causal link from money to prices, for this would provide a second and independent explanation of inflation, in addition to the original conflict theory.

How can monetary factors influence conflict over income distribution? One obvious way is through their effect on demand. As we have previously seen, conflict depends on level of demand, so, if monetary factors can alter this level, they can influence the degree of conflict and, through it, the rate of inflation. Thus, within the present analytical framework, monetary factors may influence prices through the following causal chain:

money → demand → conflict → prices.

The discussion contained in previous sections of this paper has been concerned with the middle and final links of the above chain, from demand to conflict, and from conflict to prices. Let us now extend this discussion by considering the link between money and demand.

Opinions differ widely on this subject. Some argue that money plays a purely passive role and that the private sector is never seriously affected by a shortage or surplus of money, whilst others argue that money plays a more active role and monetary factors may exert an independent influence on economic activity. In the author's opinion the latter position is correct and it is the one we shall adopt throughout this section. This view does *not* imply that money is the *only* factor which can exert an independent influence on activity. Monetary control is but one of the weapons of 'demand management', and will usually be accompanied by fiscal and other measures.

The link between money and demand is in practice very complex, but the basic principle is quite simple: a change in the supply of money leads to a change in expenditure. To explore the implications of this basic principle there is no need for sophistication, so let us simplify drastically and make some assumptions which, although not very realistic, enable us to grasp the essence of the problem. Moreover, we shall only consider the special case in which the two demand variables D^l and D^c can be replaced by the single proxy variable U.

Let us begin with the familar identity

$$MV \equiv PY \qquad (28)$$

where M is the stock of money (cash plus bank deposits) held by the private sector, Y is the gross output of this sector, P is the average price of this output, and V is the 'income velocity' of money. Expressed dynamically, this identity can be written,

$$m+v \equiv p+y \qquad (29)$$

where lower case letters denote annual rates of growth.

To convert this identity into a simple causal relationship, let us make the following assumptions.

1. The velocity of money is constant, so that $v=0$, and the

stock of money held by the private sector is always equal to the supply, which is exogenously given and grows at a rate $\bar{m}$. Thus

$$y = \bar{m} - p. \tag{30}$$

2. The supply of labour to the private sector grows at an exogenously given and constant rate $\bar{q}$. Since output per worker is by assumption constant, $\bar{q}$ is also the rate at which full employment output grows (Harrod's 'natural' rate of growth). Let E be the proportion of the private sector labour force which is currently employed $(= 1 - U)$. Then it is easy to show that

$$e = y - \bar{q} \tag{31}$$

where e is the growth rate of E.[9]

Bringing together (30) and (31) we get

$$e = \bar{m} - \bar{q} - p. \tag{32}$$

where causality runs from $\bar{m}$ to e. A more plentiful supply of money means a higher value of $\bar{m}$, which, other things being equal, means a higher e and a faster growth of employment. Conversely, a less plentiful supply of money means a lower value of $\bar{m}$ and a slower growth of employment.

Equation (32) may be written in the following alternative form.

$$e = p^{\bar{m}} - p \tag{33}$$

where $p^{\bar{m}} = \bar{m} - \bar{q}$. We shall refer to $p^{\bar{m}}$ as the *inflation ceiling*. It is positive when the supply of money is growing faster than full employment output and is negative when the opposite is true. From equation (33) it follows that $e < 0$ when $p > p^{\bar{m}}$. This means that when the economy is above the inflation ceiling, as determined by monetary factors, employment grows more slowly than the supply of labour and unemployment U rises. Conversely, $e > 0$ when $p < p^{\bar{m}}$, and thus, when the economy is below the inflation ceiling, private sector employment grows more rapidly than the available labour supply and unemployment falls.[10] So there is a feedback from prices to demand: unemployment rises when the economy is above the inflation ceiling and falls when it is below this ceiling. Prices are in their turn influenced by demand, through its effect on conflict in the private sector, so that the complete system of causality can be described by means of the following diagram:

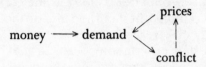

Every link in this diagram is fully specified; thus, starting from an arbitrary initial position, the behaviour of demand, conflict and prices is determined *ceteris paribus* by what happens to the money supply.[11] If this supply is under government control, it can thus be used to influence the evolution of output and prices.

Using the simple monetary theory just described, let us now analyse the long-term effects of monetary policy. The discussion will rely mainly on the method of comparative statics and the dynamic properties of the system will be described in a rather impressionistic fashion.

Steady State

Let us say that the economy is in a 'steady state' if both the rate of unemployment U and the rate of inflation p are constant. Suppose, for the moment, that there is a given long-run Phillips curve and that the supply of money grows at a constant rate $\bar{m}$. Then there is a unique steady state solution, situated where the Phillips curve intersects the line $p = p^{\bar{m}}$. Two cases can be distinguished. If the inflation ceiling $p^{\bar{m}}$ is below the expectations threshold p^{th}, the intersection point Q is on the sloping part of the Phillips curve (see Fig. 7(a)). Along this part

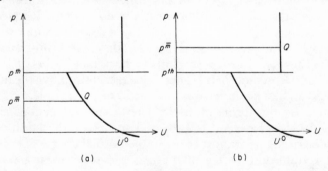

Fig. 7.

of the curve, a higher value of $\overline{m}$, and thus of $p^{\overline{m}}$, is associated with a lower value of U. Within limits, therefore, a more plentiful supply of money is associated with a higher level of economic activity. But this is only true as long as the economy remains below the expectations threshold and thus on the sloping part of the curve. When $\overline{m}$ reaches a certain value, $p^{\overline{m}}$ crosses the threshold p^{th}, and expectations begin to influence decision-making. This causes the point of intersection to shift sharply to the right, to a point on the vertical part of the Phillips curve (see Fig. 7 (b)). Thus a more plentiful supply of money, which pushes inflation over the threshold p^{th}, leads eventually to more unemployment than a less plentiful supply, which keeps inflation below this threshold.

Structural Shifts

The discussion so far has assumed a given long-run Phillips curve. Now, as we have seen earlier, there are many different factors which may cause this curve to shift. Higher taxes, worse terms of trade, greater working-class militancy, or a capitalist drive for higher profits may shift it to the right; and, conversely, lower taxes, better terms of trade, or an incomes policy may shift it to the left. Let us consider how these shifts affect prices and employment, assuming that official monetary policy prevents any change in the rate $\overline{m}$ at which the supply of money is growing. Because the money supply continues to grow at its old rate, the inflation ceiling $p^{\overline{m}}$ remains unchanged and there is no permanent change in the actual rate of inflation. Thus the economy will settle down with a different amount of unemployment, but with prices rising at the same rate as before. Two possible cases can be distinguished, and are illustrated in Figs 8(a) and 8(b): in the former, the economy is below the expectations threshold and in the latter it is above. Suppose the economy is initially at the point Q_1 and the curve is shifted to the right. The intersection point shifts to the point Q_2 where p is the same as before and U is higher. This has an intuitive meaning which can best be understood by means of an example.

Suppose the terms of trade deteriorate and neither side, capitalists or workers, is prepared to accept the additional burden of higher import costs. In the normal course of events, this would lead to faster inflation, as each side tried to pass the burden on to the other, but official monetary policy prevents

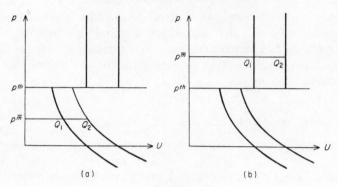

Fig. 8.

such an outcome. By refusing to provide the additional money required for faster inflation, it reduces the level of real expenditure, forcing down the level of activity and undermining the market position of the contending parties. The system stabilizes when workers and/or capitalists have become so weak that they can no longer resist the additional burden and are unable to gain compensatory increases in their money incomes. Thus, through its influence on demand, a tight monetary policy exerts a discipline on the private sector and contains the inflationary impact of worse terms of trade.

Conversely, suppose the economy is at Q_2 and the curve shifts to the left. The new intersection point is at Q_1, where prices are rising at the same rate as before but unemployment is lower than it was originally. To take an example, consider the effect of an incomes policy. In the normal course of events this might reduce the rate of inflation, but suppose official monetary policy ensures that prices continue to rise at their old rate $p^{\overline{m}}$. It does this by causing the level of activity to rise, which has the effect of weakening market discipline on the private sector. Then, on the one hand, incomes policy imposes a new institutional discipline on the private sector, but on the other hand official monetary policy leads to a reduction in market discipline. Between them, these two changes cancel out and there is no net change in the degree of discipline under which the private sector operates: the indirect discipline of demand is partially replaced by the direct discipline of an incomes policy, but that is all. The aspiration gap remains unchanged, conflict continues as before, and the rate of inflation remains at its old level. The only permanent change is a rise in the level of economic activity. Thus, a liberal monetary policy which stimulates demand may convert the price effects of an incomes policy into quantity effects, so that the system operates with less unemployment but the same rate of inflation as before.

Comparison with Monetarism

Superficially, the present analysis looks rather like that of the 'monetarists'. The money supply, through its effect on expenditure, influences demand, and demand influences prices. Moreover, the mechanism of adaptive expectations ensures that the scope for demand management is limited by the possibility of explosive inflation. But this is as far as the similarity goes. The two approaches are based on different theories of wages and prices, and yield different practical implications.

As a body of doctrine, 'monetarism' should really be called '*neoclassical* monetarism', for it is based on the assumption that capitalism still functions in a largely atomistic fashion: unions and firms are small by comparison with the whole economy; each union or firm acts independently of the others, making no attempt to act in co-operation with others or to imitate their behaviour. Moreover, unions and firms are assumed to act as calculating individuals, seeking to gain maximum advantage for themselves or their members, uninfluenced by political or ideological factors. Given these assumptions, it follows that organized power plays at most a secondary role in determining wages and prices, and politics and ideology are quite simply irrelevant. Wage and price movements are determined largely by the atomistic process of supply and demand, with monopolies and unions exercising a marginal influence on their overall movement.

The atomistic nature of conventional theory can be seen most clearly in the labour market. Wages rise primarily because they are bid up by employers seeking to attract new workers and to retain their existing work-force, and unions can have little effect on the overall wage level, although by restricting entry they can alter the pattern of differentials. This theory has several important implications for anti-inflationary policy. The trade-off between unanticipated inflation and unemployment can be best altered by measures which reduce the need for employers to bid up wages. Of these the most important are those which (1) reduce the turnover of labour and (2) reduce the length of time spent by the unemployed searching for an acceptable job. Incomes policies and changes in the terms of trade or taxation are of secondary importance in this theory because they cannot significantly shift the trade-off curve. This surprising conclusion about taxes and the terms of trade follows from the assumption that the economy consists of 'rationally' calcuating units, isolated from each other and acting independently. In such an economy, under given demand conditions, individual units are relatively powerless and an additional terms-of-trade or tax burden will not lead to a continuous inflationary spiral. At most there will be a once-and-for-all rise in wages or prices, as the burden is redistributed and a new set of marginal equalities is established.

Both the assumptions and conclusion of the present analysis are quite different from those just described. Power plays a central role in the determination of wages and prices. Individual units are not isolated from each other, as in conventional monetarism, but act in an interdependent fashion. This interdependence may be explicit, as in the case of a nationwide strike by millions of workers or a formal price agreement between a number of large firms, or else it may be implicit, as in the case of a series of imitative strikes or price increases. Moveover, political and ideological factors are extremely important. For example, capitalists may combine to restrain (or raise) prices to achieve some political objective, or workers may accept taxes for ends which they think are legitimate. The model is not, however, of the 'old' cost-push variety, because it recognizes that the exercise of power is conditioned by demand, and it postulates a trade-off between demand and unanticipated inflation. Like the cost-push models, however, it assumes that inflation can be affected by such things as the terms of trade, taxes or incomes policy, which can shift the trade-off curve up or down.

The contrasts and similarities of the two approaches are particularly clear if one considers what happens to the level of unemployment when the mechanism of adaptive expectations is in operation. Both theories predict that the rate of inflation can only be stabilized permanently at a unique level of unemployment U^0, determined by the position of the short-run trade-off curve. In conventional monetarism U^0 is the 'natural' rate of unemployment, which is primarily determined by the competitive and informational structure of the labour market. Trade unions can alter the natural rate, but only through their influence on information and job mobility, not through their combativity and fighting strength. Likewise, the influence of monopolies is marginal and they cannot significantly affect the natural rate by following an aggressive pricing policy. In the present theory, however, U^0 is the level of unemployment at which the claims of the rival parties become mutually consistent. Demand function as a regulator of class conflict. On the workers' side a low level of demand isolates militants from the mass of workers and strengthens the hand of 'moderate' leaders against dissenting elements. On the employers' side it reduces their ability to raise prices and may force them to revise downwards their target profit margins. So demand exerts a *discipline* which undermines the power of organized labour and big capital, and prevents them pressing home their rival claims. If the two sides are really powerful and determined it may require a severe economic crisis to bring prices under control, resulting in huge surpluses of labour and capacity. In the longer run, however, capitalists can escape from this situation by scrapping equipment and rationalizing their production methods so that excess capacity is eventually eliminated. This throws the full cost of adjustment onto the working class, and involves the creation of a permanent reserve of unemployed labour, sufficiently large to cow workers into submission and force them both to accept the burden of taxes and import costs, and provide a substantial surplus for profits. The required amount of unemployment may be much higher than the rather small, 'natural' rate envisaged by the monetarists.

Concluding Comments

To conclude this paper, let me stress once again some of the limitations of the foregoing analysis. Firstly, in assuming that techniques and output per worker remain constant, it ignores the effect of changing production on the movement of prices. This is clearly a serious weakness, some of whose implications are considered briefly in an appendix. Secondly, it assumes that official monetary policy has a simple and unambiguous effect on expenditure, and that demand exercises a direct influence on the market power of workers and capitalists, and thus upon their ability to raise wages and prices. In reality, of course, things are neither so simple nor so direct. Indeed, under certain circumstances monetary policy may be completely frustrated by changes in the velocity of money, and the behaviour of wages and prices may be quite unaffected by variations in demand. However, in my opinion, these are rather exceptional circumstances. In general, monetary policy does influence expenditure and demand does influence wages and prices, although rarely in quite the simple fashion which has been assumed for analytical purposes.

Appendix

This appendix discusses how the preceding analysis might be modified or extended.

Production

Throughout this paper, production is hardly mentioned; it leads a subterranean existence, influencing some of the variables but receiving no explicit recognition. For example, the relationship between the demand variables D^l and D^c depends very much on the production techniques used, and may be radically altered by the reorganization of production and the introduction of labour-saving techniques. Indeed, the historic problem of late twentieth-century capitalism is how to recreate the internal reserve of labour (low D^l) whilst maintaining a high degree of capacity utilization (high D^c). To make specific provision for this aspect of production would not require any change in the basic equations of this article, and it would complement rather than modify the present analysis.

Production may also influence through its effect on productivity and the rate at which living standards rise. Workers may be prepared to trade a lower share of output in return for a faster rise in real wages. In this case a faster rate of productivity growth leads to a reduction in working-class militancy, a smaller aspiration gap and slower inflation. Alternatively, the wage bargain may be based on *expected* productivity growth in the future, in which case capitalists can increase profits by raising productivity more than the anticipated amount. This reduces their need for higher prices and may thereby slow down the inflationary process. Naturally, if wage bargains adapt in the light of experience, this anti-inflationary aspect of productivity growth will soon disappear, bargaining will adapt to faster productivity growth and wages will rise to allow for it. Thus higher productivity can reduce the rate of inflation (a) if it has not already been anticipated in the wage bargain, or (b) if it makes workers less militant by providing them with a higher standard of living.

Exchange Rates

Exchange rates were assumed to adjust automatically so as to insulate the economy against changes in the general level of world prices. This assumption can be modified by reducing exchange rate flexibility, so that a rise in the general level of world prices leads to a rise in domestic prices, even when there is no change in the terms of trade.

The Terms of Trade

The terms of trade were taken in our analysis as exogenously given, and thus unaffected by changes in the level of domestic demand. This may be an adequate assumption in the case of a small economy which must take world prices as given, but it is hardly adequate if one is considering a large country, like the United States, whose internal state of demand exerts a major influence on the terms of trade; nor is it adequate if one is considering inflation in the world economy as a whole. To allow for this kind of interdependence the analysis can be modified as follows. Suppose trade takes place between two countries or blocs, one of which produces services and manufactured goods and the other primary products, and that the terms of trade are determined by the state of demand in the primary producing sector, which is measured by an index of capacity utilization D^f. Then the real cost of imports F is a function of D^f given by

$$F = F(D^f). \tag{A1}$$

Combining this with our earlier analysis we find that inflation in the advanced industrial country or bloc is determined by four variables: D^c, D^l, D^f and T,

$$p^u = \lambda[\Pi^*(D^c) + W^n(D^l) + F(D^f) + T]$$
$$\lambda A(D^c, D^l, D^f, T). \tag{A2}$$

It is beyond the scope of this paper to discuss the details or implications of this modification, but one comment is worth making.

In the course of a cycle all three demand variables move up or down together, and as a result the distinction between demand and burden effects becomes more subtle. Consider, for example, a boom in the world economy. This leads to a universally higher level of demand, so that D^c, D^l and D^f all rise. This has a direct impact on the rate of inflation in the advanced countries because it strengthens the market position of capitalists and workers in these countries (higher D^c, D^l), and it has an indirect impact on the rate of inflation because it makes the terms of trade worse (higher D^f) and raises the real burden of import costs which must be borne by the private sector. The former, direct, impact is what we have called a 'demand effect' in our earlier analysis, and the latter is what we have called a 'burden effect'. Thus, through its influence on the terms of trade with primary producers, a change in domestic demand has an indirect burden effect in the industrial countries. This indirect burden effect depends, of course, on how the private sector responds to changes in the terms of trade. If it is prepared to absorb higher real import costs, the indirect burden effect will be zero, but if it is not prepared to absorb these costs this indirect effect may be substantial.

BIBLIOGRAPHY

Jackson, D., Turner, H. A. and Wilkinson, S. F., 1975, *Do Trade Unions Cause Inflation?*, second edn, Cambridge, CUP.

Keynes, J. M., 1972, 'How to pay for the War', in *Collected Writings of John Maynard Keynes*, Vol. IX, London, Macmillan.

Marx, K., 1970, *Capital*, Vol. I, London, Lawrence & Wishart.

Maynard, G., 1972, *Economic development and the Price Level*, London, Macmillan.

Phillips, A. W., 1958, 'The Relation between Unemployment and Money Wage Rates in the United Kingdom, 1861–1957', *Economica*, November.

NOTES

1. Keynes (1972), Maynard (1972), Marx (1970), Phillips (1958), Jackson, Turner and Wilkinson (1975).

2. It is arguable that taxation should include not only taxes in the conventional sense, but also certain kinds of government borrowing. For example, the state can finance part of its activities by issuing money. Legally, this is considered to be a form of borrowing, and money is counted as part of the national debt. But, in fact, when prices are rising, it is a disguised form of taxation, for it involves an *unrequited* transfer of real resources from the private sector to the state. In the text, however, we ignore this 'inflation tax' and consider only taxes as they are conventionally defined.

3. Let Y be the gross output of the private sector, N the volume of imports and r the ratio of import prices to export prices (the terms of trade). Then F is given by

$$F = \frac{Nr}{Y}.$$

In this essay N/Y is assumed constant and therefore F mirrors the behaviour of r and may be taken as an index of the terms of trade. Since all imports consist entirely of raw materials and intermediate products, and state activities are financed entirely by taxation or borrowing, it follows that

real national income (excluding
income from abroad) = gross output of the private sector
       minus cost of imports
       = $Y(1-F)$.

Thus, as we should expect, a deterioration in the terms of trade raises F and reduces national income.

4. Exchange rate flexibility also insulates the domestic economy against certain kinds of inflationary pressure from abroad. A uniform rise in the *absolute* level of world prices, for example, is immediately offset by an appreciation of the local currency and thus has no effect on domestic costs or prices. On the other hand a change in *relative* prices on the world market may alter the terms of trade, causing the real cost of imports, and thus F, to increase. The result – analysed below – may well be domestic inflation (and in consequence depreciation of the local currency) as capitalists try to pass higher costs on to consumers and workers in their turn seek compensatory wage increases.

5. This rule means that prices are adjusted with a distributed lag in response to any particular cost or tax increase. Initially prices are adjusted by a fraction of the divergence between Π^* and Π^n. In the absence of any cost or tax changes, this means a different value for Π^n in the following period. In this following period prices will again change by a fraction of the (smaller) divergence between Π^* and Π^n, and so on indefinitely. Eventually, *in the absence of further cost or tax changes*, Π^n will converge to Π^*

and so capitalists will in the long run achieve their target; the size of β determines the speed of convergence. However, when costs and taxes are changing this convergence need not occur, and the share of profits may stabilize at a value different from Π^*.

6. This decomposition assumes, of course, that the parameter λ and the functional form of A remain unchanged.

7. Strictly speaking, the Philips curve gives a relationship between unemployment and so-called 'wage inflation'. Throughout this article we shall use the term 'Phillips curve' to describe the relationship between unemployment and price inflation.

   The Phillips curve may not be stable in the long run, as the relationship between unemployment U and the demand indices D^l and D^c may shift when structural change takes place. Consider the example of a severe crisis in which unemployment remains at a high level for a long period of time. At first this unemployment is of a Keynesian type, characterized by a general surplus of both labour and capacity. Both workers and capitalists are subject to severe market discipline in such a situation, and inflationary pressures are effectively contained. In time, however, structural changes may occur which lead to a reappearance of inflationary pressures, even though unemployment remains as high as ever: capitalists may reorganize their production methods and scrap equipment, eliminating excess capacity and gradually restoring utilization to its normal level; the labour market may break up into non-competing segments, so that local shortages develop despite the overall high level of unemployment. Such a transformation of Keynesian into structural unemployment strengthens the market position of capitalists or employed workers, and leads to a more intense struggle over distribution and a faster rate of inflation, even though the overall level of unemployment has not changed. The Phillips curve associated with structural unemployment is thus above that associated with Keynesian unemployment.

8. This crisis is discussed at greater length in my review of Ernest Mandel's *Late Capitalism* (see this volume, p. 95).

9. If Q is full employment output, then, since productivity is independent of the level of employment, $Y = EQ$. In growth rate form this can be written $y = e + \bar{q}$.

10. The inflation ceiling and the expectations threshold coincide when $p^{\bar{m}} = p^{th}$. This happens when $\bar{m} = m^{th}$, where

$$m^{th} = p^{th} + \bar{q}$$

So $p^{\bar{m}} \gtreqless p^{th}$ according as $\bar{m} \gtreqless m^{th}$.

11. This statement assumes that the following items are given: the tax rate, the terms of trade, the mechanism by which expectations are determined, and the functional form of $\lambda A (U, T, F)$.

7

Marx's Theory of Wages[1]

The theory of wages has for long been a subject of intense debate
between Marxists and others, and amongst Marxists themselves.
Unfortunately, there exists no satisfactory exposition or analysis of Marx's own views on the subject, at least in the English
language, and most Marxists have only the haziest idea of what
Marx actually said about wages, how his views developed, or
what relation they bore to those of his predecessors. Even works
of considerable scholarship, dealing with the character and
evolution of Marx's views, are inadequate and sometimes very
inaccurate in their treatment of wages. For example, Roman
Rosdolsky's famous book *The Making Of Marx's Capital* contains
a section entitled 'A Critical Assessment of Marx's Theory of
Wages' in which, despite its title, he merely repeats uncritically
most of the better-known passages from Marx's later writings
on the subject, and seeks to defend Marx against what he thinks
are mistaken interpretations.[2] He makes no real attempt to
consider the evolution of Marx's view on wages, nor to identify
and deal with the major theoretical difficulties raised by Marx's
writings in this field. A much better treatment is contained in
Ernest Mandel's *The Formation of the Economic Thought of Karl Marx*
which gives a fairly accurate picture of how Marx's theory of
wages developed.[3] However, Mandel gives a very inaccurate
picture of classical wage theory, and thereby greatly exaggerates
the orginality of Marx's own thought on this subject; and, like
Rosdolsky, he does not really confront the main theoretical
issues involved.

The present paper seeks to remedy these defects by providing
a fairly comprehensive exposition and genuinely critical analysis
of Marx's various writings on wages and allied questions. This is
not an easy task, as the writings concerned are often fragmentary
in character and are not always consistent with each other. Even
so, I hope that in what follows I have managed to create some
order out of the chaotic material which Marx has left us, and
that I have raised some interesting questions. The paper is

divided into three main parts which deal successively with: (1) The writings of David Ricardo, who greatly influenced Marx; (2) Marx's early writings in the period 1847-8 and (3) Marx's later writings on the question of wages. In addition, there is also a brief section dealing with Marx's views on wages and inflation.

I RICARDO

Before discussing Marx's own views on wages, it will be useful to consider in some detail the views of his classical predecessors, as exemplified by David Ricardo whose *Principle of Political Economy and Taxation* exerted a great influence on Marx. This will make clear Marx's enormous debt to the classical economists and place his theory in historical perspective.[4]

Market Price and Natural Price

Ricardo's theory of wages is based on the proposition that labour is a commodity whose price is determined like that of any other commodity. And, as in the case of any other commodity, he distinguishes between *market* price and *natural* price. The market price of a commodity is the price which is actually observed at any moment of time; it is determined by the interplay of supply and demand, is subject to a wide variety of different influences, and in particular is affected by the presence of gluts or shortages. By contrast, the natural price of a commodity may never be observed in practice, but is rather a point of attraction towards which prices have a tendency to gravitate. In the words of Adam Smith: 'The natural price . . . is the central price, to which the prices of all commodities are continually gravitating. Different accidents may sometimes keep them suspended a good deal above it, and sometimes force them down even somewhat below it. But whatever may be the obstacles which hinder them from settling in this centre of repose and continuence they are constantly tending towards it'.[5]

This gravitational tendency is the result of a quite specific mechanism, namely the long-run adaptations in supply which, under competitive conditions, occur wherever market price exceeds its natural level. The natural price of a commodity is simply the price which must be paid, under competitive conditions, to guarantee the production of this commodity on some given scale. As Ricardo says, it is 'such a price as is necessary to supply constantly a given demand'.[6] For this reason it is called by Marx 'price of production', and later by Marshall 'supply price'. If a commodity is scarce, its market price exceeds its natural price and, under competitive conditions, production increases; and supply expands until the orginal scarcity is eliminated and market price is brought into line with natural price. Conversely, when there is a surplus of a particular commodity the opposite occurs: production falls, and supply contracts until the surplus is eliminated and the market price and natural price again coincide. Thus, under competitive conditions, supply gradually adapts in response to demand and thereby pulls the market price towards its natural level.[7]

Now, the natural price of a commodity is itself influenced by the material conditions under which it is produced. Roughly speaking, the more difficult a particular commodity is to produce, the greater is the amount which must be paid to ensure its production on the requisite scale and the higher is its natural price. In this sense, the natural price of a commodity is the monetary expression of its *value*, and the gravitation of market price towards natural price is an expression of the 'law of value' through which prices are *automatically* regulated by the conditions under which commodities are produced.

Notice that the natural price of a commodity is not the empirical average of observed market prices, nor is it the normal or usual price of this commodity. It is the price which is required under competitive conditions to ensure production on a given scale. Thus market price may remain permanently above the natural price if: (a) demand is growing so fast that supply fails to keep up with it and there is a permanent scarcity, or (b) if there is a monopoly which restricts competition and maintains an 'artificial' scarcity.

Wages

Ricardo defines wages as the price of labour. Assuming a competitive labour market, he expresses the relation between market and natural price as follows.[8]

> The market price of labour is the price which is really paid for it, from the natural operation of the proportion of the supply to the demand; labour is dear when it is scarce, and cheap when it is

plentiful. However much the market price of labour may deviate from its natural price, it has, like commodities, a tendency to conform to it (p. 94).

The mechanism which establishes this tendency for the market price of labour to conform to its natural price is change in population. When wages are high population expands, and when they are low it contracts. When wages are exactly at the natural level, the population is stationary and the workforce is just replaced from one generation to the next. Ricardo describes this mechanism as follows.

It is when the market price of labour exceeds its natural price, that the condition of the labourer is flourishing and happy, that he has it in his power to command a greater proportion of the necessaries and enjoyments of life, and therefore to rear a healthy and numerous family. When, however, by the encouragement which high wages give to the increase of population, the number of labourers is increased, wages again fall to the natural price, and indeed from a reaction sometimes fall below it.

When the market price of labour is below its natural price, the condition of the labourers is most wretched: then poverty deprives them of those comforts which custom renders absolute . . . necessities. It is only after their privations have reduced their numbers, or the demand for labour has increased, that the market price of labour will rise to its natural price, and that the labourer will have the moderate comforts which the natural rate of wages will afford (p. 94).

Notice that this is not a crude physiological theory of population, for Ricardo recognizes the social character of needs. Indeed, just a little further on from the paragraphs just quoted he states this quite explicitly:

It is not to be understood that the natural price of labour, estimated even in food and necessaries, is absolutely fixed and constant. It varies at different times in the same country, and very materially differs in different countries. It essentially depends on the habits and customs of the people. An English labourer would consider his wages under their natural rate, and too scanty to support a family, if they enabled him to purchase no other food than potatoes, and to live in no better habitation than a mud cabin; yet these moderate demands of nature are often deemed sufficient in countries where 'man's life is cheap', and his wants easily satisfied. Many of the conveniences now enjoyed in an English cottage, would have been thought luxuries at an earlier period of our history (pp. 96-7).

The reaction of population to wages is a typical example of the automatic mechanisms which operate on the supply side in Ricardo's system. If the market price of a commodity deviates from its natural price, then under competitive conditions supply adapts in the course of time so as to pull this market price back towards its natural level.

Automatic mechanisms also operate on the demand side. Wages influence both the form and pace of accumulation, and thereby affect the way in which the demand for labour evolves through time. If rising wages lead to a reduction in profits, accumulation slows down and may even cease altogether, for as Ricardo says:

> The farmer and manufacturer can no more live without profit, than the labourer without wages. Their motive for accumulation will diminish with every diminution of profit, and will cease altogether when their profits are so low as not to afford them an adequate compensation for their trouble, and the risk which they must necessarily encounter in employing their capital productively (p. 122).

This reduction in the rate of accumulation will ease pressure in the labour market, and thereby contain the growth of wages.

Ricardo also considers how the demand for labour and the evolution of wages are affected by the use of machinery. His discussion is not very coherent but the gist of the argument is as follows. At any moment of time capitalists have available to them a variety of different ways of producing, and the technique they choose depends on the relative price of machinery and labour. Other things being equal, a rise in wages will make labour relatively more expensive and cause firms to replace it with machinery. Thus, if accumulation leads to a shortage of labour and wages rise, firms respond by using more mechanised techniques of production. In Ricardo's view this will slow-down the rate at which the overall demand for labour is growing as the result of accumulation, but will not entirely prevent some rise in demand. Indeed, he is quite explicit on this point:

> The same cause that raises labour does not raise the value of machines and, therefore, with every augmentation of capital a greater proportion of it is employed on machinery. The demand for labour will continue to increase with an increase of capital, but not in proportion to its increase; the ratio will necessarily be a diminishing ratio (p. 395).

This conclusion about the demand for labour continuing to rise during accumulation, despite the installation of machinery, assumes that there are no technical innovations, and that capitalists are choosing from amongst an unchanging set of techniques. Under the influence of John Barton, Ricardo also consider what happens when an improved machine is 'suddenly discovered and extensively used'.[9] He concedes that in this case total employment in the economy as a whole may be reduced. If the new equipment is very expensive the funds, which would otherwise have been used to employ workers, will be used to purchase machinery instead and the demand for labour will fall. Under these conditions,

> the discovery and use of machinery . . . will be injurious to the labouring class, as some of their number will be thrown out of employment, and production will become redundant compared to the funds which are used to employ it (p. 390).

Notice that Ricardo is not talking just about jobs in the particular industry where new machinery is introduced, but about employment in the economy as a whole.[10] However, this reduction of total employment is, in his opinion, temporary. Mechanization leads to higher profits, and thereby stimulates accumulation and savings, so that additional jobs are 'soon' created and labour displaced by machinery is reabsorbed.

Thus, despite his clear recognition that machinery may create unemployment and reduce the overall number of jobs, Ricardo takes a fairly optimistic view. Mechanization may cause temporary unemployment, but in the long run, provided accumulation continues, the demand for labour will increase.

We can summarize Ricardo's general theory of wages as follows. Wages are determined, in the first instance, by supply and demand in the labour market. However, both supply and demand themselves adapt in the longer term so as to keep the capitalist economy viable. On the supply side, demographic forces have a tendency to pull wages back towards some historically determined subsistence level, and on the demand side the behaviour of wages is influenced by the pace and form of accumulation. In this way, the automatic mechanisms in Ricardo's system control the development of the economy and the evolution of wages. The operation of these mechanisms is quite complex and Ricardo allows for a variety of possibilities.

The Stationary State

Perhaps the most famous of Ricardo's scenarios is that of the 'stationary state' in which long-term expansion is impossible and the economy fluctuates around or settles down in a position of simple reproduction. Wages are at their subsistence level, the production is constant, there is no accumulation, and profits are low. This scenario is based on two crucial assumptions:

(a) there is no technical progress in agriculture;
(b) the supply of good land is limited and productivity declines as cultivation is extended to inferior land.

According to Ricardo, these assumptions ensure that there are diminishing returns to scale in agriculture, and that any boom is eventually brought to a standstill by the rising cost of food. His argument is as follows. Other things being equal, accumulation increases the demand for labour, and, although capitalists seek to counteract this by installing labour-saving machinery, they are not in Ricardo's opinion entirely successful. Sooner or later a prolonged boom must lead to a rising demand for workers and to the depletion of existing reserves of unemployed labour. This causes real wages to rise, so that profitability declines and the pace of accumulation slows down. But the mechanism of growing labour shortage and rising real wages is only of medium-term significance, for in the longer run population will itself change and the supply of labour will spontaneously adapt so as to eliminate shortages or at least keep them within bounds. The upward movement of real wages will therefore be checked. Thus, in the longer run, population growth ensures that sufficient labour is available for accumulation to proceed. Yet this gives rise to a second and more fundamental problem. As population and employment increase, the demand for food increases, even in the absence of any further rise in the standard of living of workers. To meet this additional demand the output of food must expand. But, by assumption, there are diminishing returns in agriculture, so as output expands food becomes more difficult to produce, its cost rises and the terms of trade shift against manufacturing industry. To compensate workers for these higher prices manufacturers are forced to raise wages and accept lower profits.[11] Thus, profitability is reduced as accumulation proceeds, in the medium-run by a shortage of labour and rising real wages, and in the long run by rising food costs as cultivation is extended to less fertile land.[12] Eventually, accumulation grinds to a standstill and the entire process goes into reverse as the economy is dragged back towards the stationary state, where population is constant and real wages are at their subsistence level.

Other Possibilities

Ricardo's discussion of the stationary state has given rise to certain misapprehensions about his analysis. Ernest Mandel for example, in his book, *The Formation of the Economic Thought of Karl Marx* implies that wages in the Ricardian system remain rigidly fixed at an unchanging subsistence minimum.[13] This is not, however, correct. Quite apart from his recognition that wages may deviate temporarily from their subsistence level, Ricardo also considers the possibility that wages may rise permanently. In fact he explicitly mentions two ways in which such a permanent rise may occur.

In the first place, the subsistence minimum is socially determined, and the working class can modify the operation of demographic forces by acquiring new needs, and refusing to reproduce at the required scale unless these new needs are met:

> The friends of humanity cannot but wish that in all countries the labouring classes should have a taste for comforts and enjoyments, and that they should be stimulated by all legal means in their exertions to procure them. There cannot be a better security against a superabundant population. In those countries, where the labouring classes have the fewest wants, and are contented with the cheapest food, the people are exposed to the greatest vicissitudes and miseries. They have no place of refuge from calamity (p. 100–1).

Thus, even within the analytical framework of stationary states, a change in habits can improve the lot of workers, by shifting the economy from one stationary state to another. Incidentally, this view of needs and their evolution is strikingly similar to that adopted by Marx in his later writing.

A second possibility is to replace the assumptions upon which the stationary state is based. Diminishing returns in agriculture, for example, can be offset by the opening up of new fertile lands, or by improvements in agricultural technique. Each of these will slow down or prevent falling agricultural productivity, permit sustained increase in the production of cheap food, and thereby check the incipient tendency of profits to fall. On the subject of improvements, for example, Ricardo says:

> The natural tendency of profits then is to fall; for in the progress of society and wealth, the additional quantity of food required is obtained by the sacrifice of more and more labour. This tendency, this gravitation as it were of profits, is happily checked at repeated intervals by the improvements in machinery, connected with the production of necessaries, as well as by discoveries in the science of agriculture which enable us to relinquish a portion of labour before required, and therefore to lower the price of the prime necessity of the labourer (p.120).

Indeed, if there is a continual stream of agricultural improvements or expansion into new territories, accumulation may continue indefinitely. Ricardo mentions, for example, the possibility of a prolonged boom in which agricultural improvements ensure a ready supply of cheap food, so that labour remains relatively inexpensive and profits are high, even though the standard of living of workers is above subsistence level and population is increasing:

> Notwithstanding the tendency of wages to conform to their natural rate, their market rate may, in an improving society, for an indefinite period, be constantly above it; for no sooner may the impulse, which an increased capital gives to a new demand for labour, be obeyed, than another increase of capital may produce the same effect; and thus, if the increase of capital be gradual and constant, the demand for labour may give a continued stimulus to an increase of people (pp. 94–5).

The key to such a boom is that accumulation proceeds at a gradual rate, so that the demand for labour, and thereby food, keeps in pace with the rate of improvement in agricultural techniques. If accumulation is too rapid, the price of labour rises steeply, in the short run because of labour shortages and rising real wages, and in the longer run because of declining productivity in agriculture and higher food prices.

Thus, a permanent rise in wages is possible in the Ricardian system if (a) the working class acquires new needs in the course of capitalist development, or (b) if improvements in agriculture or the opening up of new territories ensure a growing supply of cheap food. Although Ricardo never put these possibilities together, it is a simple matter to do so, and the picture is one of an expanding capitalism in which agricultural techniques are improving, new territories are being opened up, living standards are rising, and the working class is acquiring new needs. If one abstracts from the periodic crises which have plagued capitalist development, this is not a bad picture of what has actually happened in the advanced countries, although it ignores both the uneven pattern of world development and the wars of conquest and extermination which have accompanied the opening up of new territories, or what Ricardo delicately calls the 'discovery of new markets'. I am not sure how far Ricardo himself had such a vision, but it is certainly consistent with his own analysis and became quite fashionable amongst his followers.[14]

II MARX'S EARLY WRITINGS

Marx's first excursion into the theory of wages is to be found in his *Economic and Philosophical Manuscripts of 1844*. However, despite the profound insights contained in the rest of this work, the passages dealing with wages are quite uninspired and merely repeat, in a rather garbled fashion, the views of Adam Smith. Having completed the *1844 Manuscripts* Marx undertook a serious study of political economy and his understanding of the subject was rapidly transformed. He read and mastered Ricardo's *Principles*, and he became a close friend of Friedrich Engels whose grasp of political economy was, at this time, far in advance of his own. After a space of about three years, Marx again returned to the theory of wages, and within a few months around the end of 1847 he wrote an enormous amount on the subject, all of which reflects the very strong influence of Ricardian thought, both in terminology and analysis. Of these writings the most important are *The Communist Manifesto*, written jointly with Engels, *The Poverty of Philosophy*, *Wage, Labour and Capital*, and some brief notes which have recently been published in English in the Marx-Engels *Collected Works* entitled simply *Wages*. There are, of course, certain differences between these various works but, as far as wages are concerned, they are very similar and can be treated as part of a coherent whole.

In these writings Marx takes over the following ideas from Ricardo:

  (i)   The distinction between the market price of labour and its natural price – the market price being determined by the day-to-day configuration of supply and demand, and the natural price as a point towards which the market price has a tendency to gravitate.

 (ii)   The natural price of labour as the subsistence wage which is required to maintain the existing workforce and ensure its reproduction.

(iii)   The importance of accumulation in the demand for labour and the movement of wages.

(iv)   The role of machinery as a means of saving labour and holding down wages below what they would otherwise have been.

Despite these similarities, however, there are certain differences of emphasis and judgement which lead Marx to rather different conclusions about the course of capitalist development. To start with, he believes in unlimited technical progress, and rejects the notion of diminishing returns in agriculture which play such an important role in Ricardo's stationary state. There are no natural obstacles to accumulation in his analysis and an unlimited expansion is technically possible. In the Ricardian framework this would be of benefit to the working class, for it would result in a prolonged boom accompanied by rising population and higher wages. But Marx rejects this optimistic conclusion and paints a far more gloomy picture. Why?

In the first place, Marx does not share Ricardo's relatively optimistic views about the effect of accumulation on the overall demand for labour. As we have seen, Ricardo believed that the installation of machinery during a period of expansion will retard the upward trend of employment and may even result in the temporary displacement of labour. Even so, Ricardo was confident that in the long run accumulation will eventually increase the overall demand for labour, and that the additional demand created by expansion will more than offset any loss of jobs caused by the installation of machinery. Marx, however, is not so sure, and he is sympathetic to John Barton's suggeston that accumulation may be so heavily directed into investment in machinery that the overall number of jobs may decline permanently.

More importantly, Marx points out that, even if the overall demand for labour does increase, accumulation drastically alters the character of demand in such a way that it harms all but the poorest and most wretched of workers.[15] There are a number of reasons for this. Accumulation is accompanied by a more extensive division of labour which simplifies jobs, eliminates the need for skills, and brings skilled workers into competition with the unskilled. It is accompanied by mechanization which eliminates the need for manual strength, and allows women and children to take over the jobs of men. Finally, accumulation unifies the world economy, and through trade and migration brings workers from different countries into competition with each other. Thus, accumulation breaks down the barriers between one kind of labour and another, and creates a huge international pool from which labour can be drawn. This forces the average worker to compete with the very poorest of workers who are barely managing to survive under the most wretched of conditions. Wages are thereby equalized in a downward direction towards their lowest common denominator.

Even this is not the end of the story. New ways are continually being discovered whereby the necessities of working-class consumption can be replaced by cheaper substitutes which are less enjoyable to consume, but do not impair the productive efficiency of workers or their ability and willingness to reproduce. As Marx says in *Wages*:[16]

> Although the minimum wage is determined on average by the prices of the most indispensable provisions, it is nevertheless to be remarked:
>
> *Firstly:* that the minimum is different in different countries, the potato in Ireland for example.
>
> *Secondly:* not only that. The minimum itself has a historical . . . movement and sinks always further towards the absolutely lowest level. Example of brandy. Distilled first from draft, then from grain, finally from spirits (p. 425):

Thus, even though accumulation may increase the overall demand for labour, and Marx is by no means certain that it will, its net effect on wages is harmful. Marx asserts this quite unambiguously in the following passage, drawn once again from *Wages*:

In the course of development there is a double fall in wages:

Firstly relative: in proportion to the development of general wealth.

Secondly absolute: since the quantity of commodities which the worker receives in exchange become less and less (p. 426).

Again on the same page he says:

When wages have fallen and later rise again, they never rise, however, to their previous level.

Elsewhere, in the *Communist Manifesto*, we find the following passage

The modern labourer . . . instead of rising with the progress of modern industry, sinks deeper and deeper below the conditions of his own class. He becomes a pauper, and pauperism develops more rapidly than population and wealth.[17]

In view of these and other passages, there is no doubt that, at this time, Marx and indeed Engels believed in the thesis of absolute impoverishment, that wages would be forced down to their physiological minimum. This proposition was later popularized by Ferdinand Lassalle as the notorious 'iron law of wages', and became the subject of bitter dispute within the German Socialist movement. By then, however, both Marx and Engels had changed their opinion and were harshly critical of Lassalle.[18]

Market Price and Natural Price

When dealing with ordinary commodities Marx takes the same approach to prices as Ricardo. In the short run they are determined by the interaction of supply and demand, and in the long run by the conditions under which commodities are produced. And, like Ricardo, Marx extends these ideas to the commodity 'labour', whose price, he says, is regulated 'by the same general laws which regulate the price of commodities in general'.[19] Thus, labour has both a market price and a natural price, the former being the wage actually observed at any particular time in the market, and the latter a point towards which this wage gravitates. Marx also agrees with Ricardo that the natural price of labour is determined by its 'cost of production' which he defined as 'the cost required for maintaining the worker as a worker and for developing him into a worker'.[20] For the skilled worker, this includes the various expenses incurred during the period of his training whilst he acquires the skills of his trade. But for the unskilled or simple labourer, such expenses are minimal, and the cost of production is barely equal to what Marx calls 'the cost of existence and reproduction of the worker'.[21] It is 'almost confined to the commodities necessary for keeping him alive' when he is working, together with an allowance for depreciation, which covers 'the cost of reproduction, whereby the race of workers is enabled to multiply and to replace worn-out workers by new ones'.[22] In other words, for unskilled workers, the cost of production is the minimum wage which will enable them to stay alive and reproduce themselves.

Clearly, Marx's approach to wages has much in common with that of Ricardo. There are, however, certain differences. As we have seen, like most of his contemporaries, Ricardo was a Malthusian, who believed that population is the ultimate regulator of wages and the factor which explains why the market price of labour is pulled towards its natural price or cost of production. In Ricardo's theory, the number of children who are born and survive depends on the level of wages, and any deviation of wages from their natural level will eventually cause a change in the number of people of working age. This in turn alters conditions in the labour market in such a way that wages are pulled back again towards their natural level. In particular, if wages fall below their natural level for any length of time, fewer children are born or survive, the population of working age eventually declines, labour becomes scarce, and competition forces employers to pay higher wages. Thus, in Ricardo's theory, wages are regulated by changes in population. And, as we have seen, Ricardo concluded from this that workers can best improve their situation by limiting their numbers, and thereby creating an eventual scarcity of labour.

Marx rejects this Malthusian line of argument.[23] In the first place he considers it absurdly impractical to limit the birth rate. And he points out that, even if the birth rate could be reduced, the initial impact of such a change would be on the number of small children, and it would be a considerable time before the adult labour force was significantly affected. But these objections are really of secondary importance, for in Marx's view population is irrelevant to the determination of wages, and capital accumulation proceeds in such a way as to make sure that there is *always* an excess of labour. The progressive displacement of workers by machinery and the breaking down of barriers between one kind of work and another creates a vast pool of labour competing for employment. 'We have seen,' he says, that the more productive capital grows the more is 'the disproportion between the numbers of workers and the means for their employment' and so 'the supply of labour will always be too great for the demand for labour'.[24] Thus, any changes in the supply of labour will be swamped by the effects of accumulation, and no matter how hard workers strive to control their numbers there will always be a surplus population.

Now, these objections to the Malthusian doctrine have considerable force, but they do raise some awkward questions. If population is irrelevant to the determination of wages and there is always an excess of labour, as Marx claims, then just what is the role within his theory of such concepts as the 'cost of production' or 'natural price' of labour? Why is it that wages gravitate towards this natural price? If there is *always* an excess of labour, why do wages eventually stabilise at the subsistence level, or indeed at any other level? Why do they not fall indefinitely? Marx does not answer these questions. He gives reasons for believing that competition will drive average wages downwards, but he does not explain why this downward movement will eventually stop. Nor does he explain why wages should eventually stabilize at a level which is sufficient to cover the costs of production (and reproduction) of labour. Indeed, his references to growing pauperism suggests that wages will fall below this level, and he does not say why they should ever rise back up again.

Thus, Marx correctly rejects Ricardo's one-sided emphasis on population, but he fails to provide any alternative. Having argued that average wages will fall, he simply *asserts* that they will stabilize at their natural or subsistence level. This is clearly not a satisfactory procedure. If wages are to fluctuate around or gravitate towards a certain level, as Marx claims, it is not enough that they have a tendency to fall when above this level. There must also be some mechanism which either stops them falling when they reach this level, or else pulls them back up again when they are below it. Marx provides no such mechanism. As a result, his theory seems incoherent in comparison with the elegant, if unrealistic, symmetry of the Ricardian system.

In his later writings Marx tries to overcome these defects, and he provides a far more comprehensive treatment of the subject. Although still rejecting Ricardo's one-sided emphasis on population, he concedes that demographic forces may have some effect on wages, and he lays particular stress on the need for capital to have a healthy and efficient labour force. He also considers how wages are influenced by conditions in the non-capitalist sectors of the economy, and by the presence of trade unions. As we shall see, these later modifications create new problems of their own, but they do at least eliminate some of the more obvious weaknesses in Marx's earlier writings.

Concluding Remarks

The preceding comments really bring us to the later writings of Marx, but before going on to these let us conclude with a few brief remarks.

Trade Unions and the organized power of workers play very little part in the determination of wages and conditions in the early writings of Marx. He cites the Ten Hours Bill as a victory and concedes that 'workers' associations' may raise wages temporarily, but his general view is that:[25]

> In the long run they cannot withstand the laws of competition . . . If the combinations were to succeed in keeping the price of labour so high in one country that profits fell significantly in relation to the average profit in other countries, or so that capital was held up in its growth, stagnation and recession of industry would be the consequence and the workers would be ruined together with their masters.

Despite their inadequacy on the economic front, however, Marx welcomes trade unions because they are valuable training schools and prepare workers for the eventual overthrow of bourgeois order.[26]

Starting from the idea that trade unions are weak and that competition against workers is increasing, Marx concludes, as we have seen, that real wages will fall. There is, however, one isolated passage in which he recognizes that this prediction may be wrong, and concedes that real wages may actually rise. But he warns that, even if this does occur, profits will still rise faster than wages and the *relative* position of workers will decline.[27] The significance of this passage is unclear because it contradicts everything else written by Marx in this period. He obviously did not believe real wages would rise permanently, and he was probably just covering himself against what he regarded as a conceivable but unlikely possibility. Unfortunately, this passage in *Wage Labour and Capital* is often used to 'prove' that Marx never really believed in the doctrine of absolute impoverishment. Such a claim flies in the face of an overwhelming weight of evidence to the contrary, and is not to be taken seriously.

III   MARX'S LATER WRITINGS

Marx's later writings on wages use much the same basic analytical framework as his earlier writings, although there are certain differences of terminology and judgement, and his treatment of the subject is far more complex than before.

The main change in terminology concerns the commodity which workers sell when they agree to work for a capitalist enterprise. In his earlier writings Marx follows Ricardo in calling this commodity 'labour', but in his later writings he prefers the term 'labour-*power*' which he considers to be both more scientific and more accurate. To explain the reasons for and significance of this change would require an entire paper in itself, and we shall not attempt the task here. Suffice it to say that, from a qualitative point of view, the change is of great importance, for it makes explicit key features of capitalist production which are not brought out very clearly in Marx's early writings; and it also tidies up some loose ends in the Ricardian theory of value.[28] From a purely quantitative point of view, however, this change is not so important and does not provide any new insights into the determination of wages. Indeed, Marx himself concedes this point in his popular pamphlet *Wages, Price and Profit* where he reverts to the older terminology and talks of 'labour' rather than 'labour-power'.

The main change of judgement in Marx's later writings concerns the long-run behaviour of wages. The experience of mid-nineteenth-century development, which brought some improvements in living standards in Britain, must have shaken his confidence in his earlier prediction of a long-run decline in

real wages; and instead of a simple grand vision he now provides
a more varied and qualified analysis.[30] In places he even reverses
his earlier argument and suggests there may be a similar
tendency for real wages to rise. In the *Grundrisse*, for example, he
talks of workers being able to 'participate in civilization' and, on
numerous other occasions, he allows for a permanent rise in the
standard of living by stressing the historical and moral and
social elements in subsistence.[31] However, Marx does not
commit himself firmly on this question, and in places he still
talks as though things are getting worse and will continue to do
so. On balance, though, it does seem that he expected wages to
rise.

Marx's later writings on wages extend his analysis in at least
three directions. He considers in much greater depth the
interdependence between wages and the supply of labour; he
makes a serious examination of trade unions which were
brushed aside in his earlier writings as ineffectual; and he
discusses at much greater length the relationship between wages
and accumulation.

So much, then, for the major changes which are to be found
in Marx's later writings on wages. Unfortunately, it is not easy to
analyse or even summarise these writings, as Marx nowhere
provides a clear and consistent statement of his mature views,
and the latter must be inferred from a variety of different and
often fragmentary sources. In the section which follows I have
concentrated on a number of main themes which seem
particularly important and, although the coverage is by no
means complete it does include most of the points which really
matter. These themes are: (1) the supply of labour; (2)
subsistence and the value of labour-power; (3) trade unions and
monopoly; and (4) wages and capitalist development.

The supply of Labour

Marx's view on wages and the supply of labour are not always
easy to interpret. In places he suggests that the supply of labour
is of secondary importance in the determination of wages, and
yet in *Wages, Price and Profit* he declares that:[32]

> As to the *limits* of the *value of labour*, its actual settlement always
> depends upon supply and demand, I mean the demand for labour
> on the part of capital, and the supply of labour by the working man.

The supply of labour to the capitalist sector depends on a number of factors. Firstly, there are the opportunities available for work elsewhere, in other modes or forms of production, as a peasant, artisan, or state employee for example. Marx lays great stress on this factor in his discussion of primitive accumulation and the destruction of non-capitalist modes of production. He also explains the high level of wages in the United States by pointing to an open frontier which enables workers to set themselves up as independent farmers.[33] The existence of such alternatives sets a minimum below which wages cannot fall, for if they do workers will simply leave the capitalist sector and seek work elsewhere.

The supply of labour available to the capitalist sector also depends on what may be loosely called 'demographic' factors such as the size of population and its age and sex composition, or the physical fitness and skill of actual and potential workers.[34] Marx does not pay very much attention to the former aspects of population, but he does stress the importance of both physical fitness and skill. For example, *Capital*, contains a long chapter on the working day in which he describes in harrowing detail the terrible effect of overwork on the health of the working class and shows how capitalism, through the unfettered pursuit of self-defence, squanders its reserves of labour power.[35] In the earlier phases of the industrial revolution this does not really matter, for healthy new workers can be imported from the countryside or abroad, and capital can afford to be wasteful without regard to the future. But, according to Marx, this cannot go on for ever and external sources of labour must eventually dry up. Citing evidence to show this is already happening, he claims that 'even the country labourers, in spite of fresh air and the principle of natural selection, that works so powerfully amongst them, and only permits the survival of the strongest, are beginning to die off.[36] From this he concludes that capital, in its own interest, must take measures to improve the conditions of the working class, for otherwise the result will be a degenerate and stunted labour force which is incapable of performing the hard and consistent work which is required. However, individual capitalists are, by their very nature, more concerned with their own immediate profits than with the longer term interests of their class. Left to themselves, they are unwilling to make the necessary improvements and to compel them to do so an external force is required. As an example of such a force Marx cites the Factory Acts which regulate hours and conditions of work, and restrict the employment of women and children. He recognizes, of course, that legislation of this kind is often a response to working-class pressure, but he stresses that the resulting changes are really in the long-term interest of capital itself, and the argument he uses is strongly demographic in tone. Capitalism is ruining the health of its own workers, and improvements are required to ensure an adequate supply of healthy labour power in the future.

Now, although Marx's chapter on the working day is primarily concerned with what takes place within the labour process, his discussion does have a bearing on the question of wages. Basing himself perhaps on some notion of collective subsistence, he tacitly assumes that the total income of the average working class family is given independently of the amount of work its members jointly perform. This means that any reduction in working hours, brought about by for example, the Factory Acts, will be accompanied by an equivalent increase in the hourly wage rate so as to prevent a fall in total income. Likewise, if women or children are barred from employment, the pay of other members of the family will be increased to compensate for any loss of earning. So, in a roundabout way, Marx's argument establishes a link between demographic forces and hourly earnings: to ensure a minimum standard of health in the labour force, restrictions are placed on working hours and on the employment of women and children, and these restrictions must be accompanied by a rise in hourly earnings so as to prevent a reduction in the total income received by the average working class family.

Marx takes up this demographic theme again later on in Volume I of *Capital* in a section entitled 'Illustrations of the General Law of Capitalist Accumulation' where he describes in some detail the situation of British and Irish workers.[37] He argues that, with the exception of a few members of the so-called 'aristocracy of labour' workers live under appalling conditions and their health is being ruined not just by overwork but by bad diet and terrible housing. He also points out that even amongst the labour aristocracy conditions may be very bad during periods of economic recession when they are thrown out of work and have only their meagre savings to fall back on.

However, this section of *Capital* is really just an exposé of the conditions under which workers live, and Marx does not consider how their poverty and consequential ill-health will eventually affect the supply of labour and the accumulation of capital. Yet, applying the same logic Marx used when discussing the working day, one can infer that capital cannot allow the health of the working class to continue declining through poverty, and that eventually it will be compelled to raise wages, just as it is being compelled to reduce working hours and restrict the employment of women and children.

Marx also points out that wages depend on the abilities which are required in a particular trade. Any normal physically fit person can acquire within a few days or hours the skills and habits required by the casual labourer, but there are other jobs where a prolonged period of training or habituation is required. To cover the costs of such training or habituation, and to encourage people to enter such work, employers must pay a premium over and above what they pay the ordinary labourer, and unless they do so supplies of skilled labour will eventually dry up. This fact points to an important differences between skilled and unskilled workers, at least in the early stages of the industrial revolution. The knowledge possessed by skilled industrial workers is often acquired on the job, or from parents already possessing this knowledge or, more rarely in Marx's day, in special educational institutions. It is not usually possessed by new immigrants from outside the capitalist sector whose skills are of a more agrarian kind and whose patterns of work are very different from those of the skilled industrial worker. In consequence, for its skilled workers, capitalism has always depended to a large extent on its own *internal* supplies of labour, and has not been able to supplement these at will with supplies from elsewhere. Thus, skilled workers have always been *relatively* scarce and capital has never been able to exploit them as ruthlessly as it exploited ordinary unskilled labour in the earlier phases of the industrial revolution.[38]

This simply illustrates an obvious point, running through much of Marx's discussion, that where capital relies on its own internal supplies for a particular kind of labour power, it cannot afford to be too rapacious, and must on average pay the full 'cost of production' of this labour power. If it does not do so, the quality or quantity of available supplies will diminish and a scarcity will develop. On the other hand, where there are vast *external* reserves of a particular kind of labour power, capitalism operates under no such constraint and must pay only the minimum wage required to induce those concerned to accept employment. This minimum wage may be far less than the full cost of production of the labour power in question, and the result may be a rapid decline in the quantity or quality of the existing labour force, but this does not matter as new supplies can always be imported from elsewhere.

So long as capital is operating under conditions of virtually unlimited supplies of unskilled labour the question of total population is of secondary importance, as there is always a large pool of unemployed or semi-employed people seeking work. The health or skills of these people may be inadequate, but at least there is no shortage of absolute numbers. The situation changes, however, when external sources of labour become seriously depleted, and capitalism is forced to rely upon its own internal labour force to provide future generations of workers. Absolute numbers then begin to matter, and the overall size of the population becomes as important as its physical fitness or level of skill.

Marx did not devote much attention to the question of population size, perhaps because of his extreme hostility to Malthusian ideas. Yet there is one significant passage in the Third Volume of *Capital* where he recognizes that population may play an important role in the determination of wages.[39] The passage concerned deals with the way in which economic crises reconstitute the reserve army of labour and lay the basis for a new period of profitable accumulation. Marx argues that during a crisis the reserve army is reconstituted by a double movement – the demand for labour diminishes and the supply of labour increases. The demand for labour diminishes because production stagnates whilst productivity is raised by 'new machines, new and improved working conditions, new combinations'. On the supply side the mechanism is more subtle, and depends on the existence of a Malthusian link between population and real wages. During a period of prosperity, Marx argues, the birth rate increases and there is a substantial rise in the number of children. By the time economic expansion has come to an end and crisis occurs, many of these children will have reached working age. Thus, the supply of

labour available for work increases just at the time when
depressed business conditions reduce the demand for labour,
and in consequence there is a sharp increase in unemployment.
This is, as far as I know, the only place in his later writings that
Marx explicitly recognizes any kind of interdependence between
wages and total population.[40] As a rule, he concentrates on
other demographic factors such as the health or skill of the
labour force.

From the above discussion it is clear that Marx recognizes the
importance of supply factors in the determination of wages, and
he realizes that on occasion the accumulation of capital may be
hampered by the inadequate quantity or quality of available
supplies of labour. How then are we to interpret his often
expressed and often cited view that capital can always overcome
labour shortages by adapting its rhythm of work and methods of
production? In *Capital*, Volume I, for example, he says that
capital can always reorganise production so as to reduce its
demand for labour, and thereby create what he calls a 'relative
surplus population' of unemployed workers. This surplus of
unemployed workers serves to hold down wages and permit the
continual accumulation of capital:[41]

> Relative surplus population is therefore the first upon which the law
> of supply and demand works. It confines the field of action of this
> law within the limits absolutely convenient to the activity of
> exploitation and to the domination of capital.

The intention of this, and other similar passages, is not, in my
opinion, to deny that the supply of labour is important, or that
capital is sometimes hampered by a shortage of labour. The
intention is merely to emphasize the adaptability of capitalism.
Although shortages of labour may cause problems in the short
run, these can eventually be overcome by reorganizing methods
of production and mechanizing or redesigning the work process
so that the need for labour is reduced. If there are not enough
skilled workers, new ways of producing with unskilled labour
can be found. If there is a shortage of healthy and strong male
workers, or their wages are too high, production can be
mechanized so as to allow their replacement by cheaper or
weaker child or female labour.

Thus, *given time*, capital can adapt itself to whatever supplies
of labour are available. This does not mean that adaptation is

easy or rapid. To restructure capital in the appropriate way may take a considerable time, involve a long period of depression before it is achieved. It may also involve bitter conflicts with entrenched and well-organized workers who resist the deskilling, loss of control or redundancy which is often implied. Indeed, capital may actually lose many of these battles, but in one way or another it will eventually adapt. Just how it does so is in no way predetermined, and depends amongst other things on the strength and character of working-class organization. All that can be said is that, unless it is actually overthrown, capitalism can sooner or later adapt itself to whatever supplies of labour are available. However, even the very term 'available supplies of labour' must be interpreted with care, for these supplies are themselves subject to modification. If there is a shortage of skilled labour additional skilled workers can be trained either directly by firms themselves or by the state. If there is a shortage of unskilled labour, firms can migrate to new locations where labour is more plentiful, or can import new workers from elsewhere. Naturally, such changes cost time and money, and often meet with resistance from those who benefit from existing shortages, or from those whose life will be disrupted by the penetration of capital into new areas. Even so, the scope for change is always considerable and, provided the incentive is great enough, capital can usually find ways of augmenting its supply of labour. Thus, the adaptability of capitalism must be understood in a dual sense. Where there is a shortage of labour, capital acts on both sides of the equation at once, both reducing its own demand for labour and increasing the supply available.

Subsistence and the Value of Labour Power

Marx's writings on wages contain numerous references to terms such as 'subsistence', 'need', and 'cost of production' or 'value' of labour-power; and their use by later writers is usually seen as the hallmark of a Marxist theory of wages. Unfortunately, the meaning of these terms is sometimes rather obscure, and their use often leads to confusion. For example, anyone who reads his famous pamphlet *Wages, Price and Profit*, with a critical eye, cannot fail to recognize that Marx defines the value of labour-power in a number of different ways, none of which is equivalent to any of the others, and by the end of this pamphlet the reader is left in a state of confusion, wondering just what Marx is really getting at.

Marx begins by saying that the value of labour-power

like that of every other commodity . . . is determined by the quantity of labour necessary to produce it. The labouring power of a man exists only in his living individuality. A certain mass of necessaries must be consumed by a man to grow up and maintain his life. But the man, like the machine, will wear out, and must be replaced by another man. Besides the mass of necessaries required for *his own* maintenance, he wants another amount of necessaries to bring up a certain quota of children that are to replace him on the labour market and to perpetuate the race of labourers. Moreover, to develop his labouring power, and acquire a given skill, another amount of values must be spent . . . the *value of labouring power* is determined by the *value of the necessaries* required to produce, develop, maintain and perpetuate labouring power.[42]

A similar passage can be found in *Capital*.[43] Apart from the fact that Marx uses the term 'labour *power*' instead of 'labour' the above definition is really no different from that given by classical economists such as Ricardo. It is clearly demographic in inspiration and starts from the notion that, like any other commodity, labour-power is an object produced under definite conditions which determine its long-run supply price, or that is to say, its cost of production. If wages are insufficient to cover this cost of production, then something will happen to the supply of labour power; either its quantity will decline or its quality will deteriorate. Thus, in the above definition, the value of labour-power is simply the minimum wage which must be paid to ensure that labour-power is produced in the right quantity or quality.

Now, although a minimum wage is set by 'demographic' forces, it is not purely physical or biological in character, and depends very much on historical conditions. A few examples will make this clear. In a country where there is no public or shared transport, a private car or motor-cycle may be an indispensable requirement, without which it is impossible to get to work. Wages, therefore, must on average be sufficient to cover the cost of running a car or a motor-cycle, and if they are not the amount of available labour-power will decline. Or to take a rather different example, suppose workers are very strongly attached to a form of life which includes television, tobacco or alcohol. Such items may not contribute to the productive capacity of workers, and may even be harmful to it. Yet they may be widely regarded as necessities. Faced with a choice, workers may refuse to economize on these items, and may instead reduce their expenditure on things which directly contribute to their productive capacity, such as food, clothing or technical literature. Or they may simply decide to have fewer children and to reduce their expenditure on the education of existing ones. To prevent this happening, wages must be sufficient to cover both the items which directly contribute to the productive capacity of workers, and those items which workers regard as particularly important, even though the latter may have no beneficial impact on their productive capacity and may actually be harmful. If wages fall below the required level, there will be a decline in the quantity or quality of available labour-power, even though wages remain well above any purely biological or physiological minimum. This decline, it should be stressed, is not the result of moral outrage because wages have fallen below some anticipated level, nor is it the result of sanctions by organized groups of workers. It is simply the result of normal everyday decisions by individual producers (and reproducers) of labour-power in response to market forces.

In each of the preceding examples, despite the influence of historical factors, the basic principle is the same as that which operates in the case of commodities other than labour-power: if the price falls below a certain minimum, individual producers cut back their output or lower its quality. Thus, in giving a demographic definition of the value of labour-power, based on its cost of production, Marx is referring to a real process of production (and reproduction), just as he does in the case of ordinary commodities for which value regulates price through its long-term influence on supply.

Having defined the value of labour-power in demographic terms, as the minimum was 'necessary' to ensure the production and reproduction of labour-power, Marx next defines it as the wage which is just sufficient to provide workers with their 'traditional standard of life'. Citing the work of William Thornton, he describes their traditional standard of life as follows:

It is not merely physical life, but it is the satisfaction of certain wants springing from the social conditions in which people are placed and reared up. . . . The important part which historical tradition and social habitude play in this respect, you may learn from Mr. Thornton's work on *Overpopulation*, where he shows that the average wages in different agricultural districts of England still nowadays differ more or less according to the more or less favourable circumstances under which the districts have emerged from the state of serfdom.[44]

Marx clearly believes that this new definition of the value of labour-power is equivalent to his earlier one, and that he is merely paraphrasing what he originally said. This is not, however, correct. Although both definitions are similar in stressing the historical character of human needs and desires, they are otherwise very different. The first definition of value, with its emphasis on what is 'required' to 'produce, develop, maintain and perpetuate labouring power' is clearly demographic in character, it implies something quite specific. If workers receive less than the 'value' of labour-power, then labour-power will be produced in less than its usual quantity or quality. By contrast the second definition with its emphasis on the 'traditional standard of life', is not intrinsically demographic in character, and is simply a description of what workers are accustomed to. It implies nothing about the forces which have established or are maintaining this traditional standard of life, nor does it suggest what will happen if workers receive less than the 'value' of their labour-power.

Under certain circumstances, the traditional standard of life may be just equal to the cost of production of labour-power, in which case the two definitions coincide, and a reduction in wages below their traditional level will indeed produce a decline in the quantity or quality of available labour-power. Under other circumstances, however, the traditional standard of life may be considerably higher than this cost of production, in which case a reduction of wages below their traditional level will have no effect on either the quantity or quality of available labour-power: there will be just as many actual or potential workers as before, and they will be just as strong, healthy and skilled. Of course, the absence of harmful demographic consequences, when wages are reduced, does not mean that such a reduction is actually possible. Workers may resist very bitterly any attack on their living standards and employers may be afraid to reduce wages; or political pressure may be so intense that the state is forced to intervene and prevent any reduction. These examples, and it easy to think of others, illustrate how non-demographic forces may keep wages permanently above the level which, under given historical conditions, is required to ensure that the existing stock of labour-power is reproduced.

It is now clear that, although the two may sometimes be quite close together in practice, the traditional standard of life is conceptually distinct from the cost of production of labour-power. The latter is a demographic concept whilst the former is not. It is interesting to note that Thornton, who is cited in the above passage in *Capital*, was well aware of the difference between these two concepts. He shows how the traditional wage in some parts of Britain is well below the cost of production of labour-power of 'normal' quality, and how in consequence the local work-force is chronically weak and undernourished.[45] Yet, even after reading Thornton's lucid and well-written work, Marx continues to talk as though the traditional standard of life enjoyed by workers coincides with the cost of production of labour-power of 'normal quality'. Unfortunately, this habit has plagued Marxist economics to the present day, and it is still common to use demographic language, and to talk as though the cost of production of labour-power includes everything normally consumed by workers.[46]

In a passage, already quoted in part above, concerning the role of the labour market in determining wages, Marx provides yet a third definition of the value of labour-power:

> As to the limits of the value of labour, its actual settlement always depends upon supply and demand, I mean the demand for labour on the part of capital, and the supply of labour by the working man. Hence the relatively high standard of wages in the United States. Capital may there try its utmost. It cannot prevent the labour market from being continuously emptied by the continuous conversion of wage labourers into independent self-sustaining peasants.[47]

This passage suggests that the value of labour-power is the minimum wage required to induce people to seek work or remain working in the capitalist sector. Such a wage must provide a standard of living at least equal to that obtainable elsewhere, in non-capitalist sectors of the economy. Clearly this new definition of value is very different from the others.

To sum up, Marx defines the value of labour-power in three different ways, basing himself successively on: (1) the cost of production of labour-power under given historical conditions, (2) the traditional standard of life to which workers are accustomed, and (3) the standard of living which prevails in non-capitalist modes or forms of production. Although they may sometimes coincide in practice, these definitions are not conceptually equivalent to each other, and no single one of them can be regarded as the unique and authentic expression of Marx's views. On the other hand, there is a common thread running through all of them – the idea of a minimum standard of life which wages must be sufficient to provide. This minimum may be determined in a variety of ways, but in each case the principle is the same. If the standard of living falls below the minimum level, there are very serious consequences: either the supply of good quality labour-power declines, as workers fail to maintain and reproduce themselves properly, or leave the capitalist sector altogether; or else there is conflict and disruption as workers fight for what they consider is their just reward. Which of these actually occurs, when the standard of living falls below its minimum, depends on concrete circumstances. In general, demographic forces will be less important in advanced countries, where workers are well organized and receive fairly high wages, and more important in poorer countries where wages are lower and workers are not so powerful. But this is not always the case, and even in advanced countries there may be sections of the workforce which are on the demographic margin, and whose labour-power will decline in quantity or quality if their standard of living is reduced.

The idea of a minimum wage, based on the notion of a minimum acceptable standard of living, may seem rather vague when stated in general terms, but Marx uses it to great effect in his analysis of capitalist development. To start with, the existence of such a minimum limits the freedom of action both of individual capitalists and of capital as a whole. It means that, beyond a certain point, problems such as declining profitability cannot be overcome by reducing the standard of living of workers, and some other solution must be found. There are many possible solutions, ranging from imperialism to cuts in state expenditure, but the most important, and indeed most characteristic, are those which involve some change in the sphere of production. On the one hand, capital may seek to extract more labour from workers, by making them work harder or longer for the same pay. This is called by Marx the creation of *absolute* surplus value, and he considers it to be a highly conservative response. Moreover, such a response may not always be practical, for the same forces which prevent a reduction in the standard of living may also prevent firms from increasing the length or intensity of the working day. On the other hand, firms may be able to reorganize their methods of production, so that productivity is increased and less labour is needed to provide workers with the minimum acceptable standard of living. Marx called this the creation of *relative* surplus value, and he considered it to be a highly revolutionary response on the part of capital. Although it may be resisted and may take time, its potential is unlimited.

In this context, we should mention the question of social expenditures by the state, which in Marx's day were not very large, but have assumed gigantic proportions in advanced capitalist countries. Many of these expenditures are used to finance the public provision of services which could, in principle, be provided by private capital and purchased directly by workers and their families. However, it is often cheaper and more efficient to provide things collectively, and the taxes required to finance the services concerned may be considerably less than the additional wages required to purchase the same services privately. Thus, by transferring certain activities to the state sector, the total resources required to provide workers with a given standard of living are reduced and, provided the resulting savings are appropriated by capital, profits are increased. Such a transfer of production from the private to the state sector is clearly analogous to the creation of relative surplus value which occurs when production is reorganized within the private sector itself. In each case, the amount of labour required to provide workers with a given standard of living is reduced.

The idea of a minimum standard of living takes on particular significance when it is seen against the wider background of capitalist development. As we have already stressed, this minimum standard is not something given once and for all, but is itself a creation of history and shows a marked tendency to increase through time. There are various reasons why this is so. During periods of boom wages usually rise and the pattern of life changes: workers develop new wants and become accustomed to a new standard of living. Moreover, the whole structure of output changes so that items which were cheaply and readily available a few years before became expensive and difficult to obtain – witness the decline of public transport in modern times. These subjective and objective changes make it very difficult to reduce wages by any substantial amount, partly because workers resist and partly because of the harmful demographic consequences which ensue. Thus, the 'minimum standard of life' tends to rise in booms and this establishes something of a ratchet effect, so that capital cannot overcome its problems simply by reducing wages and returning to the old pre-boom situation. It must solve its problems in a new way and produce more efficiently. Indeed, one of the mainsprings of capitalist dynamism is precisely the fact that it cannot easily go backwards, and that a revolution in production is often the only way out of difficulty. The relation between development and the standard of living is, of course, far more complicated than this example suggests, particularly on a world-scale where the phenomenon of 'combined and uneven development' creates an extremely confused picture. Even so, it does illustrate the basic point that the minimum standard of living which capital must provide tends to rise in step with productivity, and that capital is in consequence under continual pressure to revolutionize its methods of production.

To sum up, even though Marx himself never gave a simple and unambiguous definition of the value of labour-power, his various attempts all embody the idea that at any time there is a minimum standard of life which capital must provide for workers and their families, and unless it does so there will be very serious economic or political consequences. The existence of such a minimum, which has a tendency to rise through time, limits the freedom of action of capital and is one of the factors responsible for capitalism's long-term dynamism.

Trade Unions and Monopoly

In Volume I of *Capital* Marx assumes that wages and prices are determined competitively, by the blind interaction of supply and demand. Buyers and sellers are powerless to alter the terms upon which exchange takes place, and everyone must accept the competitively determined wages and prices which face them in the market. Marx mentions some exceptions to this rule, and admits that in practice things do not work in such a mechanical fashion. For example, he points out that more efficient producers will reduce their prices so as to undercut their rivals and capture their markets; and, in passing, he also mentions that workers may combine so as to restrict competition and raise wages.[48] But these are casual asides which are never fully integrated into the main argument. For most of the time, he ignores the question of market power, and assumes that wages and prices are determined competitively. On the subject of wages, for example, he has this to say:

> Taking them as a whole, the general movements of wages are exclusively regulated by the expansion and contraction of the industrial reserve army, and these again correspond to the periodic changes of the industrial cycle. They are, therefore, not determined by variations of the absolute number of the working population, but by the varying proportions in which the working class is divided into active and reserve army, by the increase or diminution of the relative amount of surplus population, by the extent to which it is now absorbed, now set free.[49]

Clearly, if the broad movement of wages is *exclusively* regulated by what happens to the reserve army of labour, then trade unions can have no effect on the average wage level, although they might affect the pattern of differentials between one group of workers and another. And, indeed, this is more or less the picture one obtains throughout the whole of *Capital*. Real wages rise and fall automatically in response to supply and demand, without any intervention on the part of unions. They rise when labour is scarce and employers are forced to bid wages upwards so as to attract the workers they need; and they fall when labour is plentiful and workers are forced to bid wages downwards so as to get a job. Thus, in the main argument of *Capital*, unions have no direct effect on wages, whose movement is for the most part determined automatically and competitively by supply and demand. This does not mean that workers are helpless and can do nothing to improve their situation – Marx himself points out how they can affect the hours, intensity and conditions of work. Such changes will inevitably affect both the supply of labour and the demand for labour, and will thus have an indirect influence on wages.[50] Even so, the fact remains that this influence is indirect, and that in *Capital* class struggle is not as a rule directly concerned with wages, but with other aspects of economic life.

The competitive picture of wage determination, which Marx gives in *Capital*, is modified in the pamphlet *Wages, Price and Profit*, the text of which is an address originally delivered to the General Council of the International Working Men's Association in 1865. In this pamphlet Marx sets out to rebut the views of Citizen Weston who argued that trade unions cannot permanently affect the level of real wages. Marx provides a long list of the circumstances under which trade unions may have some effect: when prices rise they may defend living standards by obtaining compensatory money wage increases; when productivity increases they may gain a corresponding rise in real wages and thereby maintain what Marx calls the 'relative social position' of workers; when capitalists extend the length of the working day, or increase its intensity, unions may force them to pay higher wages in compensation; and finally, they may resist attempted wage reductions during a period of depression. All of these are in a sense *defensive* struggles in which workers react 'against the previous action of capital'.[51] Even when workers demand higher wages to match higher productivity they are merely reacting to previous actions by capital, and seeking to defend their relative position and prevent a rise in the rate of exploitation. Marx considers that virtually all trade union action is of this reactive or defensive kind, although he concedes that, 'in one case out of a hundred', trade unions may undertake genuinely offensive actions.

Now, Marx is well aware that the ability of unions to influence wages depends on economic circumstances: when unemployment is high their bargaining position is much weaker than when unemployment is low. Thus, as in *Capital*, the reserve army of labour exerts a considerable influence on the movement of wages. However, the link between the two variables is considerably more flexible than in *Capital* where, as we have seen, Marx claims that the general movement of wages is '*exclusively* regulated' by changes in the reserve army of labour. In *Wages, Price and Profit* the relationship between these two variables is more subtle and Marx merely asserts that 'the value of labour *depends* upon supply and demand'.[52] In using the expression 'depends upon' rather than the expression 'exclusively regulated by', Marx is adopting a much weaker formulation, which allows for factors other than supply and demand to influence wages. It also allows for market forces to exert their influence in a less direct fashion than in *Capital*, where wages are determined mechanically by the atomistic process of competitive bidding in the labour market. In *Wages, Price and Profit* Marx recognizes the importance of power and conflict, and that for the most part wages are determined by a process of bargaining between Capital and Labour, the outcome of which depends upon the relative power of the two sides. Market forces still influence wages, of course, but they do so in a roundabout way, through their effect on the relative bargaining position of the two sides.

This difference between the two works probably does not reflect a shift in Marx's own views, but more a difference in emphasis and purpose. In *Capital*, he certainly considers power and conflict, but he is primarily concerned with their role within the production process itself, and he makes no attempt to provide a systematic analysis of their role in wage determination. In *Wages, Price and Profit* he tries to remedy this defect, and the entire pamphlet is devoted to the question of how trade unions influence wages. By combining the analysis contained in these two works, one can arrive at a fairly comprehensive picture of how the activities of trade unions are conditioned and constrained by the wider laws of capital accumulation. Trade unions can certainly influence wages, and more generally the length and intensity of the working day or conditions of work. But their ability to do so depends upon economic circumstances, and in particular upon conditions in the labour market. When labour is relatively scarce the bargaining position of unions is strong, for workers are less frightened of losing their jobs, and employers have greater difficulty in replacing them. Conversely when labour is more plentiful, their bargaining position is relatively weak, for workers who lose their jobs will have difficulty in finding new employment, and employers can more easily find replacements.

Thus, the greater is the reserve army of labour the less able are trade unions to achieve their objectives, although the link is not a purely mechanical one, for a militant consciousness and good organization can do much to offset the debilitating effects of unemployment on union power.

Through its effect on the reserve army of labour, capital accumulation places certain limits on the effectiveness of purely economic struggle by trade unions. Capitalists will not invest unless they get a certain 'normal' rate of profit and, if the action of trade unions prevents them achieving this normal rate, the result is an economic crisis in which accumulation comes to a standstill and workers lose their jobs. The possibility of crisis is a constant threat which disciplines the working class and helps keep its 'pretensions' in check. Moreover, when it does occur, a crisis is the mechanism by which capital demoralizes the working class and re-establishes its hegemony. Marx never spelled all this out in detail but it follows naturally from his writings.

Marx recognizes that the ability of unions to raise wages depends on their ability to restrict competition between employed and unemployed workers, that is, on their ability to establish some degree of monopoly in the labour market.[53] In Volume III of *Capital* he also points out that the same considerations apply to competition amongst firms, and that capitalists can raise prices by establishing a monopoly in the product market. This points to an interesting problem. Does the presence of monopoly in the product market affect real wages and thereby the rate of surplus value? Or does it leave real wages unaffected, and simply redistribute surplus value from one capitalist to another? When firms restrict competition and raise their prices, do they benefit at the expense of the working class or at the expense of other firms? Many Marxists take the latter position, and insist that real wages are given independently and are not affected by the presence of monopoly. Yet Marx himself was by no means so certain, and concedes that monopoly may on occasion reduce real wages. For example, he says that a monopoly

could depress wages below the value of labour power, but only to the extent that the former exceed the limit of their physical minimum. In this case the monopoly price would be paid by a deduction from real wages (i.e. by the quantity of use values received by the labourer for the same quantity of labour).[54]

Clearly this argument could be extended beyond goods entering directly into workers consumption, and could include any commodity entering even indirectly such as steel or oil. Thus, Marx is in effect conceding that a monopoly in any 'basic' commodity, to use Sraffa's term, may depress real wages and thereby increase the rate of surplus value.

Now, it is clear that monopoly is rarely absolute, and that monopolistic firms are still subject to market forces. Unfortunately, Marx says very little on this question, and his writings contain no systematic discussion of either monopoly power or its limitations. In the years following his death, Marxists have tried to fill this gap, and there is now a vast literature dealing with the theoretical and empirical aspects of monopoly. However, we shall not consider the literature here, as it would be beyond the scope of the present essay.[55]

Wages and Capitalist Development

Although Marx never seriously considers the long-term behaviour of wages, his analysis of accumulation implies that living standards should rise in the course of time. As we have seen, he modifies his earlier view that accumulation inevitably leads to an ever growing surplus of labour, and admits that there may be periods in which labour is relatively scarce and employers are forced to pay higher wages. Indeed, in Volume I of *Capital* he considers the possibility of an indefinitely prolonged boom in which labour remains fairly scarce and wages keep rising at a modest pace, yet expansion continues because accumulation remains profitable.[56] But this is not, in his view, the typical case. What normally happens is that after a time profitability begins to decline until a point is reached where capitalists refuse to accumulate and expansion comes to an end. In Volume I of *Capital* this reduction in profitability comes about because wages rise faster than productivity and the rate of surplus value declines. Marx mentions this possibility again in Volume III of *Capital*, but he also describes another and perhaps longer-term mechanism which may cause the rate of profit to fall even in the absence of any change in the rate of surplus value.[57] When wages begin to rise during the boom, capitalists respond by adopting new methods of production, designed to save labour and hold down costs. This reduces the demand for labour and thereby slows down the rate at which real wages are rising; it also raises labour productivity and thereby helps offset the effect of any wage increases which do occur. So, the adoption of new methods of production helps maintain the rate of surplus value by keeping down unit costs. Indeed, if capitalists adopt new methods on a large enough scale, the rate of surplus value may actually rise in the course of a boom. But this is not the end of the story. New production methods may be highly 'capital intensive' and the resulting reduction in unit costs may be small in comparison with the additional investment they involve.[58] If this is the case then, although capitalists may be making greater profits than before, these profits will have to be spread over an even greater amount of capital, and the rate of profit will be correspondingly lower. Thus, capitalists can certainly keep up the rate of surplus value by adopting new methods of production, but the cost of doing so may be prohibitive, for it may involve a disproportionate expenditure on equipment, buildings and other items of 'constant' capital. The rate of profit may therefore fall despite a higher rate of surplus value.

When the rate of profit falls below a certain 'normal' level, whose determination is left rather vague by Marx, accumulation grinds to a standstill and there is a crisis. Production falls, people are thrown out of work, and the upward movement of wages is checked. However, after a period of depression and reorganization, it becomes profitable to accumulate once again, production picks up, and the whole cycle begins all over again.

To restore profitability to the level required for accumulation does not necessarily mean reducing wages to their pre-boom level. Indeed, it may not require any reduction wages at all, and it may be sufficient merely to check the previous growth of wages. The answer all depends on what happens to productivity, for higher productivity enables capitalists to increase the rate of surplus value without reducing real wages or, for that matter, increasing the length or intensity of the working day. Provided higher productivity can be achieved without an enormous investment in fixed capital, the result will be a higher rate of profit. During the boom itself, productivity is raised through the adoption of more advanced productive techniques but, as we have already mentioned, this may be very expensive and require a large capital outlay. In a depression the same result can often be achieved more cheaply by reorganizing production within existing enterprises, driving unprofitable firms out of business, and merging existing enterprises into new and bigger units.

There are several reasons why depression may facilitate such restructuring: it threatens backward firms with bankruptcy or takeover, and forces them to accept unwelcome changes; and it may also undermine the ability and willingness of workers to obstruct the designs of capital, although this is by no means certain, as the prospect of mass unemployment and stagnant or falling living standards may cause workers to resist changes which they would accept in more prosperous times. By allowing productivity to be increased cheaply, without a heavy investment in fixed capital, depression facilitates what Marx called the creation of 'relative' surplus value, and provides an alternative to wage reductions. Indeed, given a sufficiently radical reorganization of production, the rate of profit can be restored to its 'normal' level without any reduction at all in real wages. And, even in the absence of such radical changes, some improvements in production will inevitably occur during the depression, and accumulation may become profitable before wages have sunk back again to their old, pre-boom level. Thus, recovery may begin whilst wages are still relatively high, and workers will then keep some or all of the gains they have made in the previous boom. If this ratchet effect operates in every cycle, the long-term movement of wages will be upwards, with workers gaining more in booms than they lose in the intervening slumps.

Although not described explicitly by Marx, the above process is implicit in the analysis of *Capital* and provides powerful support for the view that real wages have a long-run tendency to rise. As it stands, the argument does not depend on the existence of trade unions. Wages may rise in booms because labour becomes extremely scarce, and competition forces employers to *offer* higher pay to their workers, and technical progress may ensure that accumulation picks up again in slumps before competition has forced wages down again to their old pre-boom level. Thus, provided there is technical progress and labour becomes sufficiently scarce in the boom phases of development, competition itself will lead to a secular rise in wages even in the absence of trade unions.

What then is the effect of trade unions? To answer this we must start from Marx's belief that unions modify the link between wages and the reserve army of labour, although they do not destroy this link altogether. By restricting competition between the employed and the unemployed, they can raise wages above the level which would prevail in a competitive labour market. During a boom this is likely to mean that wages rise faster than they would otherwise, and this in turn may reduce the rate of profit and bring the boom to a premature end. During a slump, by contrast, the role of trade unions is more defensive and their main effect is to prevent or limit a reduction in real wages. At first sight it might appear that the refusal to accept lower wages will reduce the rate of profit still further, and thereby make the slump even worse than it already is. However, there are several reasons for doubting this conclusion, and it does not seem to accord with Marx's views about the nature of crisis and technical progress. Every crisis, no matter how it begins, soon becomes a 'realization' crisis in which markets collapse and even firms which would be highly profitable under normal conditions are placed in great difficulty. To reduce wages under these circumstances will cause enormous dislocation and make an economic recovery even more difficult. Workers' incomes will be reduced and they will purchase fewer consumer goods; the firms which supply these consumer goods will not easily find new markets, and will be forced to lay off more workers and cut back their purchases of material and equipment; this in turn will affect other firms in the economy and there will be a further collapse in markets and economic activity.

The second reason for believing that wage reductions are not the answer during a slump has already been mentioned in our discussion of the value of labour-power.[59] Up to a certain point, high wages are a spur to technical progress, and the refusal of unions to accept a cut in real wages means that capitalists are forced to seek other, more creative ways of reducing costs and restoring profitability. Paradoxically, therefore the inability of capitalists to cut wages may be a factor which force them to revolutionize their techniques of production, and thereby contributes to a more secure and sustained recovery from the slump.

The above remarks about the role of unions in capitalist development are, of course, rather speculative in nature, and Marx himself did not say much on the subject. Even so, they are very much in the spirit of his writing and merely spell out some of the implications of his wider theory of capitalist development.

IV WAGES AND PRICES

Throughout his entire writing Marx thinks of wages in real terms, as a bundle of commodities which workers receive in return for their labour-power. Workers are of course, paid in money and not directly in consumable commodities, but Marx assumes that this is a minor detail which makes no difference to the real wages they ultimately receive after spending the money they have been paid. With the exception of a few casual asides, he does not consider how real wages may be affected by inflation, and he assumes that the future purchasing power of money is accurately known at the time wages are paid. This has a number of implications, of which perhaps the most important concerns the role of trade unions. Most people, before and after Marx, have claimed that trade unions cannot affect the distribution of income between capital and labour, on the grounds that any rise in the average level of money wages will be followed by an equivalent rise in prices, so that in real terms workers will be back where they started. Marx explicitly rejects this view in *The Poverty of Philosophy*, where he criticizes Proudhon, and again later in *Wages, Price and Profit*, where he criticizes Citizen Weston.[60] He argues that a rise in money wages does not lead to a permanent rise in prices, although it will cause some temporary disturbance to prices as output adjusts to the new pattern of demand which results from higher wages.

Marx's objections to Proudhon and Citizen Weston are not the outcome of mere prejudice, but are the logical consequence of his assumptions about money and the way it functions. For analytical purposes he assumes that money is a commodity, say gold, which is produced under given technical conditions and thus has a given 'value', namely the labour directly and indirectly required to produce it. He further assumes that all other commodities are also produced under given technical conditions and thus have given values. And finally, he assumes, without making it explicit, that organic compositions of capital are uniform throughout the economy. The above assumptions ensure that a rise in money wages has no permanent effect on prices. Organic compositions are uniform, and in equilibrium, when profit rates are equal in different sectors, all commodities, including gold, must therefore exchange at their values. And, since values are given independently of wages, it follows that the equilibrium price of each commodity is also independent of wages.[61] This means, of course, that a rise in wages cannot permanently affect prices. When it first occurs such a rise may disturb equilibrium and cause prices to change, but competition will gradually restore equilibrium and bring prices back again to their old level.

The basic point of Marx's argument is quite simple. Gold is a commodity produced under given technical conditions which regulate its exchange with other commodities. Its use as money acts as a *discipline* on capitalists and prevents a permanent rise in prices in response to higher wages. Marx recognizes, of course, that in practice things are not quite as simple as this argument suggests. For example, workers are not usually paid in commodity gold (specie), but in some form of national currency such as Sterling or francs. However, he assumes that the currency in question is convertible into gold at a fixed rate of exchange. The price of gold in terms of national currency is therefore fixed, and each unit of the currency 'represents' a given and unchanging amount of gold. This means that, for analytical purposes, the distinction between currency and gold can be ignored; and that gold continues to exert a discipline over capitalists and limits their ability to raise prices, even where it no longer functions directly as money.

Although logically correct, Marx's argument makes a number of assumptions which may not hold in practice. For example, in assuming equal organic compositions of capital, he is ignoring the problems raised by the deviation of prices from values. However, the validity of his conclusion does not depend on this assumption, and his argument can easily be modified to take account of unequal organic compositions.[62] Furthermore, in assuming that gold is produced under constant technical conditions and has a given value, he is ignoring the well-established fact that in reality gold is often produced under diminishing returns to scale – costs may rise when output is increased because less fertile seams or alluvial deposits are brought into use. The existence of diminishing returns may undermine the disciplinary role of gold and permit prices to rise, even though the national currency remains convertible into gold at a fixed rate of exchange. This possibility had already been pointed out by Nassau Senior in the early nineteenth century, but Marx does not even mention it and his entire discussion is based on the assumption of constant returns to scale.[63]

But these are really minor points. The main criticism of Marx's argument is concerned with his assumptions about the national currency itself. As we have seen, in replying to Proudhon and Citizen Weston, he assumes that this currency is convertible into gold at a fixed rate of exchange. He thereby ensures that gold continues to exert a discipline over capitalists and limits their ability to raise prices. However, elsewhere in his writing, Marx himself points out that the rate of exchange between gold and currency may not be fixed, and may be influenced by government policy. For example, suppose that the national currency consists of inconvertible paper money issued by the state, and that all domestic payments are made in this money. Then according to Marx, the state can raise the price of gold in terms of currency by creating additional paper money and 'forcing' it into circulation. This in turn, he argues, will lead to a general rise in the price of all commodities.[64] So in the case of inconvertible paper currency, Marx himself concedes that the state can undermine the discipline of gold, by 'forcing' additional money into circulation, and thereby causing the currency to depreciate and prices to rise.

It follows that, in the case of inconvertible paper currency, the validity of Marx's reply to Proudhon and Citizen Weston depends entirely on the monetary policy of the state. If the state follows a restrictive policy and issues just enough money to keep the general price level stable, then obviously Marx is correct, and capitalists cannot offset higher money wages with higher prices. Suppose, however, that the state deliberately promotes inflation by issuing additional currency whenever trade unions gain an increase in money wages. Then, according to Marx's own theory, prices will rise and workers will not get the full benefits they anticipated. Indeed, prices may rise so much that the benefits of higher money wages are completely wiped out, and workers are right back where they started from. This may be an extreme case, but it is certainly possible when the currency is inconvertible, and cannot be ruled out on *a priori* grounds.

Of course, the state is not entirely a free agent in choosing its monetary policy, and there are economic and political limits to its use of inflation as a device for maintaining profits. For example, suppose the state decides that, no matter what happens to wages, it will allow prices to rise to the level required to maintain some given rate of profit. Then, if trade unions are in a militant mood, the result may be an explosive inflation. After the first round of wage increases the state will create additional money, and prices will rise. Workers will not passively accept these higher prices and will defend themselves by seeking and obtaining new wage increases. The state will then respond by creating even more money, and prices will rise for a second time. This will provoke a further round of wage increases, to offset which will require yet another round of price increases, and so on indefinitely. In this way an accelerating wage-price spiral may develop, in which at each stage workers obtain higher money wages, only to find themselves repeatedly frustrated by a monetary policy which causes (or allows) prices to rise at an ever faster rate. The economic and political consequences of such an accelerating spiral are so harmful that eventually the state will be forced to recognize that inflation is no longer a viable way of defending profits. At this point it will abandon its liberal monetary policy, and will refuse to sanction price increases on the required scale. So, at a certain point the state will modify its inflationary policy and reimpose some degree of monetary discipline on prices. This will mean, of course, that capitalists are unable to pass on the entire cost of higher money wages, and trade unions will achieve their objective of raising real wages.

To sum up, if workers are paid in inconvertible currency, then, according to Marx's own monetary theory, the state can raise prices by depreciating this currency, and thereby maintain profits in the face of trade-union pressure. To this extent, there is a germ of truth in the argument of Proudhon and Citizen Weston when they claim that trade-union pressure leads to higher prices. On the other hand, a policy of currency depreciation and higher prices is not a viable long-term answer to persistent trade-union pressure, for it involves an accelerating and ultimately unacceptable rate of inflation. Sooner or later the state must reimpose monetary discipline and halt, or at least contain, the depreciation of its currency. At this point real wages will rise and Marx will have been proved right.

V CONCLUSION

This brings us to the end of our discussion of Marx's theory of wages. It would be both difficult and pointless to summarize what has been said, but a few remarks are in order.

Firstly, it is clear that Marx's debt to Ricardo is enormous, and even his later work reveals a strong Ricardian influence. Secondly, Marx's writings on wages are extremely uneven and do not form a coherent and consistent whole. This is partly due to the fact that they were written over a long period of time during which his views changed considerably. But, even if we confine ourselves to the later so-called 'mature' works, such as *Capital* or *Wages, Price and Profit*, we find the same incoherence and inconsistency. Finally, despite their weaknesses, Marx's writings on wages are a fertile source of ideas, provided they are approached in a critical fashion and their limitations are honestly recognized.

NOTES

1. This is a revised version of a paper originally given at a seminar at Oxford in June 1978. I am grateful to Noboharu Yokokawa for many stimulating discussions about Ricardo's theory of wages and accumulation, and also to David Vines and John Wells for their many useful comments.
2. R. Rosdolsky, *The Making of Marx's Capital*, London, 1977.
3. E. Mandel, *The Formation of the Economic Thought of Karl Marx*, London, 1971.
4. The exposition of Ricardo's theory which follows may seem unduly long and talmudic, but is necessary in order to establish what Ricardo really said.
5. Quoted by Marx in 'Wages, Price and Profit', Marx-Engels, *Selected Works*, London, 1966, Vol. I. pp. 422–3.
6. P. Sraffa (ed.), *The Works and Correspondence of David Ricardo*, Cambridge, 1957, Vol. II, p. 227.
7. The convergence between market and natural price may involve a change in both kinds of price, for the natural price itself may depend on the scale

of production. For example, suppose the demand for corn increases because of a sudden change in the pattern of consumption. At first there will be a shortage of corn and the market price will rise very high. After time, however, new land will be brought into cultivation, the supply of corn will increase, and the market price will fall until it eventually coincides with the natural price. If the newly farmed land is less fertile than the old, costs of production will be greater than before and the natural price will therefore be higher than it was originally. Market price will never return to its old level. This example illustrates how natural prices are determined by the conditions which, under competition, regulate the *flow* of newly-produced commodities. By contrast market prices are determined by the demand for currently available *stocks* of commodities. Thus, when Ricardo says that natural price regulates market price, he is merely saying that in the long run the movement of prices is regulated by the conditions under which commodities are produced. In the short run prices are determined by the stock of commodities actually in existence at any particular moment, but the behaviour of this stock through time itself depends on the production of new commodities, and in the long run it is therefore production which really counts. This is also, in my opinion, what Marx meant when he said that prices are regulated by values.

8. All page numbers given in the text refer to the third edition of Ricardo's *Principles* in P. Sraffa (ed.), *The Works and Correspondence of David Ricardo*, Cambridge, 1951, Vol. II.

9. The third edition of Ricardo's *Principles* pays explicit tribute to J. Barton's *Observations on the Circumstances which Influence the Condition of the Labouring Classes of Society*, London, 1817.

10. In a footnote, criticizing John Barton, Ricardo seems to suggest that accumulation is *never* accompanied by a reduction in the total demand for labour:

> It is not easy, I think, to conceive that under any circumstances, an increase of capital should not be followed by an increased demand for labour; the most that can be said is, that the demand will be in a diminishing ratio (p. 396).

Just why Ricardo says this is not entirely clear, for taken literally it contradicts everything else he says about machinery. Barton was concerned with the effects of 'the sudden discovery and extensive use' of improved machinery, which is exactly the case in which Ricardo himself concedes that accumulation may be accompanied by a decline in total employment. The most probable explanation for Ricardo's statement is that he is forgetting that an 'increase of capital' may induce the discovery or more extensive use of improved machinery.

11. One apparent answer is for manufacturers to raise their own prices after raising wages. However, there are several reasons why this is no solution. In the first place, money is linked to gold in the Ricardian system and this imposes a discipline which limits the ability of firms to raise prices. But, even if money were not linked to gold, and prices could be raised, this method would still not provide a permanent answer. Manufacturers can only raise prices and restore profits at the expense of somebody else. If

they do so by reducing the standard of living of their own workers, the supply of labour available to them will not grow at the rate required for sustained accumulation, and if they raise prices at the expense of the agricultural sector the output of food will decline and this too will eventually limit the supply of labour.

12. Many expositions of Ricardian economies stress the tendency of rent to rise at the expense of profit during the course of accumulation. This is, however, of secondary importance when one is considering the stationary state. Even if capitalists were able to eliminate rent and appropriate to themselves the whole surplus value, accumulation would still be brought to an eventual standstill by falling productivity and rising costs in agriculture!

13. op. cit., p. 58.

14. There is some dispute over Ricardo's views about the prospects for sustained accumulation. In his book *Ricardian Economics* (New Haven, 1958, pp. 31–2) Mark Blaug claims that Ricardo was optimistic, whereas Maurice Dobb in *Theories of Value since Adam Smith* (Cambridge, 1973, p. 90) disputes this. More recently in her Ph.D. Thesis entitled *The Machinery Question* (Oxford, 1976), Maxine Berg has supported Blaug's interpretation and also shown that most of Ricardo's followers were optimistic about the potentialities of technical improvement and foreign trade.

15. The clearest exposition of the argument which follows is contained on pages 422–6 of *Wages* in Marx-Engels, *Collected Works*, London, 1976, Vol. 6. This argument probably reflects the influence of Engels's earlier work *The Condition of the Working Class in England* which contains a brilliant analysis of how accumulation affects the structure of the labour market. Indeed, most of the broad outlines of Marx's own vision of capitalist development are already foreshadowed in the early writings of Engels, and the conventional judgement which sees Marx as the original thinker and Engels as the populariser is extremely inaccurate. Engels was a highly original thinker, and much of Marx's more famous economic writings are really an attempt to systematize, under the influence of Ricardian thought, the earlier insights of Engels.

16. A similar passage is also to be found in 'Speech on the Question of Free Trade' in Marx-Engels, *Collected Works*, Vol. 6, p. 463.

17. Marx-Engels, *Collected Works*, Vol. 6, p. 495.

18. The historical origin of Lassalle's 'iron law of wages' is explicitly acknowledged by Engels in the following footnote to the 1885 edition of Marx's *Poverty of Philosophy*:

> The thesis that the 'natural', i.e. normal price of labour power coincides with the minimum wage, i.e. with the equivalent in value of the means of subsistence absolutely indispensable for the life and procreation of the workers, was first put by me in *Outlines of a Critique of Political Economy* (Deutsche Französische Jahrbücher, Paris, 1844) and in *The Condition of the Working Class in England*. As seen here, Marx at that time accepted the thesis. Lassalle took it over from both of us (Marx-Engels, *Collected Works*, Vol. 6, p. 125).

19. *Wage Labour and Capital* in Marx-Engels, *Collected Works*, London, 1975, Vol. 9, p. 204.

20. ibid., p. 204.

21. ibid., p. 204.

22. ibid., p. 204.

23. This line of argument, in fact, predates both Malthus and Ricardo, and goes back at least to Adam Smith's *Wealth of Nations*. However, it has become associated in the popular mind with the name of Malthus, and it is fair to call Ricardo a Malthusian, even though their views on population differed in certain respects. It is interesting to note that both Marx in *The Economic and Philosophical Manuscripts* (1844) and Engels in *The Condition of the Working Class in England* (1845) explicitly accept Adam Smith's argument that changes in population tend to pull wages back towards a subsistence minimum. In the latter work Engels tries, rather unsuccessfully, to square this with other more complex theories of wage determination.

24. *Wages*, op. cit., p. 433.

25. *Wages*, op. cit., p. 435.

26. *Wages*, op. cit., p. 425.

27. *Wage, Labour and Capital*, op. cit., pp. 218–19.

28. Some of these issues are explored in my essay *Neo-Classicism, Neo-Ricardianism and Marxism*, reprinted in the present collection (see p. 7). Unfortunately the essay concentrates on the coercive aspects of capitalist production and emphasizes the creation of absolute surplus value. It neglects the creation of relative surplus value and the revolutionary impact of capitalism on productive techniques. For Marx labour-power was the concept which allowed him to unify all these various aspects of capitalist production within one coherent framework, and its importance was even greater than is suggested in the essay just mentioned.

29. *Wages, Price and Profit* in Marx–Engels, Selected Works, Moscow, 1962, Vol. I, p. 430.

30. Cf. Engels's letter to Bebel in 1875 in which he wrote:

> Our people have allowed the Lassallean 'iron law of wages' to be foisted upon them; and this is based on a quite antiquated economic view, namely, that the worker receives on average the *minimum* of the labour wage, because, according to Malthus's theory of population there are always too many workers (this was Lassalle's argument). Now Marx has proved in detail in *Capital* that the laws regulating wages are very complicated, that sometimes one predominates and sometimes another, according to circumstances, that therefore they are in no sense iron but on the contrary very elastic, and the the matter can by no means be dismissed in a few words, as Lassalle imagined (quoted in R. L. Meek, *Marx and Engels on Malthus*, p. 106).

31. *Grundrisse*, London, 1973, p. 287.

32. *Wages, Price and Profit*, p. 444.

33. ibid., p. 444.

34. The term 'demographic' is normally used in a rather narrow sense to cover the more physical attributes of population such as size, health and age or

sex composition; more social attributes such as skill or education are excluded. However, in the present context, this seems artificial, and the term has been extended to cover skill and education.

35. *Capital*, London, 1967, Vol. I, pp. 231–302.
36. ibid., p. 269.
37. ibid., pp. 612–712.
38. There is a brilliant discussion of this subject in Engels's *Condition of the Working Class in England* (Marx-Engels, *Collected Works*, Vol. 4); his observations are still relevant today in many underdeveloped countries where the industrial revolution has barely taken hold, and there are virtually unlimited supplies of cheap casual labour power available.
39. *Capital*, Moscow, 1966, Vol. III, p. 254.
40. Cf. the passage in Volume II of *Theories of Surplus Value* (Moscow, 1968, p. 122) where Marx gives qualified approval to John Barton's view that population rises in times of prosperity because there is more employment available, and not because wages are higher.
41. op. cit., p. 639.
42. *Wages, Price and Profit*, pp. 425–6.
43. *Capital*, Vol. I, pp. 171–2.
44. *Wages, Price and Profit*, p. 443.
45. William Thomas Thornton, *Overpopulation and Its Remedy*, London, 1846. Thornton shows how agricultural wages differ greatly from one part of Britain to another, being much higher in the North than in the South-West. However, there is much less variation in the cost of production of labour-power, and there are regions where the normal wage is not even sufficient to maintain workers and their families in a strong and healthy condition. In such regions the traditional standard of life is well below the local cost of production of strong and healthy labour-power, whereas in certain other regions the two are approximately equal.
46. Modern Marxists often speak of 'reproduction cost' when talking of labour-power, but all they mean by this term is what Marx called 'cost of production'.
47. *Wages, Price and Profit*, p. 444.
48. *Capital*, Vol. I, p. 317 and p. 640 respectively.
49. ibid., p. 637.
50. Cf. the preceding discussion on pages 199–205 of this essay.
51. *Wages, Price and Profit*, p. 441.
52. ibid., p. 444 (italics added).
53. *Capital*, Vol. I, p. 317.
54. *Capital*, Vol. III, p. 861.
55. Some of these questions are considered in the article 'Conflict, Inflation and Money', reprinted in the present collection (see p. 148).
56. *Capital*, Vol. I, p. 619.
57. This is the famous 'Law of the Tendency of the Rate of Profit to Fall' which is discussed at length in Part III of Volume III of *Capital*.
58. This is merely another way of expressing Marx's view that the creation of relative surplus value may invove a disproportionate increase in the organic composition of capital.

59. See pp. 205–12 above.

60. *The Poverty of Philosophy*, pp. 144–52 and pp. 206–7, and *Wages, Price and Profit*, pp. 401–6.

61. For example, suppose that to produce 1 unit of corn requires directly and indirectly 2 units of labour, and to produce 1 unit of gold requires 8 units of labour. Then 1 unit of corn has the same value (labour content) as $\frac{1}{4}$ unit of gold. If commodities exchange at their values it follows that 1 unit of corn exchanges for $\frac{1}{4}$ unit of gold, and thus its price in terms of gold is $\frac{1}{4}$. Note that this price does not depend on the level of wages, which has not even been specified.

62. When there is no joint production Marx's argument can always be extended to cover differing organic compositions of capital, and can usually be extended even where there is joint production. Only in a few bizarre cases of joint production can it happen that higher wages in terms of gold are associated with lower real wages and a higher rate of profit. For practical purposes such cases can be ignored.

63. Nassan W. Senior, *Three Lectures on the Value of Money*, London, 1840. Briefly, Senior's argument is as follows. If the state issues additional paper money, for example notes which are convertible into gold at a fixed rate of exchange, then the *monetary* demand for gold is reduced. This reduces the overall demand for gold, which in turn leads to a reduction in the output of gold. As gold output falls, the margin of production shifts. The least fertile seams and alluvial deposits are abandoned, and only the more fertile sources are exploited. In consequence the cost of production of gold falls and so too does its *value*. Since commodities exchange at their values, a fall in the value of gold will lead to a rise in the price (in terms of gold) of other commodities. Thus, even when the currency is freely convertible into gold at a fixed rate of exchange, a rise in its quantity may lead to higher prices, because it leads to a change in the conditions under which gold is produced.

64. *A Contribution to a Critique of Political Economy*, Moscow, 1970, pp. 119–22, and *Capital*, Vol. I, p. 128. It is worth pointing out that when dealing with *inconvertible* paper money Marx adheres to a rigid version of the Quantity Theory of Money. If the state 'forces' an additional x per cent of such money into circulation, all prices, including that of gold, will rise by x per cent.

8

Skilled Labour in the Marxist System[1]

Ever since the appearance of *Capital* there has been controversy about the implications of skilled labour for the Marxist system of thought.[2] In *Capital* Marx argues that skilled labour creates more value than unskilled labour, and that each unit of skilled labour can thus be regarded as equivalent to so much unskilled labour. Having 'reduced' skilled to unskilled labour in this way, he then defines the value of a commodity as the total amount of unskilled labour, or its equivalent, which is directly or indirectly needed to produce one unit of the commodity in question. He also argues that the reduction of skilled to unskilled labour, and thus the determination of values, does not depend on the wages which various kinds of worker receive. Indeed, in a well-known passage in *Capital*, he explicitly states that values can be determined before wages have even been specified:[3]

> We are not speaking here of the wages or the value the labourer gets for a given labour-time, but of the value of the commodity in which that labour-time is materialized. Wages is a category that, as yet, has no existence at the present stage of our investigation'.

Marx has been criticized by a whole series of writers who, following Böhm-Bawerk, have claimed that skilled labour can *only* be reduced to unskilled labour on the basis of the higher wages it receives.[4] If a particular kind of labour receives x times the wage of unskilled labour then, in their opinion, it creates x times as much value. Clearly, if this claim is correct, then Marx is wrong, and values cannot be determined independently of wages.

Marxist responses to these criticisms fall into two groups. One group, taking its lead from Marx himself, bases itself on the idea that each particular type of labour power has a 'cost of reproduction', defined as the sum total of expenditures which are required, under certain ideal conditions, to educate and maintain workers of the type in question.[5] Skilled labour is reduced to unskilled labour by assuming that the value-creating capacity of each kind of labour-power is proportional to its cost of reproduction. Thus, if skilled workers cost x times as much to educate and maintain as unskilled workers, they create x times as much value as unskilled workers, and one unit of skilled labour is thus 'equivalent' to x units of unskilled labour. Unfortunately, this approach suffers from several major defects. To begin with, it does not provide an adequate response to Böhm-Bawerk's original criticism of Marx. The proposed method of reducing skilled to unskilled labour depends on the average level of wages in the economy, and a change in wages may therefore cause the values of individual commodities to alter.[6] Moreover, this approach completely ignores the educational process by which skilled labour-power is actually produced, and focuses exclusively on the cost of such labour-power to the capitalist sector. As a simplifying device for laying bare the basic mechanisms of exploitation and accumulation, this is a legitimate procedure. It does not, however, provide an adequate foundation for understanding the educational sector and its relations with the rest of the economy. In modern capitalism this sector is of great importance and deserves explicit recognition in any discussion of skilled labour and the creation of value.

For a more satisfactory treatment of skilled labour we must turn to the writings of Hilferding and his followers.[7] Their starting point is Marx's observation that the value of any commodity is determined by 'the amount of labour socially necessary for its production'. They argue that the term 'socially necessary' should be interpreted widely, to include not just the labour of workers actually engaged in the production of commodities, but also the labour of anyone who directly or indirectly helps educate these workers and provide them with the skills they need. Such people range from teachers to cleaners, from the makers of school text-books to the drivers of school buses, and all of them contribute in some way to the eventual creation of value. The extent of this contribution is estimated by Hilferding as follows.

Skilled workers may be regarded as unskilled workers who happen to possess acquired skills. Each of these skills embodies a definite amount of socially necessary labour, and when these skills are put to use the labour contained in them is gradually transmitted to some new product. So, because skills are the result of labour performed in earlier periods, skilled workers contribute to value in two ways. In the first place, they expend so much of their own effort and, provided this effort is utilized with normal efficiency, its expenditure will count as the performance unskilled of labour of normal quality. In the second place, these workers make use of their skills, and in doing so they transform the labour embodied in these skills into labour embodied in some new product.[8]

Thus, skilled labour is equivalent to so much unskilled labour performed in the current period *plus* so much labour embodied in the skills of the worker concerned. Some of the labour embodied in skills is itself skilled and can in turn be decomposed into unskilled labour *plus* labour embodied in skills produced in each earlier period. By extending this decomposition indefinitely backwards one can eliminate skilled labour entirely, replacing it by a stream of unskilled labours performed at different points in time. Each skilled labour is thereby equated to a whole stream of unskilled labours, some performed in the current period, some performed in the preceding period by the worker whilst a trainee and by his or her educators, and some performed even earlier by the educators of these educators and by workers who produce educational means of production. Naturally, these various labours lead to the creation of value only to the extent that they are socially necessary. Highly trained musicians working as ordinary labourers, for example, do not create value commensurate with the labour embodied in their musical skills, for these skills are not socially necessary for the job in question.

Once this approach of Hilferding is adopted, the reduction of skilled to unskilled labour can be performed quite independently of the level of wages and the analysis avoids Böhm-Bawerk's charge of circularity. Also, from this starting-point, one can analyse properly economic relations both within and between the educational and non-educational sectors. Before undertaking such an anlysis, however, it will be useful to give a more formal exposition of Hilferding's method which from now on we shall call the 'indirect labour method'. For convenience, the exposition is based on simultaneous equations, and skilled labour is never explicitly expressed as a stream of past and present unskilled labours. However, provided techniques of production remain unchanged through time, this is merely a difference in exposition and not of substance. And, moreover, when techniques of production do change, the use of simultaneous equations is to be preferred.

I THE REDUCTION OF SKILLED TO UNSKILLED LABOUR

To approach this problem let us first consider how the values of ordinary commodities are determined when there is skilled labour involved in their production. Marx defines the value of a commodity as the amount of unskilled labour, or its equivalent, which is socially necessary for its production. However, the meaning of this definition is not entirely clear, for he uses the term 'socially necessary' in two rather different ways. In places he uses it to denote the *minimum* labour required using the best available techniques of production, and elsewhere he uses it to denote the amount of labour which is on *average* required using a mixture of both good and bad techniques. Throughout this paper we shall adopt the latter interpretation, and use averages.

To find an expression for the value of a commodity assume there are no joint products and that all production processes require one unit of time. Assume also that there are n different commodities labelled $1, 2 \ldots n$; and $m+1$ different types of labour, labelled $0, 1 \ldots m$, of which labour of type 0 is unskilled and the remainder are skilled. Suppose that to produce one unit of commodity j requires an average l_{rj} units of labour of each type r, and a_{ij} units of each commodity i. Then, if one unit of labour of type r is equivalent to φ_r units of unskilled labour, the total value created by the various kinds of labour is equal to $\varphi_0 l_{0j} + \varphi_1 l_{1j} + \ldots + \varphi_m l_{mj}$, or $\sum_r \varphi_r l_{rj}$ for short. And, if one unit of commodity i contains the equivalent of σ_i units of unskilled labour, the total value contributed by means of production to the final product is $\sigma_1 a_{1j} + \sigma_2 a_{2j} + \ldots + a_{nj}$, or $\sum_i \sigma_i a_{ij}$ for short. Adding together these various contributions we find that the value of one unit of commodity j is given by,

$$\sigma_j = \sum_r \varphi_r l_{rj} + \sum_i \sigma_i a_{ij} \qquad (1)$$

for $j = 1, 2, \ldots n$. In matrix form these equations can be written as follows:

$$\sigma = \varphi L + \sigma A.$$

where σ and φ are respectively the vectors $(\sigma_1, \sigma_2, \ldots \sigma_n)$ and $(\varphi_0, \varphi_1, \ldots \varphi_m)$, and L and A are matrices (l_{rj}) and (a_{ij}).

The above equations are not sufficient to determine the values σ_j, for the reduction coefficients φ_r are as yet unknown. To determine the latter let us recall that, in the present approach, one unit of skilled labour is equivalent to one unit of unskilled labour *plus* a certain amount of the labour embodied in the skills of the worker concerned. Suppose that workers work for one period of production, during which they perform one unit of labour, and then retire. This implies, of course, that their skills are used up within the space of one period, and that all of the labour embodied in these skills is transmitted to a new product within the space of this period. Let σ_s^* be the amount of unskilled labour contained in one unit of skill of type s. Then one unit of labour of this type is equivalent to one unit of unskilled labour, representing the effort put in by the worker concerned, *plus* σ_s^* units of unskilled labour embodied in the skills of this worker. Thus,

$$\varphi_s = 1 + \sigma_s^*. \qquad (3)$$

To find σ_s^* one must consider the process by which skills are produced. Let us ignore any training which workers receive from their families or on the job, and assume that all skills are learned in formal educational establishments. Assume also that education lasts for one period only, and that there are no joint products in the educational sector. Suppose that to produce one unit of skill of type s requires t_s^* units of unskilled labour by the person being trained, *plus* l_{rs}^* units of labour of each type r by other people, *plus* a_{is}^* units of each commodity i. Since each unit of labour of type r is equivalent to φ_r units of unskilled labour, and each unit of commodity i contains σ_r units of unskilled labour, it follows that the total labour required to produce one unit of skill of type s is equivalent to

$$\sigma_s^* = t_s^* + \sum_r \varphi_r l_{rs}^* + \sum_i \sigma_i a_{is}^* \qquad (4)$$

units of unskilled labour. Note that the method of calculation used here is almost identical to that used to derive the values of ordinary commodities in equation (1). The only difference is that the labour of the trainees has been separately identified.

To fit unskilled labour into the present notational framework we may regard an unskilled worker as someone who possesses a negligible learned skill which embodies a negligible quantity of labour. For such a worker $t_0^* = 0$, $l_{r0}^* = 0$ for all r, $a_{i0}^* = 0$ for all i, and thus,

$$\sigma_0^* = 0 \qquad (5)$$

From equations (3) and (4) we can obtain the reduction coefficients:

$$\varphi_s = (1 + t_s^*) + \sum_r \varphi_r l_{rs}^* + \sum_i \sigma_i a_{is}^* \qquad (6)$$

for $s = 0, 1, \ldots m$. In matrix notation this can be written,

$$\varphi = (u + t^*) + \varphi L^* + \sigma A^* \qquad (7)$$

where $u = (1, 1, \ldots 1)$, $t^* = (t_0^*, t_1^* \ldots t_m^*)$, and L^* and A^* are respectively the matrices (l_{rs}^*) and $a_{is}^*)$. Note that the above equation implies that,

$$\varphi_0 = 1 \qquad (8)$$

which is what we should expect as one unit of unskilled labour is by definition equivalent to one unit of itself.

Taking (1) and (7) together we now have $m + n + 1$ equations which under most conditions will be sufficient to determine both the values σ_j and the reduction coefficients φ_r. In matrix notation the complete set of equations can be written,

$$(\sigma, \varphi) \left[I - \begin{pmatrix} A & A^* \\ L & L^* \end{pmatrix} \right] = (0, u + t^*) \qquad (9)$$

and providing the matrix on the left hand side is invertible we get,

$$(\sigma, \varphi) = (0, u + t^*) \left[I - \begin{pmatrix} A & A^* \\ L & L^* \end{pmatrix} \right]^{-1} \qquad (10)$$

It is clear from the form of this solution that the calculated reduction coefficients do not depend on the wages which workers receive. Indeed, in deriving equation (10) we have not even mentioned wages.[9]

II SURPLUS VALUE AND EXPLOITATION

Having reduced skilled to unskilled labour and therefore defined the value of any commodity or bundle of commodities, we are now in a position to discuss exploitation and the creation of surplus value.

The first difficulty we face is the possible presence of more than one set of production relations. Unless education is organized on a capitalist basis, teachers and other workers in this sector will stand in a different relationship to capital from those employed by the capitalist firms of the non-educational sector. To use Marx's term, they will not be 'productive' workers, they will not be directly employed by capital. Under these circumstances, it would be misleading for us to talk of educational workers as creating surplus-value. We can, however, talk of them performing surplus labour. Surplus labour is a quite general category which can be applied to any mode or type of production. Workers perform *surplus* labour when the labour content of the products they receive is less than the labour they actually perform. The form and significance of surplus labour will, of course, vary from one mode or type of production to another. The surplus labour of a personal servant, for example, takes the form of a direct use-value for the customer. The surplus labour of the productive worker, on the other hand, takes the form of surplus value for capital.

In the present case we need to consider the surplus labour performed by two groups of workers: those employed in the non-educational sector, which we shall assume is capitalist, and those employed in the educational sector which we shall assume is run by the state. In each case we shall estimate surplus labour in the same way, and the outcome will depend only on the amount of labour the workers in question perform and what they are paid. It will not depend on who employs them.

Consider workers of type s. Over the course of their lives as trainees and later employees, such workers perform a total of $(1 + t_s^*)$ units of labour. Let us call this their 'own labour':

$$\text{own labour} = (1 + t_s^*) \qquad (11)$$

In return for this labour these workers receive a certain collection of commodities for their own personal consumption.[10] Suppose that in return for each unit of labour they perform, as trainees or employees, workers in this category receive *on average* a bundle of commodities $(b_{1s}, b_{2s}, \ldots b_{ns})$. Since these workers perform a total of $(1 + t_s^*)$ units of labour, this implies that their lifetime reward, including both wages and any payment they receive as trainees, consists of $(1 + t_s^*)b_{1s}$ units of commodity 1, $(1 + t_s^*)b_{2s}$ units of commodity 2, and so on. The total amount of labour contained in this collection of commodities is equivalent to $(1 + t_s^*)\sum_i \sigma_i b_{is}$ units of unskilled labour. Let us use the term 'paid labour' to denote this quantity:

$$\text{paid labour} = (1 + t_s^*)\sum_i \sigma_i b_{is} \qquad (12)$$

There is the amount of other peoples' efforts that workers of type s receive in return for their own expenditure of effort. Hence the term 'paid labour'. In practice, of course, workers usually perform more labour than they receive in payment, and in consequence they perform 'surplus' or 'unpaid' labour. Thus,

$$\text{unpaid labour} = \text{own labour} \cdot \text{paid labour} \qquad (13)$$

If we denote the unpaid labour of a worker of category s by u_s, we get:

$$u = (1 + t_s^*) - (1 + t_s^*)\sum_i \sigma_i b_{is} \qquad (14)$$

To indicate how far workers of any particular category, whether employed in the educational or non-educational sector, perform surplus labour one can define the 'rate of surplus labour' as follows:

$$\text{rate of surplus labour} = \frac{\text{unpaid labour}}{\text{paid labour}} \qquad (15)$$

and using e_s to denote this ratio we get from (12) and (14)

$$e_s = \frac{1 - \sum_i \sigma_i b_{is}}{\sum_i \sigma_i b_{is}} \qquad (16)$$

The meaning of e_s is quite simple. The personal expenditure of effort by workers of type s during their working life is equal to $(1 + t_s^*)$ units in return for which they receive consumption goods containing the equivalent of $(1 + t_s^*)\sum_i \sigma_i b_{is}$ units of other peoples' effort. The relationship between these two magnitudes determines how far workers in this category perform surplus labour. Thus e_s is an index of exploitation. The higher e_s the more exploited are the workers concerned. In general, unskilled workers receive very low wages in return for the work they do, and are thus more exploited than the average worker. Conversely, skilled workers often enjoy an above-average standard of living and, even if we take into account their low incomes during training, they emerge as relatively well paid. This is particularly true for professional and managerial workers who often enjoy earnings twice or three times the national average, and yet do no more work, and often less, than many unskilled labourers. Such an inequality would be clearly indicated by the index e which we have just defined. It is interesting to note that in a perfectly competitive labour market with free access to education, the rate of surplus labour would be uniform, apart from minor differences caused by differences in taste regarding the timing and pattern of consumption.

III THE CONVERSION OF SURPLUS LABOUR INTO SURPLUS VALUE

What happens to labour performed in the education sector and in particular to surplus labour performed in this sector? Initially it is embodied in the skill of the skilled worker. If education is organized privately on a profit-making basis, educational workers produce a commodity with a value just like that of any other commodity. Educational labour is then 'productive' in the sense understood by Marx. When education is not part of the capitalist sector, however, educational labour is not productive in this sense. Surplus labour does not take the immediate form of surplus value, nor do educational workers perform their labour under the direct control of capital. Nevertheless, surplus labour performed in education may be *transferred* to the capitalist sector where it appears as surplus value, apparently originating there. In reality, however, this surplus value is merely the converted form of surplus labour performed outside of the capitalist sector.

To demonstrate this formally let us assume that education is organised by the state and is financed by taxes levied on the capitalist sector. Let c_s denote the total cost to capital *in value terms* of labour-power of type s, including both the wages which are required to hire this kind of labour-power and any taxes required to finance its education. The magnitude of c_s is determined as follows. Firstly, there is the consumption of the

workers themselves during both training and subsequent
employment! As we have seen this consists of $(1 + t_s^*)b_{1s}$ units of
commodity 1 $(1 + t_s^*)b_{2s}$ units of commodity 2 and so on. The
total value of these commodities is equal to $(1 + t_s^*)\Sigma_i\sigma_i b_{is}$.
Secondly, to produce a unit of labour power of type s requires
the employment of l_{rs}^* units of labour-power of type r in the
educational sector $(r = 0, 1, \ldots m)$. The total cost in value terms
of this educational labour-power is $\Sigma_r c_r l_{rs}^*$. Finally, there are the
means of production used in the educational process and their
total value is $\Sigma_i \sigma_i a_{is}^*$. Adding together these various costs, we find
that,

$$c_s = (1 + t_s^*)\Sigma_i\sigma_i b_{is} + \Sigma_r c_r l_{rs}^* + \Sigma_i \sigma_i a_{is}^* \tag{17}$$

This tells us the total cost to capital of one unit of labour-power.
It is the value or unskilled labour content of the commodities
which are required to support the education and maintenance of
a worker of type s.

Now, we know that where such labour power is put to work it
'creates' value equivalent to φ_s units of unskilled labour, where
according to equation (4),

$$\varphi s = (1 + t_s^*) + \Sigma_r \varphi_r l_{rs}^* + \Sigma_i \sigma_i a_{is}^* \tag{18}$$

Subtracting (11) from (18) we find the total amount of surplus
value which capital gains from each unit of labour power it
employs in producing ordinary commodities:

$$\varphi_s - c_s = (1 + t_s^*) - (1 + t_s^*)\Sigma_i\sigma_i b_{is} + \Sigma(\varphi_r - c_r)l_{rs}^* \tag{19}$$

Using equation (14) above the first two terms can be replaced by
u_s to give,

$$\varphi_s - c_s = u_s + \Sigma_r(\varphi_r - c_r)l_{rs}^* \tag{20}$$

The first term u_s on the right hand-side represents the surplus
labour performed by the worker himself or herself during
training and subsequent employment. And the second term
represents the surplus labour of everyone employed in the
educational sector who directly or indirectly contributes to the
education of the worker concerned. This can be seen more
clearly by expressing (20) as an infinite series of terms:

$$\varphi_s - c_s = u_s + \Sigma_r u_r l_{rs}^* + \Sigma\Sigma_{qr} u_q l_{qr}^* l_{rs}^* + \ldots \text{ etc.} \tag{21}$$

The first term represents the surplus labour performed by the worker himself or herself; the second term represents the surplus labour performed by those who educated this worker; the third term represents the surplus labour of those who educated these educators, and so on. Thus, the total surplus value appropriate by capital represents a whole string of surplus labours, some performed by workers employed in the capitalist sector itself, and the rest performed by workers employed in the state educational sector.

IV   A SIMPLE ILLUSTRATION

To illustrate the way in which surplus labour performed in the state educational sector can contribute to surplus value in the capitalist sector let us consider the following simple example. Education is run by the government and financed by taxes on the capitalist sector. The entire educational sector is devoted to the formation of skills used by capitalist firms. In each sector labour is the only input and in education all labour is unskilled. Trainees acquire their skills effortlessly and as a result perform no labour in the educational sector. Suppose that E_G units of unskilled labour are performed in the government educational sector, which are just sufficient to provide a steady stream of new workers to replace those retiring from the private sector whose labour force E_P remains constant through time. Every worker in the economy performs one unit of labour and then retires. Finally, in return for their labour, workers in the private sector receive wages containing the equivalent of V_P units of unskilled labour and those in the state educational sector receive wages containing the equivalent of V_G units of unskilled labour. According to our earlier definitions, this means those workers in the capitalist sector perform $E_P - V_P$ units of surplus labour and those in the government sector $E_G - V_G$ units. Denote these amounts by U_P and U_G respectively.

Using Hilferding's method of reduction we can determine the value of capitalist output as follows. Because no constant capital is used, the value of output is equal to the total amount of labour performed in this sector E_P reduced to its unskilled equivalent. Since E_G units of unskilled labour are embodied in the skills used by the E_P workers of the capitalist sector, it follows that one unit of skill contains on average E_G/E_P units of unskilled labour. Thus, the average skilled worker in the capitalist sector creates

$1 + E_G/E_P$ units of value. Since there are E_P such workers employed in this sector the total value of output is therefore E_P $(1 + E_G/E_P)$ which is, of course, equal to $E_P + E_G$. This result could have been obtained directly by regarding all labour performed in the economy as unskilled, and then simply adding up the labour performed in the two sectors.

Capitalist output may be divided into two parts. One part E_P represents the value genuinely originating in the capitalist sector. And another part E_G represents educational labour in the state sector which is transformed into value when workers in the capitalist sector put their skills to use. This is shown in the first part of Table 1.

TABLE 1

Value of Capitalist Output

Source

Labour in state sector	$V_G + U_G$	$(= E_G)$
Labour in capitalist sector	$V_P + U_P$	$(= E_P)$
Total	$E_P + E_G$	

Destination

1. Cost of labour power:
   taxes paid by capitalist sector V_G
   wages paid in capitalist sector V_P
2. Surplus value retained by capital $U_P + U_G$

Total $E_P + E_G$

Capitalist output is distributed in various ways. One part V_P goes to workers in the capitalist sector as wages, and another part V_G goes as wages to workers in the state sector. The rest $U_P + U_G$ remains as surplus value in the hands of capital. This is shown in Table 1.

If we look at flows of embodied labour, independently of whether they take a value form or not, it is clear that there is a net flow from the state sector to the capitalist sector. Embodied labour E_G in the form of skills is transferred to the capitalist sector, where it is converted into an equal amount of value. After subtracting the value V_G which capital must pay for its labour power, a residual U_G remains in the capitalist sector as surplus value (see Diagram 1). If, on the other hand, we look only at the value flows the picture appears quite the reverse. It is the capitalist sector which appears to be supporting the government sector by paying V_G in the form of taxes. There is no corresponding flow of value from the state to the capitalist sector.

DIAGRAM 1

Flows between Sectors

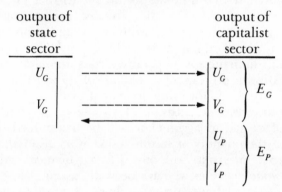

Key: value flows ——————▶, non-value flows – – – – – – –▶

net transfer of embodied labour to capitalist-sector $= V_G$
net transfer of value to state sector $= U_G$

The above example is, of course, quite artificial. The point of including it is to dispel some of the confusion surrounding the notions of 'productive' and 'unproductive' labour and the role of the state sector. The example shows clearly that an unproductive sector such as state education may subsidize the productive (capitalist) sector. Naturally, not all state activity can be viewed in this light. Much of it really does represent a subtraction from capitalist surplus value.

This conclusion seems less surprising when one remembers that Marx used the word 'productive' quite specifically to describe workers employed directly by capital. In this sense, other employees can never be productive – no matter how much surplus labour they perform indirectly for the capitalist class as a whole or for some section of it. Even when they perform a crucial economic function they are not productive.

Until now we have considered the impact of the state sector only from the point of view of its direct effect on the amount of surplus value remaining in capitalist hands. This is not, however, the only way in which the state can affect the ability of capital to accumulate. To expand production capitalists must be able to convert their surplus value into productive capital, they must be able to purchase the appropriate use-values. In particular, they must be able to purchase labour-power. Now, other things being equal, the greater the amount of labour-power purchased by the state sector, the smaller the amount available for purchase by the capitalist sector. Potentially, therefore, state activity constitutes a limitation on the accumulation of capital. When labour-power is in plentiful supply this limitation is inoperative. Mass immigration or the destruction of pre-capitalist modes of production in the domestic economy, for example, may provide capital with all the labour power it needs. Under these circumstances, the ability of capital to accumulate will be determined by such factors as the quantity of surplus-value at its disposal and the post-tax rate of profit, both of which may be increased by the kind of state activities we have been discussing. Thus, under conditions of labour surplus, those 'unproductive' state activities which result in a net transfer of embodied labour to the capitalist sector may help capital accumulate.

When labour-power is in short supply the overall impact of these same activities, however, may be quite different. They will, of course, continue to subsidize the capitalist sector in the way we have described. On the other hand, in employing workers the state is reducing the labour-power available to the capitalist sector, thereby inhibiting the accumulation process as capitalists find themselves unable to expand because of the labour shortage. To some extent capitalists may be able to overcome this problem by investing in machinery and other forms of constant capital. However, to the extent that these measures fail to reduce the demand for labour power, capitalists will be forced to look for new sources of labour-power. If they cannot find these new sources, the accumulation process will be held back and the system may enter a period of crisis.

It is against this background that shifts towards more 'capital' intensive methods of teaching, medicine, and other activities of the State sector must be considered. The replacement of teachers, doctors and other state employees by machinery affects the accumulation of capital in two ways: it may reduce the cost of the goods and services provided; and it may reduce the number of workers employed in the state sector, thereby releasing labour power for exploitation in the capitalist sector. At times of acute labour shortage the latter affect may be the more significant.

It is, unfortunately, not possible for us to discuss this problem any further within the confines of the present paper. We have, however, said enough to show that educational and certain other state sectors, although 'unproductive', may compel workers to perform surplus labour, some or all of which is transferred to the capitalist sector where it appears as surplus value in the hands of capitalists. The extent to which this process helps or hinders the accumulation of capital depends upon the amount of labour-power available. When labour-power is in plentiful supply state activities of the kind we have described may be of unambiguous benefit to capital. When, on the other hand, labour-power is in short supply this is not the case, and the pre-emption of labour-power by the state may seriously inhibit the accumulation of capital.

APPENDIX:

REDUCTION BASED ON REPRODUCTION COST

In this section we show how skilled labour may be reduced to unskilled labour on the basis of its higher 'cost of reproduction'. The reproduction cost of a particular kind of labour power is the expenditure which is required, under certain ideal conditions, to ensure the provision of this kind of labour-power. These ideal conditions are as follows:

1. The personal consumption requirement of workers can be clearly distinguished from any special consumption requirements associated with their work, and the latter can therefore be classified under the heading 'means of production'.

2. For each unit of labour they perform, during both training and subsequent employment, all workers receive the same

bundle of commodities for their own personal consumption.[12]

Thus, roughly speaking, the reproduction cost of a particular type of labour-power is what it would cost to educate and maintain a worker of the type in question, if all workers in the economy enjoyed the same average standard of living throughout their entire lives.

To estimate reproduction costs let us make the same assumptions about educational and non-educational production as we have used in the text. Let $\bar{c}_s$ be the reproduction cost in value terms of one unit of labour-power of type s. This consists of three parts. First, there is the personal consumption of the worker concerned, assuming that, in return for each unit of labour he or she performs, this worker receives the *average* consumption bundle which we shall denote by $(\bar{b}_1, \bar{b}_2 \ldots \bar{b}_n)$. Since workers of this type perform $(1 + t_s^*)$ units of labour altogether, including the labour they perform whilst training, each of them receives in all $(1 + t_s^*)\bar{b}_1$ units of commodity 1, $(1 + t_s^*)\bar{b}_2$ units of commodity 2, and so on. Since commodity i has value σ_i the total value of this collection is $(1 + t_s^* \sum_i \sigma_i \bar{b}_i$. Secondly, there are the costs of reproduction of the various kinds of worker employed in the educational sector. Since there are l_{rs}^* workers of type r and their individual reproduction cost is $\bar{c}_r$ their total cost in value terms is $\sum_r \bar{c}_r l_{rs}^*$. Finally, there are the educational means of production whose aggregate value is $\sum_i \sigma_i a_{is}^*$. The total of these various expenditures is[13]

$$\bar{c}_s = (1 + t_s^*)\sum_i \sigma_i \bar{b}_i + \sum_r c_r l_{rs}^* + \sum_i \sigma_i a_{is}^* \qquad \text{(A 1)}$$

The next and most crucial step is to assume that each category of labour creates value in proportion to the cost of reproduction just defined. Thus, for some number $\bar{e}$

$$\varphi_s = (1 + \bar{e})\bar{c}_s; \text{ for } s = 0, 1, \ldots m \qquad \text{(A 2)}$$

for all s. To determine $\bar{e}$ we need merely consider unskilled labour-power, whose reduction coefficient φ_0 is by definition unity and whose reproduction cost $\bar{c}_0$ according to (A 1) is simply $\sum_i \sigma_i \bar{b}_i$. Substituting in (A 2) we get

$$1 = (1 + \bar{e})\sum_i \sigma_i \bar{b}_i \qquad \text{(A 3)}$$

and therefore

$$\bar{e} = \frac{1 - \sum_i \sigma_i \bar{b}_i}{\sum_i \sigma_i \bar{b}_i} \qquad (A\,4)$$

Thus $\bar{e}$ is simply the average 'rate of surplus labour' in the economy.

Multiplying (A 1) by $1 + \bar{e}$, and using equations (A 2) and (A 3) we can easily derive the following equations:

$$\varphi_s = (1 + t_s^*) + \sum_r \sigma_r l_{rs}^* + (1 + \bar{e})\sum_i \sigma_i a_{is}^* \qquad (A\,5)$$

for all s. These are identical to equations (4) given in the main text, except that the terms representing means of production are multiplied by $(1 + \bar{e})$. In matrix notation these equations can be written,

$$\varphi = (u + t^*) + \varphi L^* + (1 + \bar{e})\sigma A^* \qquad (A\,6)$$

where $u = (1, 1, \ldots 1)$, and L^* and A^* are the matrices (l_{rs}^*) and (a_{is}^*).

Equations (1) of the text, which give the values of commodities, are still valid, and therefore

$$\sigma_j = \sum_r \varphi_r l_{rj} + \sum_i \sigma_i a_{ij} \qquad (A\,7)$$

for all j. Which in matrix notation can be written.

$$\sigma = \varphi L + \sigma A \qquad (A\,8)$$

where L and A are the matrices (l_{rj}) and (a_{ij})

For given e equations (A 6) and (A 8) can be solved as follows:

$$(\sigma, \varphi) = (0, u + t^*) \left[I - \begin{pmatrix} A & (1 + \bar{e})A^* \\ L & L^* \end{pmatrix} \right]^{-1} \qquad (A\,9)$$

If, on the other hand, we take $\bar{b} = (\bar{b}_1, \bar{b}_2 \ldots b_n)$ as given the solution is more complicated for we must solve,

$$(\sigma, \varphi) \left[I - \begin{pmatrix} A & A^*/\sigma \bar{b} \\ L & L^* \end{pmatrix} \right] = (0, u + t^*) \qquad (A\,10)$$

In either case it is clear that the values σ and reduction coefficients φ depend on the level of real wages as given by $\bar{e}$ or $(\bar{b}_1, \ldots \bar{b}_n)$.

Comparing equation (A 10) with equation (10) of the text, we see that this method of reduction yields results identical to those obtained by the indirect labour method of Hilferding, if either $\bar{e}=0$ or $A^*=0$. In the first case there is no surplus value at all created in the economy, and in the second case there are no means of production employed in education.

NOTES

1. This is a revised version of a paper of the same name originally published in the *Bulletin of the Conference of Socialist Economists* in 1973.
2. For a survey of this controversy see Harry Meier, 'Historisches zum Reduktionsproblem' in *Wirtschaftswissenschaft*, Heft 12/1965, Berlin (GDR).
3. *Capital*, Vol. 1, London, 1967, p. 44.
4. E. Böhm-Bawerk, *Karl-Marx and the Close of his System*, Ed. P. Sweezy, Clifton, 1973.
5. This approach is followed by most of the writers in *Materialen zur Politischen Ökonomie des Ausbildungssektors*, ed. E. Altvater and F. Huisken, Erlangen, 1971.
6. This proposition is established formally in an Appendix to the present article.
7. R. Hilferding *Böhm–Bawerk's Criticism of Marx* reprinted as an Appendix to Sweezy's edition of Böhm-Bawerk (see note 4). For a mathematical treatement see N. Okishio 'A Mathematical Note on Marxian Theories', *Weltwirtschaftliches Archiv*, Heft 2/1963, pp. 287–98.
8. There is an obvious parallel between skills and means of production. When means of production are used the labour embodied in them is gradually transmitted to some new product. The difference between skills and means of production is, of course, that skills are an integral part of the workers who possess them, whereas means of production have an independent material existence. In the present context this is not an important distinction, although it is very important in other contexts.
9. Note that the reduction coefficients φ given by equation (10) normally depend on the techniques of production used to make ordinary commodities, for the latter are normally required as means of production in the education sector. However, if education is carried out without means of production, then reduction coefficients are independent of the methods by which ordinary commodities are produced, and depend only on the educational process itself. This follows immediately from equation (5). It is also interesting to note that in this peculiar case the method of reduction based on reproduction costs coincides with that of Hildferding based on indirect labour (see the Appendix).
10. This discussion ignores the fact that workers have families and other dependents. It also assumes that they do not save, and ignores differences in the intensity or unpleasantness of different kinds of labour.

11. See note 10.
12. See note 10.
13. Equation (A 1) is, of course, very similar to equation (16) in the text. The only difference is that $\bar{c}_s$ is calculated on the *hypothetical* assumption that all workers enjoy the same average level of consumption, whereas c_s is calculated on the basis of their actual consumption.

9

Rosa Luxemburg and the Political Economy of Militarism[1]

The final chapter of Rosa Luxemburg's *The Accumulation of Capital* is entitled 'Militarism as a Province of Accumulation'. It is perhaps the most difficult part of what is, by any standards, an obscure and confusing book. Her enemies have dismissed this chapter out of hand, whilst her friends have usually given it a rather 'Keynesian' interpretation, which sees Rosa Luxemburg as an illustrious forerunner of modern theories of effective demand.[2] According to this interpretation, Rosa Luxemburg was trying to show that military expenditure raises demand, increases employment and helps stave off the realization crisis with which capitalism is continually threatened. However, as the more critical of her friends have pointed out, Rosa Luxemburg's own analysis does not actually establish these results. The numerical example, forming the core of her chapter, is based on assumptions which ensure that military expenditure has no effect on total demand: such expenditure is financed entirely out of taxes on the working class, and any rise in military demand is offset by an equivalent reduction in working-class consumption, so overall demand is unaffected. Now, if Rosa Luxemburg really was trying to show that military expenditure raises demand, as these friends claim, then her argument is obviously defective and must be modified. Several modifications along Keynesian lines have been suggested. For example, taxes may be levied not on the working class, as Rosa Luxemburg assumes, but on the rich or some other section of the population which saves a large part of its income. Or the money required for military purposes may not be raised through taxation at all, but by borrowing from the private sector. According to orthodox Keynesian theory, either of these modifications will ensure that military expenditure stimulates demand by mobilizing private savings and making use of income which would not otherwise be spent.

The Keynesian approach to Rosa Luxemburg does have some justification. She often talks as though the basic problem is a shortage of demand, and it is certainly true that her argument can be modified along Keynesian lines to ensure that military expenditure really does stimulate demand. Indeed, various comments by Rosa Luxemburg herself foreshadow the suggested modifications.[3] On the other hand, these comments are never developed systematically and, for the most part, she seems fairly hostile to the idea that military expenditure raises demand.[4] Moreover, in the chapter dealing specifically with militarism she hardly considers the question of total demand, and is more concerned with other economic aspects of militarism. In fact she provides a whole catalogue of the ways in which militarism may help the accumulation of capital, none of which depend on its effect on overall demand. Firstly, it undermines antiquated modes of production and clears the way for capitalist expansion. Military expenditure is in part financed by taxes on the peasantry and, to pay these taxes, peasants are compelled to market some of the produce they would otherwise consume themselves or barter amongst each other. In this way, they are forced to participate in the monetary economy and commodity relations are forcibly extended in the countryside. Pre-capitalist modes of production are further undermined by the shift in the pattern of demand which accompanies militarism, away from peasant and artisan products in favour of arms and ancillary products made by large-scale industry. Secondly, militarism causes beneficial changes within the capitalist sector itself. It creates a secure and growing market for arms producers and their suppliers, and the presence of such a secure and dynamic group of industries acts as both a stabilizer and an engine of growth for the capitalist sector as a whole. Finally, militarism may increase the average rate of profit by allowing capitalists to depress wages and exploit their workers more ruthlessly.

It is clear from the above outline that Rosa Luxemburg had a very broad vision of militarism's role in the accumulation of capital, as a factor aiding the development of dynamic and technically progressive branches of production and clearing away internal obstacles to capitalist expansion. Such a vision is very different from a Keynesian approach which stresses the short-term conjunctural problem of effective demand

and ignores more fundamental problems of long-term development.

Military Expenditure and the Working Class

In the central part of her chapter on militarism Rosa Luxemburg assumes that military expenditure is financed out of taxes levied on the working class, and she asks how this will affect the capitalist sector? The answer, she says, depends on the form this expenditure takes. If taxes are used to pay the wages of a regular army drawn from the ranks of peasantry or unemployed, it will have no affect on the capitalist sector at all. Working-class consumption will be reduced by a certain amount, and in its place there will be an exactly equal amount of consumption by soldiers. Neither the scale nor pattern of demand for capitalist products will change, and the rate of profit will be the same as before. Thus, the capitalist class will gain no direct economic benefit from a transfer of purchasing power from workers to soldiers.

On the other hand, if the money is spent on arms then, according to Rosa Luxemburg, the capitalist sector will derive substantial benefits. Modern industry will be guaranteed a secure market for its products and the overall rate of profit will be increased. To see how she arrives at this latter conclusion let us go through her argument step by step, making use of the numerical example she herself employs.

Rosa Luxemburg considers an economy in which wage rates, organic compositions of capital and profit rates are uniform, and commodities exchange at their values. Arms expenditure is financed by means of a sales tax levied on working-class consumption, and profits are not taxed at all. The capitalist sector of the economy is divided into two parts, which we shall call the 'arms sector' and the 'civil sector', although Rosa Luxemburg herself does not use these terms. The arms sector produces weapons and the means of production directly and indirectly used in making weapons. All other commodities are, by definition, produced in the civil sector.[5] The gross output of the civil sector is equal to 9,000 units, of which pre-tax wages V and profits S each account for 1,285 units, and the rest consists of constant capital C used up in production (depreciation, materials and so on). The pre-tax wage rate $V/(V + S)$ is equal to

0.5 and the 'rate of profit' $S/(C + V)$ is equal to 16.7 per cent.[6] This is all shown in line (1) of Table 1.

Rosa Luxemburg now assumes that an additional tax of 100 units is levied on working-class consumption, the proceeds of which are spent on arms. This has no affect on the scale of demand or output, but it does affect their composition. The demand for consumer goods, and for those means of production directly and indirectly used in making them, is reduced; and in its place comes a demand for arms and the means of production directly and indirectly employed in making arms. Productive capacity is therefore transferred to the arms sector and the output of the civil sector declines. Rosa Luxemburg estimates the extent of this decline as follows: consumer goods 100 units and means of production 71.5 units. The gross output of the civil sector thus falls by a total of 171.5 units, from its original value of 9,000 units to a new value of 8,828.5 units.

To calculate the rate of profit in this new situation requires some assumption about income distribution. As a preliminary step, Rosa Luxemburg assumes that arms expenditure has no effect on the *pre-tax* distribution of income in the civil sector: capitalists receive the same profit per unit of output as they did originally, and workers receive no extra pay to compensate for the additional taxes levied on them. The *pre-tax* wage rate $V/(V + S)$ is the same as before, and so V and S are again equal to each other. The resulting breakdown of gross output into C, V and S is shown in line (3) of Table 1 which reproduces Rosa Luxemburg's own calculations.[7]

From a worker's point of view the new situation is, of course, worse than before because taxes have raised prices and reduced the purchasing power of their wages. But, from a capitalist point of view, things have not changed very much, and the new civil sector is merely a scaled-down version of the old one. Output is now smaller, but the rate of profit is exactly the same, namely 16.7 per cent. For each unit of output they produce, capitalists advance exactly the same amount of constant capital and wages as before, and they receive exactly the same profit in return.

This is clearly a very embarrassing conclusion for Rosa Luxemburg, who wants to show that expenditure on arms increases the rate of profit. However, she does not give up. She goes back over her reasoning to see where she has gone wrong, and identifies what she claims is a mistake. The above calculations assumed that arms expenditure has no affect on the *pre-tax* distribution of income and that any reduction in the output of the civil sector is matched by an equivalent reduction in total profits in this sector. These assumptions, she now argues, are incorrect. The contraction of the civil sector is caused by the removal of workers directly or indirectly engaged in the production of goods for working-class consumption. Such workers, she now claims, do not create surplus value, and their removal from the civil sector should not, in her view, affect the amount of surplus value created in this sector, or the amount of profit received by its capitalists. She concludes that her calculations were wrong, and should be corrected by restoring profits to their original figure of 1,286. To achieve this result she simply raises S by 24·5 units and then, for arithmetical consistency, reduces V by the same amount. Her adjustment and its effect are shown in lines (4) and (5) of Table 1.

The effect of the adjustment is, of course, to increase the rate of profit. Capitalists in the civil sector now receive as much profit as they did originally, before the transfer of resources into arms production, but they advance less constant capital and wages. In fact, according to Rosa Luxemburg's own figures, the rate of profit has risen from 16·7 per cent to 17 per cent. Naturally, the capital released from the civil sector does not remain idle. It is transferred to the arms sector where it is used to extract surplus value from the workers now employed there, and earns a profit just like any other capital. Thus, profits in the capitalist sector as a whole are greater than before. They have remained unchanged in the civil sector, despite a reduction in its size, and additional profits are now being earned in the arms sector.

Note that Rosa Luxemburg's 'demonstration' that arms expenditure increases the rate of profit depends entirely on a shift in the pre-tax distribution of income. Although she does not seem to realize it, in raising S at the expense of V, Rosa Luxemburg is in effect reducing the pre-tax wage rate $V/(V + S)$. Indeed, as her own figures show, $V/(V + S)$ falls from 0·5 to 0·49, and it is this fall which explains why the rate of profit increases from 16·7 to 17 per cent. Thus, her new version of the argument, the standard of living of workers is reduced in two ways: taxes are levied on the goods they consume and money wages are reduced. The taxes are used to finance arms expenditure and the

TABLE 1

Rosa Luxemburg's Numerical Example

1. Original civil sector	$6,430C$	$+,285V$	$+1,285S$	$=9,000$	$V/(V+S)=0\cdot5o, S/(C+V)=16\cdot7\%$
less					
2. Transfer to arms sector	$122\cdot5C+$	$24\cdot5V+$	$24\cdot5S=$	$171\cdot5$	
3. New civil sector	$6,307\cdot5C+1,260\cdot5V+1,260\cdot5S=8,828\cdot5$				$V/(V+S)=0\cdot5o, S/(C+V)=16\cdot7\%$
plus					
4. Income redistribution	—	$24\cdot5V+$	$24\cdot5S=$	0	
5. Final civil sector	$6,307\cdot5C+1,236V$	$+1,285S$	$=8,828\cdot5$		$V/(V+S)=0\cdot49, S/(C+V)=17\cdot0\%$

Definitions: $V/(V+S)=$ pre-tax wage rate, $S/(C+V)=$ 'profit rate'.

reduction in wages is used to boost profits. So, the rate of profit increases because workers are more intensely exploited, and produce enough extra surplus value to finance both arms expenditure *and* a higher rate of profit.

Evaluation

Rosa Luxemburg's discussion of arms expenditure has caused widespread confusion, partly because it is obscurely presented, and partly because her numerical example uses inconsistent methods of approximation and contains a major error of calculation. However, the mathematical defects of her presentation are of secondary importance, and do not affect the essence of her argument. We shall not discuss them here and will confine our remarks to points of real substance. For anyone who is interested, a mathematically correct and consistent version of her calculations is given in an Appendix to the present chapter.

In the course of her argument Rosa Luxemburg either assumes or attempts to prove the following propositions:

1. If arms expenditure is financed by levying taxes on the working class, there is no change in the overall level of demand and output, although there is a change in their composition when arms replace consumer goods.
2. If arms are produced in the capitalist sector, the labour involved in making them creates surplus value and is productive in the Marxist sense.
3. If arms expenditure is financed by taxing the working class, the average rate of profit in the capitalist sector as a whole will increase.

The first of these propositions rests on a *static* analysis which ignores possible dynamic effects of militarism, such as a faster rate of technical innovation, or the disruption caused by shifting resources from one use to another. However, within such a static framework, her proposition is correct and by stressing the impact of militarism on the structure of production, rather than its overall level, she provides a useful antidote to the Keynesian approach with its almost exclusive concern with the problem of effective demand.

Productive Labour

Let us now consider whether or not the labour involved in making arms is productive. The question of productive labour is a thorny one and this is not the place for an extended treatment of the subject.[8] Even so, a few comments are in order. Labour is productive in the Marxist sense if it satisfies two conditions: (a) it produces a commodity which is sold in the market and has value, and (b) the workers who perform this labour are employed in the capitalist sector and, therefore, operate under the direct control of capital. Thus, productive workers are those who sell their labour power to a capitalist enterprise and, having done so, work as their employers direct and create value. Provided they create sufficient value in return for the wage they receive, such workers automatically create *surplus* value. So, one can equally well define a productive worker as anyone from whom capital extracts or, rather, seeks to extract surplus value in the process of production.

Several points can be made about the above definition. In the first place, for people to be productive workers, it is not sufficient that they perform surplus labour and thereby contribute to capitalist profit. They must also be employed in the capitalist sector itself where they work under the direct control of capital. In other words, they must be exploited by capital in production itself. This latter condition excludes many kinds of people who would otherwise be classified as productive workers. For example, capitalist firms may obtain enormous profits by purchasing the output of peasant farmers at well below its value. Or the state may tax the peasantry and use the proceeds to subsidize capitalist firms. In each case peasants will contribute to profits, but will not be productive workers, for their productive activity will not be performed under the direct control of any capitalist enterprise.

A second point to notice is that the definition of productive labour makes no reference to what kind of object is produced, who buys it or what it is used for. The only thing which matters is that this object is a commodity, and as such is produced for sale and has value. The aim of capitalist production is not the creation of any particular kind of wealth, but of wealth in general, and for this purpose all saleable commodities are equivalent, no matter who buys them and what they are used for. This indifference on the part of capital, to the actual nature of what is produced, is mirrored in the definition of productive labour, which makes no reference to the nature of the commodity in question.

It is now simple to evaluate Rosa Luxemburg's view that the labour involved in making arms is productive. In her analysis arms are a commodity with a value like any other commodity, and the workers who make them therefore create value. Moreover, these workers are employed by capitalist enterprises and, provided they create sufficient value in return for the wages they receive, they must of necessity create *surplus* value. Rosa Luxemburg is therefore correct in believing that the labour making arms is productive.

In a recent article Tarbuck has criticized Rosa Luxemburg's view that making arms is productive on the grounds that the 'labour-power expended on arms production is exchanged for the revenue of the state, and thus as such is *not capital*'.[9] This objection, however, is mistaken. In Rosa Luxemburg's example, arms are produced by capitalist firms and it is these firms which purchase the necessary labour-power and control its use. The state does not purchase labour-power, as Tarbuck implies, but arms. And it is precisely this fact which ensures that the labour involved in making arms is productive. If arms were produced by the state, for its own use, then the labour-power of the workers concerned would, as Tarbuck claims, exchange for the revenue of the state and be unproductive. But this is not the case. The workers who produce arms are employed by capitalist firms, and their labour-power therefore exchanges for the capital of these firms and not for the revenue of the state. Naturally, the *arms* they produce exchange for the revenue of the state, as military expenditure is financed out of taxes, but this has no bearing on the issue of whether or not the labour they perform is productive.

The Rate of Profit

This brings us to Rosa Luxemburg's third conclusion regarding the rate of profit. In her example, working-class living standards are depressed by a dual mechanism: taxes are levied on the goods they consume and pre-tax wages are reduced. The taxes are used to buy arms and the reduction in wages is used to boost capitalist profits. Thus, the rate of profit rises because the rate of exploitation is increased by an additional amount over and above what is needed to pay for the weapons purchased by the state. This raises several questions. Is Rosa Luxemburg's justification for assuming such an increase in the rate of exploitation acceptable? And, if it is not, can her assumption be justified on some other grounds? Let us consider the first of these questions.

As we have seen, Rosa Luxemburg assumes that the total amount of profit in the civil sector does not change when this sector shrinks in size and workers are transferred to the arms sector. She justifies this assumption by saying that the workers transferred were originally making consumer goods for the working class, and were not *therefore* creating surplus value. And, since they were not creating surplus value, their removal from the civil sector has no effect on the amount of surplus value or profit received by capitalists in this sector. The passage in which Rosa Luxemburg makes this argument is not very long and is worth quoting in full.

> The value of the aggregate social product may be defined as consisting of three parts, the total constant capital of the society, its total variable capital, and its total surplus value, of which the first set of products contains no additional labour, and the second and third no means of production. As regards their material form, all these products come into being in the given period of production – though in point of value the constant capital had been produced in a previous period and is merely being transferred to new products. On this basis, we can also divide all the workers employed into three mutually exclusive categories: those who produce the aggregate constant capital of the society, those who provide the upkeep of all the workers, and finally those who create the entire surplus value for the capitalist class.
>
> If, then, the workers' consumption is curtailed, only workers in the second category will lose their jobs. *Ex hypothesi* . . . these workers had never created surplus value for capital, and in consequence their dismissal is therefore no loss from the capitalist's point of view but a gain, since it decreases the cost of producing surplus value.[10]

This passage reveals an extraordinary confusion and its reasoning is quite fallacious. It confuses use-value with value, and surplus product with surplus value. As we have already seen, all workers employed in the capitalist sector to make commodities are productive and may contribute to the total pool of surplus value, irrespective of the particular commodity they make or who buys it. Workers who make goods for working-class consumption may create surplus value, and contribute to capitalist profit, just like any other workers, and Rosa Luxemburg is incorrect in claiming they are unproductive. Indeed, she is making much the same mistake as Tarbuck who, as we have seen above, also tries to classify labour as unproductive or productive according to who purchases the resulting output.

Thus, Rosa Luxemburg is wrong in claiming that workers who make goods for working-class consumption are unproductive. Once this claim is rejected her entire argument falls to the ground. She gives no other reason for believing that the establishment of an arms sector will raise the average rate of profit. Does this mean that her conclusion itself is wrong, or is there some other way in which it can be justified? In my view, Rosa Luxemburg's logic is faulty but, as so often in the case of great thinkers, her intuition is sound. There are good reasons for believing that militarism may increase the overall rate of profit and thereby facilitate the accumulation of capital, especially when it involves the establishment of a modern arms industry which can act as an engine of growth and economic transformation.

In essence Rosa Luxemburg's argument depends on one single premiss, namely that militarism is accompanied by a shift in the distribution of income in favour of capital. In her numerical example this shift comes about through a reduction in money wages, but the same result can be achieved in many other ways. For example, taxes may be levied on workers or peasants, and the proceeds used to subsidize the capitalist sector or to purchase some of its output at grossly inflated prices; or wages may be held down whilst prices or productivity are increased. However, no matter what the precise mechanism involved, an increase in the rate of profit requires a shift in the distribution of income in favour of capital, and this in turn is only possible under certain economic and political conditions. The real question, therefore, which Rosa Luxemburg never tackles directly is, does militarism help redistribute income towards profits by creating economic and political conditions which are favourable to capital? There are two reasons for believing the answer to this question is yes.

In the first place, militarism involves more than just expenditure on weapons and the armed forces. It is part of a whole system of power in which the ruling bloc, often composed of capitalists and landlords, maintains its position and intensifies its exploitation of the rest of society. If this power is used to hold down popular living standards, the result may be a huge increase in the rate of exploitation. The additional surplus value which is thereby made available may be sufficient, even after the subtraction of military and other expenses of the state, to provide additional profits for the capitalist class. If this is the case, then militarism will raise the rate of profit, even though it involves a massive waste of resources. In the second place, militarism may be accompanied by a hot-house development of technology and the productive forces, so that productivity increases rapidly and a growing surplus can be produced even without a reduction in living standards.

Both of the above factors were clearly at work in pre-1914 Germany. Rapid technical advance, spearheaded by the arms industries and their suppliers, led to a huge increase in national income; and an extensive system of taxes and protective tariffs ensured that a substantial part of this additional income was appropriated by the state, capital and landed interests. Popular living standards rose, it is true, but this rise was kept within certain limits, so that despite large military expenditures, German industry prospered. Thus, in pre-1914 Germany, militarism aided the accumulation of capital, both by fostering modern industry and keeping the working masses in a state of subordination. It was precisely the success of this imperialist and militarist system of power which made the tasks of Left social democrats such as Rosa Luxemburg and her close collaborator Karl Liebknecht so difficult, and paved the way for the capitulation of the Social Democratic Party during the First World War.

Concluding Remarks

Given that militarism is part of a system of power with far-reaching consequences for both the distribution of income and the organization of production, one can easily see how it may lead to a higher rate of profit, and why it may be extremely desirable from a capitalist point of view. This does not mean, of course, that militarism is an ideal solution even for capital, as it involves a huge waste of resources which could otherwise be used for accumulation and consumption, and carries with it the risk of war. A more pacific solution is clearly in the interests of capital, *provided* the conditions for profitable and fast accumulation can be ensured. Modern Japan, for example, illustrates very strikingly how capitalist development may, under the appropriate conditions, take place in a non-militarist way. But these conditions are not always satisfied, and militarism may provide the only practical way in which capital can establish its internal and external hegemony, and ensure a favourable distribution of income and organization of production. Or, even where militarism is not the only practical answer, it may still provide a solution which is viable from a capitalist point of view and permits a satisfactory rate of accumulation.

The broader aspects of militarism, as part of a system of power and economic organization, were a familiar theme in the writings of left-wing social democrats before the First World War. They pointed out how it reinforced the power of capital over labour, favoured big industry at the expense of smaller producers, and helped the accumulation of capital in a host of other ways. Indeed, to anyone living in pre-1914 Germany, or Japan for that matter, it was only too obvious that militarism was part of a coherent system of social and economic organization.[11] Imperialist and militarist ideas were prevalent in sections of the working class, especially those directly and indirectly involved in the production of arms, and were widespread amongst the peasantry and other strata of the population which might have allied with the proletariat.[12] The army played a major role in politics both as a pressure group and as a moulder of public opinion.[13] And the state took an active role in promoting the development of the modern industries associated with the production of armaments. In these and a variety of other ways militarism and, more generally, imperialism served to keep the masses in check and speed the development of both German and Japanese capitalism. Rosa Luxemburg was well aware of this fact and, despite its shortcomings, *The Accumulation of Capital* reveals a keen understanding of the basic issues involved. It contains in rudimentary form the elements of a general theory of 'forced match' industrialization in the era of imperialism.

APPENDIX

In this Appendix a corrected and consistent version of Rosa Luxemburg's numerical example is derived. She begins with the following schema for the non-military part of the capitalist sector:

$$
\begin{array}{llll}
\text{Department I} & 5{,}000C + & 1{,}000V + & 1{,}000S = 7{,}000 \\
\text{Department II} & 1{,}430C + & 285V + & 285S = 2{,}000 \quad \text{(A\,1)} \\
\hline
\text{Civil sector} & 6{,}430C + & 1{,}285V + & 1{,}285S = 9{,}000
\end{array}
$$

Where department I produces means of production, Department II produces consumer goods, C is constant capital used up in production, V is pre-tax wages and S is profit. The above schema is clearly based on the assumption that the 'ratio of dead to living labour' $C/(V+S)$ is equal to $2 \cdot 5$, which implies that the ratio $C/(C+V+S)$ is equal to $5/7$.

The figures given by Rosa Luxemburg are rounded to the nearest five. Recalculating them on the assumption that $C/(V+S)$ is equal to $2 \cdot 5$, we get:

$$
\begin{array}{llll}
\text{Department I} & 5{,}000C + & 1{,}000V + & 1{,}000S = 7{,}000 \\
\text{Department II} & 1{,}428 \cdot 6C + & 285 \cdot 7V + & 285 \cdot 7S = 2{,}000 \quad \text{(A\,2)} \\
\hline
\text{Civil sector} & 6{,}428 \cdot 6C + & 1{,}285 \cdot 7V + & 1{,}285 \cdot 7S = 9{,}000
\end{array}
$$

Rosa Luxemburg assumes that the output of consumer goods in Department II is reduced by 100 units, and that all the resources directly and indirectly used in making these consumer goods are used to make arms instead. Since $C/(C+V+S)$ is equal to $5/7$, it follows that to produce 100 units of consumer goods

Department II requires $5/7 \times 100 = 71 \cdot 4$ units of constant capital. Rounding to the nearest quarter, Rosa Luxemburg argues that the output of means of production for Department II will therefore fall by $71 \cdot 5$ units when consumer goods production falls by 100 units. She concludes that the gross output of the civil sector $(C + V + S)$ will fall by $171 \cdot 5$ units, made up as follows:

Department I	$51 \quad C + 20 \cdot 5(V + S) =$	$71 \cdot 5$	
Department II	$71 \cdot 5C + 28 \cdot 5(V + S) =$	100	(A 2)
Total transfer	$122 \cdot 5C + 49 \cdot 0(V + S) =$	$171 \cdot 5$	

This argument is correct, as far as it goes, and Rosa Luxemburg correctly calculates the quantity of means of production which are directly used by firms making consumer goods. But she forgets that these means of production are themselves produced using other means of production, which are in their turn produced using other means of production, which are in their turn produced using still other means of production, and so on *ad infinitum*. Thus when expenditure is switched from consumer goods to arms there is a whole chain of effects in Department I, all of which must be taken into account in arriving at the right answer. This is not difficult and can be done as follows.

Assume that the ratio of C to $C + V + S$ is equal to $5/7$ in each department. Then, in producing 100 units of consumer goods, $5/7 \times 100$ units of constant capital are used up. In producing this constant capital a further $5/7 \times 5/7 \times 100$ units of constant capital are used up, and in producing this constant capital a still further $5/7 \times 5/7 \times 5/7 \times 100$ units are used up. And so on. Altogether the total amount of constant capital used up is equal to,

$$5/7 \times 100 + \frac{5}{7} \times \frac{5}{7} \times 100 + \frac{5}{7} \times \frac{5}{7} \times \frac{5}{7} \times 100 \ldots$$

This is a geometric series whose sum is given by,

$$\frac{5/7 \times 100}{1 - 5/7} = 250 \qquad (A 3)$$

So, in producing 100 units of consumer goods, a grand total of 250 units of constant capital are directly and indirectly used up.

A switch in expenditure of 100 from consumer goods to arms thus involves the transfer of 250 units of output in Department I from civil to miltary uses.

The chain of direct and indirect production of constant capital involved in making 100 units of consumer goods can be displayed as follows:

$$
\begin{array}{lll}
\text{Stage 1} & 51 \cdot 0C + 20 \cdot 4(V+S) = & 71 \cdot 4 \\
\text{Stage 2} & 36 \cdot 4C + 14 \cdot 6(V+S) = & 51 \cdot 0 \\
\text{Stage 3} & 26 \cdot 0C + 10 \cdot 4(V+S) = & 36 \cdot 4 \qquad (A\,4)
\end{array}
$$

_____

$$\text{Total} \quad 178 \cdot 6C + 71 \cdot 4(V+S) = 250 \cdot 0$$

Rosa Luxemburg stops after Stage 1, and thus underestimates the extent to which Department I is affected by the switch in expenditure.

From (A 4) we conclude that the following productive capacity, previously employed in the civil sector, is transferred to arms production:

$$
\begin{array}{lll}
\text{Department I} & 178 \cdot 6C + & 71 \cdot 4(V+S) = 250 \\
\text{Department II} & 71 \cdot 4C + & 28 \cdot 6(V+S) = 100 \qquad (A\,2)
\end{array}
$$

$$\text{Total transfer} \quad 250 \quad C + 100 \quad (V+S) = 350$$

Notice that this is a miniature sub-economy in a state of simple reproduction. Department I produces a gross output of 250 units, of which 178·6 are retained for its own use, and the remaining 71·4 units are transferred to Department I where they are used to produce the 100 units of consumer goods. Moreover, the net-output or value-added $(V+S)$ of the two departments combined is equal to 100 units. This is exactly what we should expect, as the transfer of resources is induced by a switch in expenditure of 100 units.

The Distribution of Income

The above schema (A 2) makes no assumption about the distribution of income between V and S. If we accept Rosa

Luxemburg's initial assumption, that V and S remain equal, we can rewrite this schema as follows:

$$\text{Department I} \quad 178 \cdot 6C + 35 \cdot 7V + 35 \cdot 7S = 250$$
$$\text{Department II} \quad 71 \cdot 4C + 14 \cdot 3V + 14 \cdot 3S = 100 \quad \text{(A 5)}$$

$$\text{Total transfer} \quad 250 \quad C + 50V + 50S = 350$$

Subtracting this from (A 1) we find that the situation in the civil sector, after the transfer of resources to arms production, is given by:

$$\text{Department I} \quad 4{,}821 \cdot 4C + \quad 964 \cdot 3V + \quad 964 \cdot 3S = 6{,}750$$
$$\text{Department II} \quad 1{,}357 \cdot 2C + \quad 271 \cdot 4V + \quad 271 \cdot 4S = 1{,}900 \quad \text{(A 6)}$$

$$\text{New civil sector} \quad 6{,}178 \cdot 6C + 1{,}235 \cdot 7V + 1{,}235 \cdot 7S = 8{,}650$$

Comparing this with the situation before the transfer of resources (A 1) we get:

$$\text{Original civil}$$
$$\quad \text{sector} \quad 6{,}428 \cdot 6C + 1{,}285 \cdot 7V + 1{,}285 \cdot 7S = 9{,}000$$
$$\text{New civil sector} \quad 6{,}178 \cdot 6C + 1{,}235 \cdot 7V + 1{,}235 \cdot 7S = 8{,}650 \quad \text{(A 7)}$$

Thus, profits have fallen from $1{,}285 \cdot 7$ to $1{,}235 \cdot 7$. Rosa Luxemburg argues that profits should not fall in this way, and she restores them to their original level by reducing pre-tax wages. In the corrected version of her example this involves reducing V by 50 and raising S by 50, after which our figures for the civil sector will be as follows:

$$\text{Final civil sector} \quad 6{,}178 \cdot 6C + 1{,}185 \cdot 7V + 1{,}285 \cdot 7S = 8{,}650 \quad \text{(A 8)}$$

This completes our argument, and the results are summarized in Table A1 which is merely a revised version of Table 1 in the main text. Notice that, as in Rosa Luxemburg's own calculations, arms expenditure only raises the rate of profit because it is accompanied by a reduction in the pre-tax wage rate. Without such a reduction the rate of profit is unchanged.

TABLE A1

Revised Version of Rosa Luxemburg's Numerical Example

1. Original civil sector	$6,428 \cdot 6C + 1,285 \cdot 7V + 1,285 \cdot 7S = 9,000$	$V/(V+S) = 50, S/(C+V) = 16 \cdot 7\%$
less		
2. Transfer to arms sector	$250C + 50V + 50S = 350$	
3. New civil sector	$6,178 \cdot 6C + 1,235 \cdot 7V + 1,235 \cdot 7S = 8,650$	$V/(V+S) = 0 \cdot 50, S/(C+V) = 16 \cdot 7\%$
plus		
4. Income redistribution	$- \quad 50V + 50S = 0$	
5. Final civil sector	$6,178 \cdot 6C + 1,185 \cdot 7V + 1,185 \cdot 7S = 8,650$	$V/(V+S) = 0 \cdot 48, S/(C+V) = 17 \cdot 5\%$

NOTES

1. This is a revised version of a paper originally given at a Cambridge seminar for research students.
2. I have used the word 'Keynesian' because modern interpretations of Rosa Luxemburg have been very much influenced by the ideas of Keynes about the importance of effective demand and the tendency of capitalism towards global overproduction. In fact these ideas pre-date Keynes by many years and have a long pedigree in under-consumptionist writings of the nineteenth and early twentieth centuries. Amongst the many authors who have interpreted Rosa Luxemburg in a Keynesian fashion are the following: M. H. Dobb, 'The Accumulation of Capital' in *On Economic Theory and Socialism*, London, 1955; M. Kalecki, 'The problem of Effective Demand with Tugan-Baranowski and Rosa Luxemburg' in *Selected Essays on the Dynamics of the Capitalist Economy*, Cambridge, 1971; T. Kowalik, *Il Pensiero Economico di Rosa Luxemburg*, Rome, 1977; T. Kemp, *Theories of Imperialism*, London, 1967; G. Lee, 'Rosa Luxemburg and the Impact of Imperialism', *Economic Journal*, December 1971; P. Leon, *Structural Change and Growth in Capitalism*, Baltimore, 1967; G. Lichtheim, *Imperialism*, London, 1971; J. P. Nettl, *Rosa Luxemburg*, 2 vols., London, 1966; J. Robinson, Introduction to R. Luxemburg's *The Accumulation of Capital*, London, 1963; and P. Sweezy, *The Theory of Capitalist Development*, London, 1962.
3. For a comment on the effects of borrowing to finance military expenditure see page 420 of Rosa Luxemburg *The Accumulation of Capital*, London, 1963. And for a comment dealing with the taxation of savings see p. 465 of the same work.
4. For example, *The Accumulation of Capital* devotes a whole chapter to attacking the views of Vorontsov, a Russian forerunner of Keynes, especially his idea that demand can be raised by taxing profits and using the money for military purposes. Elsewhere, in an earlier piece of writing, Rosa Luxemburg dismisses as 'vulgar economy' the view that military expenditure and other kinds of waste provides 'relief' for capitalism and absorbs an unsaleable surplus of commodities (see especially her reply to Max Schiffel in 'Militia and Militarism' which is reprinted in *Selected Political Writings of Rosa Luxemburg*, Dick Howard (ed.), New York, 1971).
5. These definitions imply that the civil sector produces the goods consumed by workers in the arms sector.
6. The total amount of labour performed is equal to $(V + S)$ and, if there were no taxes on workers' consumption, wages would purchase goods with a value V. Thus $V/(V + S)$ is an index of the *pre-tax* wage rate. The formula given for the rate of profit is an approximation which assumes there is no fixed capital. Note that Rosa Luxemburg calls S 'surplus value', which is misleading when workers are taxed because V then also includes an element of surplus value. Thus, S is that part of surplus value which accrues to capital, i.e. profit. Note also that Rosa Luxemburg uses the term 'aggregate social product' to describe the gross output of the civil sector.

7. The breakdown given in lines (2)–(5) of Table 1 assumes that the 'ratio of dead to living labour' $C/(V + S)$ is the same as it was originally, namely 2·5.

8. For a more extensive treatment see I. Gough, 'Productive and Unproductive Labour in Marx', *New Left Review*, November–December 1972.

9. K. Tarbuck 'Rosa Luxemburg and the Economics of Militarism' in J. Schwarz (ed.), *The Subtle Anatomy of Capitalism*, Santa Monica, 1977, p. 157.

10. *The Accumulation of Capital*, op. cit., p. 463.

11. The effects of militarism in pre-1914 Japan are discussed at length in a remarkable series of books published under the auspices of the Carnegie Endowment for International Peace in the 1920s. Perhaps the most interesting of the series are G. Ono, *War and Armament Expenditures*, New York, 1922, and U. Kobayashi, *Military Industry of Japan*, 1922. The latter author argues forcefully that militarism helped industrial development and makes the rather exaggerated claim that 'most of the achievements which raised the Japanese industries, especially the manufacturing industry, as high as their present position at one bound within fifty years after the (Meji) Restoration, are due to no other than the military industry' (p. 259).

12. Ideological aspects of German militarism are discussed at length in K. Liebknecht, *Militarism and Anti-militarism*, Cambridge, 1973 and T. Veblen, *Imperial Germany and the Industrial Revolution*, Ann Arbor, 1968.

13. See G. A. Craig, *The Politics of the Prussian Army*, New York, 1972, especially Chapter VI.

Index